# Advance Praise for *Th*

"In this candid, emotionally nuanced, and meticulously researched memoir about growing up poor on the wind-swept shores of Cape Cod, Cynthia Blakeley brings both an academic's intellectual rigor and a seeker's openness to the interrogation of her family's complicated and fragmented history, full of secrets and traumas. Gorgeously written, *The Innermost House* is a stunning book that will make you reassess everything you thought you knew about remembering, forgetting, and storytelling."

—Adrienne Brodeur, author of *Wild Game:*
*My Mother, Her Lover, and Me*

"In *The Innermost House*, a powerful and moving meditation on the nature of memory and forgetting, and the effects of trauma on narrative self-making, Cynthia Blakeley confronts her personal history and family secrets with unflinching clarity and wisdom. In finely wrought prose, she elegantly demonstrates the way that in the act of writing—of remembering—lies the possibility for transformation, for mapping one's future, and offers readers a guide to finding a pathway into our own innermost houses. This is a book I will cherish and return to again and again."

—Natasha Trethewey, author of *Memorial Drive*

"*The Innermost House* is a clear-eyed attempt to find order and meaning in a childhood lived fifty years ago in a small town by the ocean. Cynthia Blakeley shared a house with a charismatic, eccentric, and devoted but troubled mother and the questionable men she attracted. Her book is an account of the ways in which memory operates and her effort to find a standpoint among the unspoken emotional assaults that adults practice on children."

—Alec Wilkinson, author of *A Divine Language: Learning*
*Algebra, Geometry, and Calculus at the Edge of Old Age*

"Anyone interested in memoir as a literary genre should read *The Innermost House*. This is not just a memoir but a meta-memoir, an examination of what memoir-making is about, how life story and identity are interwoven, and how memory, that slippery devil, shapes and reshapes what we tell ourselves about ourselves. Blakeley's not just telling us a life story, she's constructing one as we watch, and for me there's something eerily familiar about the process, because even though my life has been nothing like Blakeley's, I do this too—I suspect we all do."

—Tamim Ansary, author of *The Invention of Yesterday*

"*The Innermost House* is more than a memoir; it confronts existential questions about the trustworthiness of memory and how the stories we hear, the stories we tell, and maybe most especially, the stories we hide, even from ourselves, weave an evolving and complicated story of self. In a beautifully evocative depiction of life growing up in a working-class family on Cape Cod, Cynthia Blakeley struggles with forging an identity from things remembered, things forgotten, and perhaps things only dreamed or imagined. Informed by contemporary neuroscience of memory, Blakeley considers how we both live in the past and leave it behind, how we reconcile the family we love with the harrowing secrets we hold, and, ultimately, how each of us crafts a life story in the face of these ambiguities."

—Robyn Fivush, professor of psychology and *Psychology Today*'s The Stories of Our Lives blogger

"Scholars and students of women's history will benefit enormously from Cynthia Blakeley's perspective in *The Innermost House*, a gripping narrative of coming of age on Cape Cod in a working-class world marked by trauma, struggle and love. Carefully crafted and beautifully written, this work joins the canon of pathbreaking 20th and 21st century memoirs by writers such as Anzia Yezierska, Jill Conway, Mary Karr, and Rebecca Solnit."

—Mary E. Frederickson, coeditor of *Global Women's Work: Perspectives on Gender and Work in the Global Economy*

"This is a beautifully written and moving story of a young woman growing up in a working-class household on Cape Cod, but it is really a memoir of an extended family, their fraught and loving relationships as characters come and go from their saltbox home. Blakeley's mother and grandmother stand out most vividly, and the struggles of these women are at once heartbreaking and heartening. *The Innermost House* is memoir at its best."

—Elliott Gorn, author of *Let the People See: The Story of Emmett Till*

# OTHER BOOKS FROM BRIGHT LEAF

# The Innermost House

My mother and me, in our yard on Lecount Hollow Road in South Wellfleet, MA, 1961. Photo by Robert V. Blakeley.

# The Innermost House

*a memoir*

## Cynthia Blakeley

**BRIGHT LEAF**
BOOKS THAT ILLUMINATE
Amherst and Boston
An imprint of University of Massachusetts Press

ISBN 978-1-62534-814-2 (paper); 815-9 (hardcover)

Designed by Westchester Publishing
Set in Adobe Minion Pro
Printed and bound by Books International, Inc.

Cover design by adam b. bohannon
Cover photo by George H. Power, *Five Children at Lecount Hollow Beach,
Wellfleet, MA* (Vicki, Ken, Richard, Pat, and Cynthia Blakeley), 1964.
Courtesy of Leslie H. Power.

Library of Congress Cataloging-in-Publication Data

Names: Blakeley, Cynthia D., author.
Title: The innermost house : a memoir / Cynthia Blakeley.
Description: Amherst : Bright Leaf, an imprint of University of
Massachusetts Press, [2024] | Includes bibliographical references. |
Identifiers: LCCN 2024016779 (print) | LCCN 2024016780 (ebook) | ISBN
9781625348142 (paper) | ISBN 9781625348159 (hardback) | ISBN
9781685750855 (ebook) | ISBN 9781685750862 (ebook)
Subjects: LCSH: Blakeley, Cynthia D.—Childhood and youth. | Blakeley,
Cynthia D.—Family. | Blakely family. | Wellfleet (Mass—Biography. |
Wellfleet (Mass.)—Social life and customs—20th century.
Classification: LCC F74.W39 B64 2024 (print) | LCC F74.W39 (ebook) | DDC
929.20973—dc23/eng/20240808
LC record available at https://lccn.loc.gov/2024016779
LC ebook record available at https://lccn.loc.gov/2024016780

British Library Cataloguing-in-Publication Data
A catalog record for this book is available from the British Library.

*For Thelma*

# Contents

# Author's Note

The following names are pseudonyms: Ben Harrow, Willy Celms, Drew, Freya, Geoff, Jeanne, Kimi, Maggie, Nicky, Samantha Smith, Roy ("the Texas Tumbler"), Sebastian, and Ted. In rare cases, identifying details and place names have also been changed to preserve an individual's privacy.

# Preface

We were the ones who stayed past Labor Day, into the slanting, undusted light of autumn and the off-season's shivery quietude. While our parents settled into winter's sluggish pace, we hauled toboggans from our clapboard garage and tramped through woods to sled the open hills of the power lines, or yanked on rusty skates to wobble across the ice at Pinky Newcomb's, a freshwater marsh where brown reeds slashed the frozen surface. A few months later, and the pop of spring crocuses led to mayflowers, mayflowers to box turtles and frogs, some of whom met their end under the tire-crunch of tourists hurtling past our hedge come July, propelled by nine months of pent-up hunger for sand, salt water, and baby-oil sunburns.

The Outer Cape's windswept ocean bluffs, humming salt marshes, clear kettle ponds, and evening birdsong have long attracted not only summer vacationers but poets, architects, artists, and literary naturalists, including Henry David Thoreau and Henry Beston. In his classic work, *The Outermost House*, Beston describes his year in a solitary cottage on a dune overlooking the Atlantic. Contemplating his elemental surroundings, the hordes of seabirds and the crash of waves on an unsullied shore, he writes, "these sands might be the end or the beginning of a world." Indeed, they were the beginning of mine.

This is a memoir of a working-class family in a natural paradise; of the haunted house on Lecount Hollow Road in Wellfleet, Massachusetts, where I was raised and where my mother lived for over sixty years; and of the ways I have made sense of the events in my early life and the events and secrets in my family's life. But this is also a book about memory and its conjoined twin, forgetting, as well as about our curation and co-construction of the past—and with it, our shaping of the present and future.

Once I understood that memory was the crux of *The Innermost House*, I found my roadmap for navigating the thousands of pages I have written in my journals and the many stories I have collected. I love my family, fiercely, but its early fracturing left so much unknown. My tale begins with the most unknowable memories of all, our "impossible" memories, inscribed not in consciousness but the body, or experienced but perhaps not always believed. From there I venture into the revelatory and conciliatory power of oral histories, the pull of family secrets, the disorientation—and reorientation—of recovered memory, and the intervention of dreams. Later chapters shed light on the dynamic between memory and narrative identity, the organizing and sometimes coercive power of scripts, the underappreciated mercy of forgetting, and the role of forgiveness in allowing us to live more companionably with the past. Each of these larger themes is animated by personal stories of ghosts and hauntings, astonishing natural beauty and sly town politics, failures and crimes, chance turns and unconventional redemptions.

This is the story of a life and a family and not an academic treatise, but because thinking about how we remember and why we forget has helped me to understand and construct that story, I have added supplementary notes at the end of the book. Organized by chapter, these comments offer scientific support for my observations on memory and storytelling, historical contextualization, literary references, and elaboration on important points. The endnotes thus comprise a vital companion to the text, a guide that makes explicit the process of crafting—or co-crafting, as is often the case in retelling the past—a memoir out of scraps of memory.

It is my hope that as readers live through these events and scenes with me and catch glimpses of how they were brought back to life, they might consider ways to gather, perhaps even rediscover, their own fragments of personal and family memory, creating constellations and stories that add light and meaning to what the Provincetown poet Mary Oliver so rightly calls our "one wild and precious life."

# The Innermost House

Blakeley house as the South Wellfleet General Store, circa 1930, when the store was moved around the corner by a team of horses and turned into a home.

Blakeley house, late 1950s. The upstairs window is to my childhood bedroom. The summerhouse is on the right, before its move closer to the marsh.

# 1

# Impossible Memories

~

*One need not be a chamber to be haunted,*
*One need not be a house;*
*The brain has corridors surpassing*
*Material place.*
                    —*Emily Dickinson*


Two men wait outside the heavy fir door, the header so low they'll have to duck to enter. Seven months pregnant with me, my mother is somewhere inside, cooking, perhaps, at the cast iron stove in our roughly finished kitchen. The flat half of the stove stays warm year-round, taking the chill off the unheated room. Above the narrow countertops and windows, blue willow plates and mismatched wine glasses sit on shelves wedged between exposed two-by-fours, while two straw-covered bottles of Chianti dangle like buoys from a roofing nail hammered into the wall next to Mom's homemade cotton curtains.

The kitchen, added to our old wooden house in the 1930s after its conversion from a general store to a home, has gaps near the ceiling where ivy has slipped inside, its grasshopper tendrils finding easy purchase on the coarse interior walls. Mom likes the ivy and the ark-like feel of her home, with its nooks and crannies, its hand-hewn rafters, its windowpanes of wavy glass. This eccentric house, ripe for imaginings, is a welcome change after seven years of trailers and army base lodgings, each as spartan and predictable as the last.

Though it's the middle of July, the thermometer has barely cracked seventy degrees—too chilly for a dip in the ocean or even one of the kettle ponds sunk among the pitch pines of Wellfleet's back roads. So Mom is at home with her five children, none of them yet a teenager, the house no doubt pulsing with their careening and pranks.

I can't, of course, know for sure what my mother is doing. Maybe she's not in the kitchen at all but sitting at her black Singer sewing machine listening to the Everly Brothers' new hit "All I Have to Do Is Dream" on the transistor radio as she makes a shirt for one of my brothers. Or perhaps she's feeding scrambled eggs to my older sister Thelma, a toddler but the easiest of her children. Or maybe she's writing a letter to her estranged husband, stationed in Germany, to beg, again, for a divorce. Never mind; it's July 14, her thirty-second birthday, and Mom, who loves celebrations as much as her children do, likely has a cake in the oven.

While I can't know what my mother is doing, I do know what she has heard: a knock on the front door, two or three raps at once hesitant and hard. I imagine her wondering why no friendly voice has followed the knock, no *yoo-hoo!* or *Shirley!*—or why anyone would knock in the first place. There's no lock on the door, no way to bar entry, no need to. It's the Outer Cape in 1958, a salt-sprayed arm curling into the Atlantic, a string of fishing villages where tenacious year-rounders negotiate nature and summer tourists rent it. And in Mom's ancient saltbox on Lecount Hollow Road, there's little worth envying or stealing.

Perhaps she imagines one of her friends is outside the door, there to surprise her with a handful of birthday flowers or a box of chocolate fudge. No matter the draw, she would be moving more slowly than usual, and not just because of her wide belly. A month or two earlier, one doctor after another at the Hyannis hospital had dug into her right foot, prying loose the snapped tip of a sewing needle that had lodged first in the nubbly rug where Mom had dropped it and then into metatarsal bone when she stepped on it.

After the surgery, Mom had rustled up a pair of crutches but couldn't manage them on our house's narrow stairs, so if she was busy in one of the two upstairs bedrooms when the knock sounded, she would have laughed at herself as she crawled down backward, keeping her center of gravity low to stop from toppling over.

The "wittiest girl" of her high school class and a party girl long after (she once told me she kept having children because she liked the company), Mom surely hurried as best she could toward the sound and the diversion it promised, perhaps running her fingers through her short auburn curls and tossing her apron, printed with windmills and Dutch maidens, onto the back of a Windsor chair she was refinishing. Or maybe she slapped on some red lipstick and checked her teeth in the mottled, gilt-framed mirror she had wrangled from her parents' attic and hung on nicked pine walls the color of burnt honey. She knew she was attractive, even when pregnant, a card she'd played her entire life.

However well-composed Mom might be, the house was surely a mess, its flotsam and jetsam of handed-down clothes and dinged furniture strewn with random beautiful objects she had salvaged from yard sales or her parents' more orderly past.

One of the two men standing outside the door was a familiar face around town, someone Mom shared an occasional laugh with down at Al Graham's piano bar on the harbor, though I imagine he was not smiling so much as grimacing in the cool, bright sun. Perhaps he was shifting uneasily, favoring the leg that had never fully healed from a knife stab during an off-Cape scuffle. Given their friendship, it must have taken some arm-twisting to get him to Mom's doorstep, to play his part in this birthday errand.

The other man—young, raven-haired, blue-eyed—was the last person Mom expected or wanted to see. She hadn't crossed paths with him for two years, had been grateful for the ocean that lay between them, for the first of six pregnancies where she hadn't fended off his punches or cigarette burns or shoves off the bed.

But there he was, Ben Harrow, her nightmare of a husband, muscles twitching in anticipation. And next to him stood
Wellfleet's chief of police, who held a warrant for my mother's
arrest.

Though I couldn't see the violence that followed, science tells
me I could feel it, and while I can't consciously remember it, my
body surely holds its traces. Mom was in her third trimester,
when my developing brain was forming hundreds of synapses
a second. How did the furious firing of Ben Harrow's fists and
curses ricochet through the synaptic firings in my brain? As Mom's
cortisol levels spiked, were mine shooting high? As she flung her
wedding ring at him, as she shielded herself, as the chief of police
intervened to arrest Ben, as well, were the early neural networks
for extreme emotion and its correlate, extreme behavior, carving
enduring pathways in my gray matter?

This is what could be called an impossible memory: inscribed
but unreadable, a guess and a ghost. Though other ghosts popu-
late this memoir, Ben Harrow's is the most haunting, and this
early experience of him—a bodily trace I can neither consciously
remember nor touch in the physical archive of scars—remains
at once invisible and diffusely present, a radioactive element in
a constellation of phenomena that lights one of the many ways
I could describe my childhood. This episode also alludes to the
lifeblood of nascent memory, its fountainhead: who we are in
relation to our mother, first in the womb, and then during our
journey outside of it.

I did not learn about this birthday surprise until I was forty
years old, five years after I started interviewing my mother as
I raked our family's past for clues to my present. I knew she regret-
ted her first marriage. But nothing I had heard in our earlier
interviews, much less during my childhood, had prepared me
for the jealous vengeance that drove Ben Harrow to Mom's door,
for what happened in that roughly furnished kitchen, or for the
shocking arrest and trial of my mother, which lie at the heart of

the secrets it took me many years to unravel and then stitch back together in the writing of this book.

In reconstructing this kitchen scene as a kind of episodic memory, based as it is not only on the stories I have hunted down but also on legal records I have found, I am searching, of course, for another way to explain myself to myself, to relate the past to the present, and to create a personal narrative that is as coherent and as close to truth as possible.

I want to be able to point to events in my past and say, "This is why I am vigilant; this is why I gloried in beating up boys as a child and in wrestling boyfriends as an adult (and in mock pummeling my much taller and stronger husband, who laughs good-naturedly as he parries my fine-boned fists). But it's a tricky business to pin the present on the past (though where else should we pin it?), largely because memory itself is so partial, and our choices about which stories to spotlight so consequential not only for our sense of self and our internal well-being but also for the social dynamics of our life.

In the same way that memoirists select their most salient memories to illustrate the story they want to share, we all, to varying degrees, curate our memories to tell the story of who we understand ourselves to be, or who we hope to become in the future. In writing this book I can choose stories that tell a tale of victimhood or of lucky escapes. Stories of resilience or cruelty or kindness. Of a childhood besotted with the natural world, or one dreaming about what lay beyond the arched bridge latching the slip of sand I called home to the continent.

Underlying these choices is the recognition that most events in a person's history can be framed in varying ways, interpreted one way for good, another for ill, and in the telling shape a life. It's what friends do in conversation and writers do on the page. And it's what many of us do in our private stream of self-talk, those interior words, phrases, even conversations or rants that can dishearten or encourage, mislead or calm us.

To be honest, I don't want to count this bodily trauma as my first "memory," and I don't have to. I can just as easily go further back, to the first months of my mother's pregnancy with me, when she was in love with my father, a quiet, still-dashing sportsman nearly ten years older who was as impatient as she was for the divorce that would allow them to marry.

A machinist and land surveyor, Dad marked the seasons with golfing, hunting, gardening, and sailing. He had served in England as a bomber mechanic during World War II and then, during the Korean War, far inside the Arctic Circle, where he helped to build a secret air base, code-named Blue Jay, in a frigid and isolated stretch of northern Greenland accessible only by boat, plane, or dogsled. After his discharge, Dad settled in Wellfleet, where his parents and two brothers had moved from Hingham, Massachusetts, several years earlier. Floating between houses, Dad, still a bachelor in his late thirties, spent much of his time with his brother's family in the eighteenth-century, hip-roofed colonial on Lecount Hollow Road next to Mom's nineteenth-century saltbox.

It was just a few steps along the privet hedge fronting Mom's yard to her neighbors' house, as full of children as her own. When Mom met Dad on a visit next door in 1955 ("I caught him watching me over the top of his newspaper," she laughs), her husband was living on an Air Force base in Germany and had another lover. By the time Mom was pregnant with me three years later, it had been two years since she'd separated from Ben Harrow for the last time. During the spring days of her pregnancy, Dad brought her flowers, early vegetables from his garden, and bottles of wine to share after the kids went to bed.

Mom, not only the wittiest girl of Tewksbury High but also the "class flirt," no doubt sparkled as she arranged daffodils in a cut-glass vase or poured another glass of Madeira, love's signature of dopamine and oxytocin coursing through her, through us. Again, this is not a memory, but it's a beginning. A beginning of a story whose shape gives substance to a history I can't recall and yet feels vital.

My sense of those early days is, of course, reliant on the stories I've been told—or more accurately, those I wrested out of my mother, coaxed out of other relatives, and fashioned from photographs and any relevant documents I could find, from letters and diaries to travel logs and court records. Perhaps more than we like to admit, autobiographical memory is a cobbled affair, an inner phenomenon that feels personal and archival but is inherently social and malleable. We intentionally and unintentionally collaborate on our autobiographical stories all the time, adding details remembered by others around the supper table or revising our understanding of what happened, persuaded by their perspectives. Or the story changes slightly, depending on who our listeners are, and as that story evolves, the way it is encoded in our memory often follows suit.

Even the act of unspoken recall is a collaboration of different parts of the brain, with visual, auditory, and emotional elements, for example, firing together to conjure a remembered image or scene. Every memory of an event is a neural act of reconstruction, with details shifting slightly, one element dropped perhaps, another added, still another amplified.

Unsettling as this variation might seem, perhaps it can be viewed not as the enemy of truth but as a tint that changes with the light, refracting more than one true version of the same event. I have come to think of this slight remixing of memory not as pollution but as the addition or alteration of color. The point is not complete accuracy, which is a chimera, but a plausible and strong narrative that anchors us in our life and in a familial and cultural lineage, a story of self that pulses with meaning and dissipates the uncertainty that can keep us turning, half-blind, in a fog of shallow history.

In many ways, I wish I were less captivated by the past, wish I did not feel this urge to reconstruct it as faithfully as possible, to pinpoint not only names and dates but also motives and consequences, to write this story. I sometimes think of my fascination with personal narrative as a weakness, an attempt to regulate a fluctuating sense of self by fixing in place the details of my family history, my own history, and Wellfleet's history, as if they were knots on a rope suspended between the past and the future, allowing me to move backward and forward without losing my way.

This fascination also speaks, however, to my desire to know and understand, to recognize the experiences of those I have loved, to piece together a narrative that provides insights and the scaffolding on which to construct my story, our story.

Other kinds of "impossible" memories, many of them good—a few even transformative—have played a part in molding my sense of myself and of my history and future. I am thinking here of memories that beggar belief or could not have happened, such as flying from the top of a dune on towel wings to land on toasted sand before dashing toward the sea. Or seeing Santa's reindeer alight on the roof, or glimpsing elephants and giraffes among the locusts and scrub oaks of Wellfleet's back roads. This first mental image, however, I consider a dream; the second a wish fulfilment; the third a product of my imagination while bouncing with my sisters and cousins in the rusting bed of Dad's turquoise, side-step Chevrolet truck on weekend "safaris." These are happy memories, but they are not persuasive ones.

Two other "impossible" memories from my childhood are less easy to dismiss, more complicated. They indelibly marked my early years, becoming talismans that have accompanied me over the decades, images that carry a question and a promise. Both took place in the upstairs bedroom that I shared for a time during elementary school with two of my sisters, before our teenaged brothers volunteered for Vietnam.

Our small house had three bedrooms: Geoff and Ted shared a room downstairs, and we three girls slept upstairs. Our room sat across the tiny landing from our parents' room, two boxed wings attached to the staircase spine and connected at the back by a narrow bathroom. The room I shared with Thelma and Beth was messy and cozy, with knotty pine walls and windowpanes streaked with bubbles that bent and blurred the branches of the yew bush outside.

In the first memory, I am sleeping in my small twin bed under the eaves when a sound awakens me. It's not the familiar creaking of our old house, but a rustle infused with a presence, an intelligence demanding attention. I turn my head toward the hall; perhaps our cat Rusty is on a midnight prowl, or my mother is climbing to bed after an evening of sewing.

Standing in the doorway is neither cat nor mother. A tall stranger, regal and ragged, fills the frame. Her long, gray-blond hair cascades past the shoulders of a lacy dress that sweeps the floor. She is radiant, nearly translucent, all brown gold and dust. Stunned, uncomprehending, I lie mute in her gaze. A few seconds is all I can stand, and I shut my eyes. But that frightens me, too, so I chance a second glance. The doorway still shimmers with her unearthly form. Trapped in my bed, unable to cry out, I do the only thing I feel capable of: I curl toward the wall and pretend to sleep, not daring to look again.

In the morning I float toward wakefulness until, memory flooding, I open my eyes and twist to face the threshold. Empty. Rolling back onto my blue-ticking pillow, its feathers grown lumpy in the sea air, I gaze at the ceiling, its knots and swirls my private menagerie. With a thrill bordering on fright, I wonder, *could I have seen my guardian angel?*

A year or two later, during the dark blue hours of a spring night, I wake in this same room to another figure, this one watching me from the foot of my narrow bed, where she sits draped in black, a shroud covering her head. She has none of the radiance of my ghost-angel, but the curve of her back is all tenderness and care.

I stifle a cry of astonishment, my heart flailing, my skin as porous as cobwebs against the night world. Again I turn over and pretend to sleep, pulling my scratchy wool blanket over my shoulder. I then dare to look again, but this time the figure has disappeared.

An early June whip-poor-will trills familiar notes of longing as I hug myself back to sleep. In the morning, contemplating what I have seen, I decide, *someone must be guarding me.*

She was a welcome addition to my world, a different kind of adult than those around me. My parents—was it their generation or their disposition?—didn't play with us, or read to us, or even supervise us so much as open the door and shout at our backs to be home in time for supper.

While they went to work, did house chores, and drank cocktails, my sisters, cousins, and I played games and dodged dangers both small and big. We lit fires on top of the sandpit, climbed high into trees to launch pine-cone missiles at out-of-state cars, leapt from mound to mound in the medieval shades of the white cedar swamp, and hiked down the old railroad bed to Duck Pond, chanting "Kumala, kumala, kumala savesta" or swelling our small hearts with the cry of "Five Hundred Miles."

After crossing the scrubby flank of the power lines and racing down the path to the pond, we'd stash brown paper bags with bologna sandwiches and MacIntosh apples in the hollows between tree roots, then fling ourselves into the dappled water. Duck Pond's smooth, sandy bottom, edged with a golden-brown ring of softened pine needles, shimmered with ribbons of light refracted from the surface. Though barely nine or ten years old, we often dared ourselves to swim across to the other side, one of us sometimes going to the trouble of finding a raft. Like dolphins astride a boat, the rest of us slapped our way forward in a country crawl or rolled over to make water wings, pausing in the middle to take a breather and measure our gains against shifting clouds.

The ghost-angel's powers were as welcome inside our house as they were in Wellfleet's ponds and woods. My father, a patriarch with inflexible habits—supper at 5:30 p.m., golfing on Wednesdays and Saturdays, a date with Walter Cronkite every evening—had a volatile temper that Mom never seemed to notice, perhaps because she so often slipped out in the evenings.

My parents had married five months after my birth, scooting up to New Hampshire as soon as Mom's divorce from Ben Harrow was finalized. They had planned to visit the justice of the peace on Valentine's Day, a Saturday, only to find all the appointments filled. Undeterred, they married a day earlier, because as Mom laughingly points out, "there were loads of openings for Friday the thirteenth!"

In the three seconds it took Dad to sign the marriage certificate, he became not only a husband for the first time but also the acknowledged father or stepfather of six children. His mother, my Nana Lyda, was furious that her strapping son had dumped a widow with a large property on Nauhaught Bluff overlooking Wellfleet Harbor to marry a young divorcée who was too fertile and flat-out broke. Mom's charms—she was artistic and generous, with playful good looks and a figure to die for—were lost on my grandmother. Her needs were not.

With my father's two brothers in Wellfleet, I also had a dozen unsupervised cousins next door or a quick jaunt down Route 6, some of them more likely to tie me to a tree and stuff garter snakes down my shirt than play games of Red Rover.

But it was my brilliant, dyslexic half-brother Geoff who most inventively booby-trapped my play world, with frogs in my bed, plastic vomit in my bath water, and nooses slung over the living room rafters in mock execution of my dolls. Sparking with animal magnetism, Geoff built hot rods from scratch, a cigarette hanging from his mouth and a devoted team handing him screwdrivers or wire cutters. (My cousin Richard, head twirling with blond curls, knew the difference between pliers and a socket wrench when still in diapers.) Geoff made bombs from whatever he could steal during nighttime raids on the military camp at the old wireless Marconi site, crashed cars along the power lines so he could fix them, and devised electrical experiments of every sort. Most of these involved frogs, but some required human subjects.

One of these experiments took place in our garage, a clapboard cavern smelling of grease, salt, and gasoline. Much of the interior was taken up with antique furniture my mother planned to refin-ish, along with the toboggan and sleds, gardening tools, fishing tackle, saws, outboard motors, and bicycles. A huge, rusting, aqua-green freezer—another hand-me-down from my grandparents—stood immediately to the right of the garage door opening.

My father used to spread newspapers on top of this freezer to scale and fillet the striped bass and bluefish he caught in early morning retreats to the back shore, that night's supper. I loved to watch the sweep of his knife and feel the scaly, then smooth, sides of the fish. The severed head, however, always unsettled me. On hot summer days, my sisters and I would prop open the heavy lid of this freezer and fold ourselves over the edge, lowering our shoulders into the mist and dangling there for a minute or two to cool ourselves off.

In Geoff's garage trick, he rounded up my sisters, cousins, and me, none of us older than ten, and placed us in a circle, instructing us to hold hands. I usually stood with my back to the freezer, near the open garage door, while my brother, sixteen, sat on a three-legged wooden stool under a bare bulb at the opposite end, a foot pedal he had yanked from Mom's sewing machine on the cement floor at his feet. He had clipped and stripped the end of the cord leading from the pedal to the machine, exposing two wires. Plugging the cord in, he pinched one bare wire between his thumb and fingertips and passed the other to a child, saying, "hold tight." Then he stepped on the pedal.

Hands twitching and scalps tingling, we popped screams as the shocks traveled through us, watching each other's faces as we tried to catch electricity in motion. How long could we hang on? In his happy place, Geoff explored the foot pedal's range and his guinea pigs' endurance.

"If I stepped on it light, you'd get a little bit of current," he remembers. "If I stepped on it hard, you'd get a good shock. But I'd never use the full 110 volts on you kids, 'cause, you know, that could cause heart problems."

All my life tourists have told me I was raised in paradise, but even paradise can require a trip-wire vigilance given the right combination of tools, woods, and troublemakers. Small and scrappy, I was ready to fight in a spin-around second and gave as good as I got. Yet kindness, even in ghostly hue, caught my heart and imagination. I suppose that's why I was more reassured than frightened by the ghosts, whose visits hinted at an infinite, mysterious world across the everyday threshold.

What these apparitions suggested, of course, was not so much the reality of ghosts (I am still agnostic on that score, tending toward disbelief), but how I responded to the uncertain, sometimes scary, world I lived in. Even if I only imagined these events (I don't believe I did, though I don't understand how they occurred), I am glad for the way my vivid, realistic recall of these otherworldly figures helped me to hold on to forces of good in the universe, to feel myself aligned with and protected by them.

Especially for the first few years after my ghost-angel sightings, my thoughts turned toward these visitors whenever I met with unexplainable luck or small miracles, like finding extra treats in the green freezer, or having my lost shoes appear next to me on school mornings just before Dad's hurry-up voice turned dangerous. By returning to those visitations again and again, I not only fixed them in my memory but also, I now see, wove them into an interior narrative that helped form my sense of myself in the world and of the world itself.

Curiously, I have no memory of talking about these two experiences while growing up. I did record them, however, thanks to my beloved English teacher at Wellfleet Elementary School, Mrs. Winslow, who assigned us journal writing in fifth and sixth grades. Instead of telling everyone I knew about these miracles, which felt too strange to share, I mulled them over in my head and on the pages of my journal. It was not until I was in my twenties that the stories came out, prompted by my great-uncle Clyde.

Clyde was easily my favorite uncle. Childless and gruff, he had worked a hodgepodge of jobs over his long life: as a mill worker and cab driver in Lowell in the 1920s, a streetcar conductor, a dairy farmer, and a gas station attendant, smuggling contraband candy bars to my mother, his niece, while she was growing up. The last and longest job he held was as a machinist in the block-long, red-brick Dennison Manufacturing plant in south Framingham, nicknamed "tag town" for Dennison's bestselling product, shipping tags, which had guided Union military crates during the Civil War.

When my great-uncle visited Wellfleet, he'd bring us an endless store of Dennison paper products: donut-shaped stickies to go over torn notebook paper holes, gummed shipping labels with bright red borders, tabs we used to organize our schoolwork, and all manner of stationery and folders. Minutes after arriving he'd ferry my sisters and me to the First National Grocery on Route 6 in Wellfleet, where we loaded up on potato chips, pretzels, and six-packs of Coke, treats Mom seldom could afford (for years, Captain Crunch was a victory purchase). In July and August he'd drive us to the docks for ice cream at the Harbor Freeze, where as a teenager I spent two summers mixing frappes and watching boat traffic.

Though indulgent with us, my great-uncle lived off a tiny Social Security check and was frugal to the core, cutting napkins in two to make them last longer and wearing the same clothes all the time I knew him: green twill pants, a nubbly gray cardigan, and a flannel plaid shirt, switching to a short-sleeved polyester blend when the summer heat hit. He helped Mom save money by fixing things whenever he visited. He replaced windowpanes that Geoff shot out with his BB gun. Tore out rotten wood and fiddled with faucets. One afternoon he came across a tangled mass of embroidery threads my mother used for quilting and for two hours sorted them by color, wrapping odd strands around matchbook covers.

Uncle Clyde lived just a two-hour drive from Wellfleet, in a cement and tarpaper eyesore he stopped working on the day his wife, Persis, died of colon cancer in 1964. They had moved to

Ashland in the 1950s to build a home on two acres of land with a small apple orchard, a modest spread they named Meadowbrook. In every way she could, Persis threw herself into helping Clyde, who during evenings and weekends did most of the construction. Persis wielded a pickax and shovel, hauled lumber, and planted the flower garden. "Every shovelful I got out, he didn't have to lift," she wrote in her diary, which is filled not only with stories of their building Meadowbrook together, but also with clippings of the poems she published, along with recipes, humorous quotes, nature images from magazines, and swatches of fabric from family wedding dresses dating to the mid-1800s. Clyde, whose life had known precious few kindnesses, adored her.

"She'd be alive today if it wasn't for the damn doctor," Clyde wrote in one of the many letters he sent to the far-flung places I lived in after graduating from high school: Finland, France, Austria, Switzerland. "When I got his bill," he added, "I took it to his office and told him where he could shove it." Inside the envelope, Clyde, who knew I had been down with the flu, slipped a scrap of pink and white wrapping paper on which he had typed a list of "Ten Healthful Foods" for me to eat, along with their benefits. The list included "Broccoli—Vitamins A & C." and "Flounder—High in protein, Lower Saturated Fat." As was his custom, he decorated the back of the envelope with wildlife and smiley stickers.

Losing the heart of his home after Persis died, Clyde strung up sheets in place of doors and left the cinderblock uncovered, the windows untrimmed. For the next twenty-four years, no one used the front door facing the street, because it had no steps—just a four-foot drop between the door's threshold and the ground. Tacked-up plastic covered the cotton-candy insulation stuffed between two-by-fours in the guest bedroom. In the rest of the house, Sheetrocked walls stood primed and waiting.

Inside, ashtrays lay everywhere, littered with nubs of the most powerful stick of all: unfiltered Camels. As stubborn a fixture of my uncle's life as canned wax beans with fried liver, they were easy to filch during his visits to Wellfleet. I had my first smoke in elementary school, followed by an hour of nausea as I curled on my gold chenille bedspread in the upstairs pine room. Although he growled until the end that "cigarettes never did me any harm," Clyde survived a stroke and was diagnosed with lung cancer in his mid-eighties.

Years earlier, after an abdominal surgery, my great-uncle had written me, "I haven't the slightest idea what happens after you die, some say you go to heaven or hell, and some say you come back to earth in another person, they call it reincarnation, who knows or cares, I don't." But even Clyde had no interest in facing the end alone. Death notice in hand, he looked toward Mom, his beloved niece, and her house on Lecount Hollow.

It was the winter and spring of 1987, when I was twenty-eight and living at home for a year before heading to graduate school in Atlanta. Mom made Uncle Clyde comfortable in her bedroom on the ground floor, and she moved upstairs to the pine room.

Emaciated from the cancer he refused to treat, Uncle Clyde shuffled into the kitchen one morning and barked, "You've got a goddamned ghost in this house!"

"I know that, Unk," Mom replied, still half asleep. She flipped on the Mr. Coffee and sliced a Portuguese muffin, dropping it into the toaster. "But I've never seen it. I wish I would. Tell me about it?"

Weak but wired to talk, Uncle Clyde sat at the kitchen table while Mom fixed his two soft-boiled eggs. "I woke up in the night and it was standing at the foot of the bed," he said.

"What'd you do?" she asked.

"I told her, 'Get out of here!' and closed my eyes."

Mom smiled as she dunked a tea bag in a mug for Clyde, then plopped the sodden sack onto a gold-edged trinket dish to save for a second round.

"A few minutes later I opened my eyes and the ghost was still there," Clyde continued. "*Dammit*, I thought. So I yelled, 'Get the *hell* out of here!'"

That evening several of us sat at Mom's long pine supper table, laughing about Uncle Clyde's midnight meeting and for the first time sharing our own ghost stories. I described my visitor in the doorway, the most vivid of my two sightings, and Thelma said she'll never forget the night she saw a ghost in Mom's downstairs bedroom, where Clyde was now sleeping, when we three girls shared the tiny room during my preschool years. "She had long hair and a flowing dress," Thelma remembered. "She stood at the foot of Beth's cot, looked me in the eyes, then slipped out the window. I had lost a tooth and wanted to see the tooth fairy so badly, but I saw her instead!"

None of us questioned the reality of these memories, and none of us seemed surprised by them. Even before these events were voiced, they had become stitched, I believe, into the fabric of our life in that house. But these were blind stitches, invisible on the right side and hardly seen on the wrong, much like the ghosts themselves. Did the ghosts help to create that shared life or, rather, to explain it? This, I suspect, is one of the functions of "impossible memories": translating psychological truths into perceptual phenomena that allow us to externalize a struggle or hope or fear or yearning that is cutting too close to the bone and is hard to articulate, even to ourselves.

Then again, maybe Mom's house *is* haunted. Fifteen years after Uncle Clyde's passing, my brother Geoff, who left for Vietnam at eighteen and seldom looked back, heard my story and asked, "You saw a ghost, too?"

A familiar charge twitched the air.

He paused, then said in a low voice: "I saw her twice."

"You're kidding," I said, "When was this?"

"Once before I went to 'Nam and once after. Upstairs, in the doorway of the pine room."

I went very still. "My god, that's exactly where I saw her!"

"I can still see her face," said Geoff, his voice drifting across the threshold.

My scalp prickled. "Were you afraid?"

"*No*," he spat, snapping back to the present. "I told her, 'I ain't got time to fuck with you!' and rolled back over to sleep."

While others have also seen a ghost in Mom's house (or perhaps *the* ghost? I am not sure how these things work), one particular sighting seems to confirm all the others, because any priming of expectations was so unlikely.

In the way of families with secrets, I have a first cousin who was unknown to us for nearly thirty years. Raised by Sephardic Jews in Brooklyn, Lynda first began to suspect she was adopted in her early teens, when a Punnett square assignment in science class revealed her family's combination of phenotypes to be genetically improbable, if not impossible. It took years, however, and hard-won documentation, for Lynda to get her parents to admit she was adopted, then the services of a private investigator to find her biological parents, who had serendipitously married a few years after her birth. Their reunion was joyous, with blood trumping bigotry. My conservative Christian aunt and uncle couldn't have cared less that their daughter was Jewish and married to a woman, so grateful were they for their reconnection. That first phone call, in my aunt's lexicon, was the answer to a prayer she had uttered every day for twenty-seven years.

My birth-cousin Lynda managed to merge her beloved adoptive family and her newfound biological one better than anyone I know, with acceptance on both sides of the divide. Shortly after meeting her birth parents, Lynda and her wife launched a whirlwind tour to meet as many people as possible in the family, including my mother, her Aunt Shirley, in Wellfleet.

On their first night there, sleeping in the upstairs pine room, Lynda woke to the sound of footsteps on the stairs. Sensing someone else in the room, she peered over her wife's shoulder and was startled by the sight of a translucent figure dressed in an "old-timey sleeping gown" and quavering at the doorway, its arm stretched toward the door handle. Was it a man or a woman? Lynda couldn't tell. As she stared, the figure neither moved nor disappeared.

Squeezing her eyes shut, Lynda frantically tried to process the impossibility of what she had just seen. What should she do? Where could she go in a new and unfamiliar house? Should she wake her wife? Could light be leaking in from somewhere else, creating an illusion? A long moment later she opened her eyes to find the visitor still present, now just a few feet away. Terrified, she buried her head in the pillow but was too frightened not to look again. This time, the room was swathed in darkness. Unable to fall back to sleep, she nestled close to her wife and waited uneasily for dawn.

The next morning was Sunday, and I called to chat with my mother. "Lynda saw the ghost!" she announced, handing the phone to my new cousin. My arms tingled as Lynda described my early childhood vision in that same doorway, although the creature I had seen was decidedly female and, to my young eyes, regal and beautiful, whereas Lynda couldn't tell if all that hair was a man's night cap or a woman's rat nest.

"Welcome to the family," I laughed.

It seems pointless to argue that none of these, nor any of the other ghost sightings in Mom's house I've since heard about, could be "true," or that Ben Harrow's mistreatment of my mother while she was pregnant is not somehow carried in my body, influencing my being in a way not dissimilar to cognitive memories. Ben Harrow's cruelties toward my mother—which persisted for months after that scene in the kitchen—are more than information, more than a collection of events I have been told about. Most scientists would agree they had a cellular effect, and I wonder if they became a kind of implicit memory that found expression in my behavior and my understanding of the world.

This is the great seduction, of course: trying to establish lines of cause and effect so we can better know and understand ourselves. But even science, that largely trusty compass, can foil the desire for certainty. It both muddied my story and reassured me,

for example, when I learned that prenatal stress does not necessarily dictate the script of a child's life. Children whose mothers
were depressed or abused while pregnant do have an increased
risk of psychopathology, but many children are not measurably
affected, while those who suffer don't necessarily share the same
problems. And all of these effects are modulated by genetic risk.
In other words, as with most things in life, what we bring to the
table and what's already on (or missing from) it flex in tandem to
shape the cognitive and emotional lines of our lives.

It's tempting to contrast such "impossible memories" with
those we can document through photographs or corroborating
witnesses, or even to dismiss them outright, but even imagined
memories that feel real, that have that "being-there" or "from-the-
inside" quality, can affect our psyches and behavior regardless of
whether they represent actual events.

While some might argue that it's impossible that ghosts
(because they don't exist) appeared in my mother's house, it's not
impossible that I remember them. But how does one "remember"
in a visceral way something that might not have happened? What
is the relationship between belief and memory, and how blurred
is the line between them? These are complicated questions. With
the passage of time, it can become hard to distinguish between
truth and fiction, between an event we experienced and one we
heard about, especially when the latter is emotionally charged,
because emotions are so influential in encoding and amplifying
memory.

Our visual imagination also plays a role, of course. That said,
not everyone visualizes to the same degree—and that's normal.
Aphantasics, for example, are unable to visually imagine an object
or a face. They might know its features and structure and have
the language to describe it, but they can't form a picture of that
face in their mind. They are also more likely to experience what
psychologists call "severely deficient autobiographical memory."
Instead of recalling and reliving episodic moments, aphantasics rely on what they know, and this kind of semantic memory,

comprised of facts about one's past, doesn't have quite the same pull as reliving vivid or emotionally charged scenes.

Most of us produce varying degrees of visual imagery, from the fleeting and dim to the clear and moderately animated. But on the other end of the spectrum, those with hyperphantasia enjoy entire, life-like scenes in technicolor projected onto their mental screens. This vibrant "mind's eye"—which I sometimes wish I had—may well be connected to genuinely impossible memories, because the imagined scene is drawn in such detail that it feels like a sensory experience and might be recalled as such. Indeed, hyperphantasics tend to have many more fleshed-out autobiographical memories than those with weaker visual imagery.

Hyperphantasia reminds me a bit of dreaming, but nocturnal visions are crucially different, in that most of the time (except when having a lucid dream) we are completely—emotionally and perceptually—in the dream world, and we experience it as real without any kind of reality check or ability to control it. This is one of the reasons dreams can (re)produce a huge range of emotions, from mild amusement to terror to ecstasy to reconciliation. But dreams are also conceptual achievements, and many of mine have influenced decisions and deepened my understanding of situations and relationships. They have also affected my feelings toward, and even memories of, my father, and I talk about this in a later chapter.

For now I'd like to caution against too fast an adherence to what is documentable in our assessment of impossible memories. I will never be able to prove that a ghost lives in Mom's old house, despite having triangulated it, much as a historian would, with others' observations. Nor will I be able to prove, despite the support of science, that Ben Harrow's revenge on my mother when pregnant with me is inscribed on my body and affects who I am today. Proof is not the primary issue. The story we tell is.

Correspondence to actual events is of course essential; otherwise, we'd just be making up our life and living in a dissociated or delusional state. But our memory of past events is unavoidably an interpretation of "what happened." None of our memories is the thing itself but our representations of it, which can shift, both in the process of recall and as a result of what we may have learned about the situation, others' interpretations, or subsequent changes in a relationship.

The inescapably interpretive nature of perception does not make a memory untrue, but it does often make it one of several possible true versions, as siblings growing up with the same—but very differently experienced—parents can attest. Some elements in our memories might be fictions, but they're *our* fictions, and they help to construct the story we tell to and about ourselves. As time passes we might look at an experience from another angle, hold its facets to a different light, much as I did over the years with my ghost-angels and, later, with my father. The operative point is that our stories not only reflect our lived experience but also shape it, with consequences for who we are. We tend to live up to, as well as be constrained by, the stories we choose to tell about ourselves and our relationships.

To abandon my "impossible memories" because I was not able to cognitively process my experiences while in the womb and don't know how to explain ghosts would feel like trading one kind of truth (or untruth) for another, but at a loss.

It is reasonable, and in many cases freeing, to call into question details of specific memories, but to invalidate these memories altogether, to repudiate their gist, would yank threads from a tapestry I've woven over a lifetime, tearing it in ways I might not be able to repair. That's not a risk I'm willing to take. So I'll rely on the sturdiest threads I can find—not only personal memories but also diaries, oral histories, newspaper archives, photographs, court documents, and letters—as I weave this story of a life, of a family, of a house on sand.

# 2

# Proof of Other Worlds

~

"You find the damnedest questions to ask," says my mother, ripping open a pink packet of Sweet'N Low and shaking the tiny crystals into a second cup of coffee. Her blue eyes, clearer now than in her forties or fifties, scan me with an appraising look. I am home in Wellfleet on another summer visit, and we've gravitated to our favorite spots on the screen porch running the length of our two-hundred-year-old shingled house. The porch, built after Mom became sober and we started acting more like a family again, holds three chaise lounges, a dish cabinet, a full-size refrigerator, and a picnic table large enough to seat the stream of children and grandchildren, neighbors, friends, and AA pals who stop by for a chat or caffeine fix. For several months of the year this graying addition serves as Shirley-Central, the place where we play cards, share boiled ham suppers or Chinese take-out, snooze for a bit, and talk about our day. On this visit I'm after the stories, trying to get Mom to disclose more of her past and feeling like a mosquito she might swat if I circle too close.

Seldom a match for her repartee, I ignore my mother's remark and turn to look past the moldering beach towels draped over the wood railing, toward the rosa rugosa and irises she planted long ago on a hilly rise in the backyard, a green wave swelling with pastel sprays each summer. Beyond the yard's cultivated edge, I can spot the purple blossoms of money plants, pokeweed bending with magenta berries, and swamp maples lashed with poison ivy. The shiny leaves of three conjure bottles of pink calamine lotion, a staple in our medicine cabinet and balm of my childhood. Catching the direction of my gaze, Mom says, "You couldn't pay me to go down there." But it isn't the itchy pustules she fears. It's the black snakes—some as long as five or six feet—that jigger her nerves, never the steadiest to begin with.

Returning to our conversation, I float more questions, and Mom's responses begin to spark with anger, amusement, and frustration. I know I've been asking too much of her, prodding her to dredge up memories she'd rather leave mired in forgetfulness. Though the sharing of stories is, arguably, the glue that holds families together, it's not as if wanting stories means you'll get them.

While a few of Mom's reminiscences have popped out over tea, games of rummy, or runs to the Stop and Shop in Orleans, most have been harder to come by, and this particular afternoon is another round of a complicated tug-of-war we've been in for decades: me straining to yank Mom across her shifting line of silence into recounting scenes I hope will unriddle her past and clarify my present, and Mom pressing her heels into sandy ground I know will eventually give. But no matter how hard I pull, what tumbles over to my side is never enough. Perhaps my own ambivalence plays a part. I am greedy for my mother's memories, but I also want to protect her, not to hurt her.

Like a stumped crossword-solver, I've turned to others over the years to fill in some of the blanks—people like Charles, Mom's French fisherman lover for over forty years, and Nana, Mom's mother, the Puritan paragon she never managed to please. As is perhaps typical for any family sleuth tramping through memory's borderlands, I have heard some stories I now wish I hadn't but discovered others that have allowed me, finally, to trace the shape of my mother's life while more convincingly staking out the boundaries of my own.

In many ways, it feels like the task of a lifetime, this differentiation between her and me. While some daughters shape their identity through reaction against that first mirroring image, others of us fall prey to overidentification, to searching for self-understanding not only in our parents' faces but also in their histories. More than empathy, it's a kind of erasure of self, this merging with and psychically privileging a parent's life, a mother's dramas, which of course bleed into one's own.

This merging was most intense during my teenage years and twenties, the years of rapid becoming for any person. I often felt as if a double-exposed filmstrip whirred in my head: my mother's experiences superimposed on mine, or mine on hers—the order didn't really matter, since the effect was the same: a confusing melding of two lives, of two narrative arcs.

Although therapy in my mid-twenties, and again in my mid-thirties, offered some distance, it was only as I sought out details and storylines over many years of conversations and emails with Mom that I discovered that hearing, recording, and piecing together her dramas would help me to externalize them, to place them before me on the table instead of living inside them, to have them flow through my pen instead of my veins. And in this externalization taking shape on the page, a different kind of internalization was able to take place, one less shackling, one that allowed for recognition without haunting.

Mom starts by reminding me of where she grew up: in a large Victorian home on Rogers Street in Tewksbury, Massachusetts, a graceful homestead just over the Lowell line that her great-grandparents had bought in the early 1900s. Pear and apple orchards bordered the property, and a brook ran through nearby fields first planted by Wamesit Indians. Stone walls and pathways separated fields of carrots, corn, and potatoes, while ducks paddled across an irrigation pond near a huge boulder with indentations deep enough for Mom and her friends to build fires for roasting food.

My grandmother Bertha had wrangled the property into her name in exchange for caring for her grandmother

Henrietta—my great-great grandmother, who descended from Truro sea captains but whose real crew sailed off the pages of Dickens's *Hard Times*. Henrietta's stinginess was legendary: she once berated Nana for using a few teaspoons of her sugar on a Sunday when Nana had a friend over and her own meagre supply had run out.

"That woman was unbelievable," Nana says. "We lived with practically nothing, and no reason for it neither." After Henrietta's long sparring match with life ended, Nana collected her prize, and she and my grandfather Bumpa transformed the bare-bones, antiquated boarding house that Henrietta had run into the kind of home Nana had always wished for, with refinished inlaid floors, French doors, and stately windows framed with damask drapes she sewed herself.

"It was a beautiful house," Nana says, a tight note of wistfulness in her voice, "and everyone thought we had more money than we did." She hung white wallpaper dancing with blue and yellow flowers in the breakfast room and furnished it with a wooden table she painted bright blue, while upstairs she created the kind of bedroom for Mom she wished she herself had had as a child, with dreamy, orchid-colored walls and matching furniture and curtains. Mom's favorite space, however, was the attic that Nana, for good reason, hated.

"Our attic was full of the best of things," Mom says, pleasure lighting her eyes as she travels half a century back. "My grand-father's Massachusetts Militia uniform, hundreds of his books, old spool beds, big trunks. One was full of chiffon flapper dresses with handkerchief hemlines. Another had my costumes, tutus, and ballet shoes. I lived to play there on rainy days, the only time my mother would let us."

"The house on Rogers Street" has sparkled like a gold nugget in my mother's reminiscences, the touchstone of her happiest childhood memories. But it was also the place where she was con-stantly watched and diligently trained, suspected of misbehavior at every turn.

"My mother sent me to dance lessons, elocution lessons, piano lessons, and comportment lessons," Mom says, tapping out her refinement with a soft thud against the white porch tablecloth, a repurposed bedsheet. "She wanted to make me into another Shirley Temple, to be happy on her terms, not mine."

I glance at Mom's oversized rings, etched with dirt from planting impatiens in the slate-blue flower boxes along the front of the house. Her favorite gardening tool is a makeshift trowel: a wide, sterling-silver buffet spoon from the house on Rogers Street, now dented and misshapen from its move out of the house and into the yard.

After a pause, Mom adds in a low voice, "I once had a dream, a horrible dream about my mother. I'm thirteen or fourteen years old and in my bed. I hear my mother's footsteps on the stairs, and I'm terrified, because—God, I hate to tell you this—I think she's demented and coming after me. She's sure I've done something wrong, but I haven't, really. I see my mother's head and shoulders as she reaches the top landing, and I'm so terrified, I bolt awake!"

Mom shifts in her green plastic chair and crosses her legs, her knee bouncing to the beat of an old, relentless argument. "So much of the guilt in my life came from what my mother expected me to do, not what I did!" she says, angry tears starting even at seventy. "She always thought I was going to embarrass her."

Nana, essentially, agreed. "Your mother gave me so much trouble," she complained to me long before Mom told me this dream. "She was pretty as a movie star but so strong-willed we couldn't handle her."

Like many children with controlling mothers, Mom had little inkling of how Nana's chaotic childhood—so different from her own—had driven her to the kind of aspirational order Mom spent a lifetime outrageously thwarting. And like many mothers, Nana could not help but unconsciously try to heal herself, to redeem her blighted childhood, by taking the naked slate of a newborn child, her first, and cultivating her to become everything she wished she herself had been: well fed, well dressed, accomplished, sheltered in a safe home and raised in a respected family.

In a common intergenerational calculus, the magnitude of Nana's ambition for Mom was matched only by the emotional and material deprivations of her own early years. Born into an unhappy marriage that ended in separation when Nana was four, my grandmother and her two older siblings were emotionally, and often physically, abandoned, wandering a maze of relatives' and strangers' homes. One of their first stops was the home of an African American family in Providence, Rhode Island, where Nana's mother deposited her three young children on her escape from Lowell to New York City with her lover. Nana says she doesn't remember much of the weeks she, my great-uncle Clyde, and their sister stayed in Providence, apart from the shock of seeing an eel for the first time, in a frying pan.

Other than descriptions of the fabled house on Rogers Street, these and the stories that follow are not ones I grew up hearing. I knew my grandmother as an eminently practical woman, one focused entirely on the day's activities, tomorrow's projects, healthy meals, and card games (Spite and Malice was a favorite). We celebrated Thanksgivings with my grandparents in Tewksbury when I was growing up, and they visited us often in Wellfleet, but Nana was too busy for affection, too quick, especially for a grandmother, to spot a child's failings. She never sat me on her lap that I remember, but during one visit to Wellfleet she did lie back on Mom's messy bed and let me rub Oil of Olay on her cheeks. I hopped around her in my flannel nightgown, thrilled to be trusted with this evening ritual, hoping I wouldn't mess it up. I did, of course, but only a little. "Stroke upwards, not downwards," Nana instructed. "It lifts the expression."

Some of Nana's favorite stories involved her grandchildren's bad behavior. On one visit to Tewksbury when I was still in diapers, Mom was chatting with a friend across the street when it came time for me to take my nap, so Nana took my hand and led me back to her house to lay me down.

It was only when my grandmother placed me in the crib and handed me a bottle that I realized, with fury, that she was not my mother.

"I'm telling you," Nana says, warming up to the tale, "I had an awful time with you. You just looked at me, and boy, you sent that bottle flying right at me." Ever the one to deliver an amused barb, she shook her small, perfectly detailed head and said, "You were a spiteful little thing."

Things didn't improve over the years that followed—especially after I scaled Nana's new, modern shower door, breaking the towel bar attached to it—but we had an unspoken family solidarity that overrode any lack of warmth. Nana was unfailingly committed to us, whether or not she enjoyed us.

The first time I recall hearing stories of Nana's own childhood was when I was twenty-one and she and I took a three-week European tour at the end of my junior year abroad. My grandmother, then seventy-seven years old and on the safe side of two mastectomies, loved to travel, and she couldn't help but capitalize on a granddaughter in Europe who could manage arrangements in French and German and knew *Let's Go Europe* nearly by heart.

As we strolled through European parks and medieval churches, sat in train compartments and cafés, gambled in casinos (Nana never saw a slot machine lever she didn't want to pull), I began asking her the kinds of questions I had not dared to ask my parents. Nana was characteristically frank, readily telling me about Mom's childhood, Mom and Ben Harrow's marriage and infidelities, and her own earliest years, including her unkind grandmother, Henrietta. While I mostly wanted to learn more about the person I'd been studying, gauging, watching since childhood—my mother—hearing Nana's stories began to shift my understanding of her, as well as my sense of our family dynamics and the roots of some of my own traits and preoccupations.

I didn't write the stories down, however, and while over the next decade I spilled the most head-shaking ones at dinner parties, I knew I was forgetting others. Later, when Nana was nearly ninety and a bit less invincible, I asked her if she'd be willing to do recorded interviews with me. She had recently moved in with her youngest daughter, who lived in a small ranch house in Jacksonville,

Florida. I was in Atlanta writing my dissertation, and when Nana said yes, I jumped in my car.

Within hours after my arrival, Nana and I take a seat at my aunt's kitchen table, the recorder sitting between us and a fresh notepad by my elbow. The air is thick with artificial rose fragrance from outlet dispensers, and I wish I could yank out every one of them.

I start with the basic background questions about Nana's ancestors, where she grew up, and what her family did for work. She answers quickly, her mind still sharp from decades of physical exercise and a transporting stream of romance novels. Nana is the picture of self-respecting old age: colored hair styled every week, eyebrows neatly waxed, lips the color of pink dogwoods.

We soon arrive at the story that most shaped her early life, her mother's flight from Lowell. What, I ask, might have driven her mother to leave three young children with strangers—as it turns out, the relatives of a family they knew—rather than with their father, or with one of their grandparents, all four of whom were living in the Lowell area? Was it a vindictive act, or a desperate one?

Nana is not sure, but she says she at first believed her mother planned to fetch them once she got settled in New York. It didn't work out that way.

"She just didn't want us, that's all," Nana concludes, her lips flinching with grief or disgust. She takes a sip of hot tea, the used bag slumped in a saucer next to her cup, saved for one more dunking.

Nana says that it took her father, Albra, a month of asking around before he figured out where his children were hidden, and that it was ten years before she saw her mother again.

At this point, Nana's stoicism cracks and she begins to cry. She glances at my aunt, who is in the kitchen putting the finishing touches on a Cool Whip and Jell-O pudding dessert, an architectural wonder of white and black layers in a tall trifle bowl. A health-food nut, I can't believe I'm going to have to eat it, but I tell myself to take one for the team. When I do, I discover to my horror that it's delicious.

My aunt, the easy, compliant, daughter ("nothing like your mother," says Nana), tosses her chocolatey spatula into the sink as if to say, *the past is the past, Mom, let it go*. Or perhaps she is signaling, *time to wrap this up, Cynthia*.

But Nana seems eager to keep talking, so I keep asking. She describes how, after carting his three children back to Tewksbury, her father Albra moved them into the five-bedroom Victorian house on Rogers Street that he shared with his mother, Henrietta. His own father, Nana's grandfather, had been kicked out of the house decades earlier, shortly after Albra's birth. "My grandmother never cared about anybody but her son," Nana says. After Albra's marriage, Henrietta didn't make things any easier for her daughter-in-law, Nana's mother.

A black-haired, blue-eyed union man, Albra worked as an itinerant steam engineer for hospitals, schools, and mills in eastern Massachusetts. Given his long stretches out of town, he had no way of looking after his three children alone. His mother adored him but had no more use for grandchildren than she did for husbands. Saving her bedrooms for paying boarders, Henrietta wedged three mattresses between piles of junk and horsehair furniture in the attic, turning the crowded, dusty space into both bedroom and prison, locking in her grandchildren when they misbehaved. Even Nana's father occasionally slept under the rafters, though he also kept a room in town. At suppertime, Henrietta loaded his plate but half-starved her grandchildren, one of whom, Nana and Uncle Clyde's sister, died young of anemia.

Tiring of her three grandchildren—the only ones she had—Henrietta decided others should share her burden. Her first choice was to scatter them among relatives.

"Oh God," says Nana, her voice breaking, her shoulders slightly slumping, like a child's. "We were shipped around everywhere, to anyone who would take us."

But that didn't solve the long-term problem of what to do with inconvenient children, and either desperation or stinginess paved the way to the one set of doors that wouldn't close on them.

Nana doesn't say if it was her grandmother or her father who came up with the idea, but Albra did boiler maintenance at a children's home on the banks of Lowell's Merrimack River and somehow negotiated beds for Nana and Clyde there. His two children then lived in that orphanage for the next four years, despite their large, immediate family all over Middlesex County.

What did Nana see, how did her young mind and heart twist, I now wonder, on the day she left the familiar, if parsimonious, world of her relatives and entered the anonymity of the children's home? How did she make sense of this abandonment, when her parents and aunts and uncles and grandparents were all alive and had houses or apartments with room to accommodate them? In the years since our interviews at my aunt's kitchen table, I have often wished I had asked Nana for more details, but the stories were so startling—and her pain so evident—that I felt disoriented, scrambling to incorporate these harsh and baffling events into my simplistic version of family history. Like many grandchildren, I had blithely assumed I knew my grandmother, but in truth, I had known next to nothing: mainly my experience of her, and not the events and forces and feelings of her years before I existed.

The orphanage, I have since learned, was housed in a granite-trimmed home built of rubble stone that James C. Ayer, a wildly successful "maker of medicines" and majority shareholder in several mills, had bought as his private residence in 1854 with the millions he earned concocting and hawking patent drugs, some of them worse than useless but brilliantly marketed. Bestsellers included Ayer's Cherry Pectoral, a cough syrup spiked with morphine that stupefied sick children, and Ayer's Sarsaparilla, a purported cure for everything from pimples and boils to rheumatism, eczema, tuberculosis, debility, and every possible disorder of blood.

Before Ayer bought the 25,000-square-foot "Stone House," as it was known, it had served as a tavern and hotel overlooking Lowell's Pawtucket Falls, a popular stop on the stagecoach route from Boston to New Hampshire. It was also the site of the first town meeting of the newly incorporated Town of Lowell in 1826, a historic emblem of the Commonwealth's premier mill town. Ayer and his wife raised their three children in Stone House until Mr. Ayer's death from insanity in 1878, after which Mrs. Ayer abandoned Lowell's gritty streets and relocated her ménage first to New York City, then to the Duc de Mouchy's former mansion near Esplanade des Invalides in Paris, where she sparkled for the remainder of her life.

In Paris, Mrs. Ayer's lavish spending, brilliant jewels, and magnificent parties made her the talk of the faubourgs and the preeminent American socialite in France, outshining, as one journalist gushed, even the famed Mrs. Astor. A year or two after moving to the City of Light, Mrs. Ayer, perhaps soothing her conscience or simply ridding herself of reminders, transferred Stone House to a struggling local orphanage. Adding the family name to the charity, Mrs. Ayer won effusive praise for providing a home for Lowell's destitute and troubled, many of them, no doubt, ground into penury and illness on the floors of her family's wildly prosperous medicine factories.

On her death in 1898, Mrs. Ayer, who purportedly controlled the largest fortune held by any woman in the world, bequeathed $100,000 to Lowell's Ayer Home for Young Women and Children, the cold mansion which, just fifteen years later, Nana and my greatuncle Clyde entered, clutching a bag with their few belongings. Mrs. Ayer's children and grandchildren, on the other hand, were bequeathed millions each, making them, as one newspaper crowed, the richest children in the world.

Traveling back in my imagination, I try to picture Nana, ten years old, as she approached the massive building of irregular gray, black, and brown stone. What was she thinking as she passed under the home's imposing portico? Did she reach out and touch one of the four fluted columns standing guard before the door? Crane her neck toward the Doric entablature decorated with vertical stripes resembling prison bars, or squint into one of the façade's forty windows, behind which she would march each morning in two straight lines of girls? Did her knees quiver as she ascended the tall staircase and wandered through rooms lined with beds, enough for 125 children? Reach for her brother's hand when their father, a weak man she loved, turned his back and walked out the door? At my aunt's kitchen table, I am too astonished by Nana's story, too hesitant to press on still half-healed wounds, to ask for more. And now there's no more asking.

I also never learned if Albra resented his mother for refusing to care for his children, but as Nana beelines toward other details of her childhood, she says that even as a grown man, her father never left the house without his mother's permission and never picked up a newspaper without first casting an eye to where she sat, checking to see if he was permitted to read it silently instead of aloud. "He was a thirty-two-degree Mason," says Nana, assuming I'd understand how many secret rituals and handshakes it took to reach such lofty heights in the fraternal organization, "but he could not call his soul his own." I wonder if this vision of her father helped her to endure his abandonment, to fault her miserly grandmother instead of the father who, though he failed to protect her, she would care for and nurse until the day he died.

Nana's family didn't completely cast her aside, though. Her grandfather Charles, I discovered by hunting through Lowell city directories from the 1910s, gave up his job as a guard and fireman to become a janitor at the orphanage, staying there for four years—surely the four years that his grandchildren were residents. He couldn't force his wife to look after them, but he must have found a way to do so himself, if only from a distance. But neither Nana nor Uncle Clyde, who described the children's home to me in a letter after I asked him to tell me more about his childhood, ever mentioned their grandfather's presence there. Nana never got over the shame of her abandonment, and both brother and sister hated to talk about their internment there.

When she turned fourteen in 1917, Nana, instead of attending high school, was packed off to the Ingleside Home School for Girls, a charity institution in Revere that she says was "paid for by wealthy people in Boston." Housed in a stately Second Empire–style building, the boarding school, writes the *Boston Daily Globe*, took charge of around twenty "young, neglected girls" who were "in danger of falling into evil ways if left in their existing surroundings." A Christian publication from that time describes the Ingleside pupils as at-risk girls who, while "threatened by the undertow of life, had not yet been swept out into the sea of shame, ruin and lifelong misery." Founded in the mid-1890s, the school initially sought to rescue young prostitutes from the social evil of sex work, then pivoted to a mission of preventing marginalized girls from turning to such work in the first place. The school trained its residents to become instead "a power for good in the world," primarily through careers as reliable domestic servants. The curriculum was light on academics, organized instead around household arts such as cooking, washing, darning, and dressmaking. Nana, eager and competent, thrived.

"A lot of the girls didn't like it because it was very strict, but I slept in a dirty attic full of junk at home, and I had a decent bed to sleep in down there," she says, her voice regaining its steadiness over her tea. "Every Saturday our mattresses went out and we beat them. It was *immaculate*," she says, her stressed "*mac*" and crisp "*t*" the sound of all that is right in the world.

As for love, I think she found some semblance of it in the school's director, Miss Margaret Forbes, whom Nana continued to visit well into adulthood. Unusual for its time, and for Nana personally, Ingleside believed that showing love and kindness to children was as important as their practical care. Nana would remember that kindness for the rest of her life. "It was the best home I ever had as a child," she says of her four years there.

Once she started her own family, Nana sometimes brought my mother, trussed in large hair bows, finely sewn dresses, and white gloves, to visit the inestimable school director. Now securely middle-class and the mother of a pretty, precocious daughter, Nana, ever grateful, delighted in showing Miss Forbes that the school's investment had proved good, that she had escaped a fate in the streets or in one of the cotton mills that the Sarsaparilla King had snatched up with his patent medicine profits.

When she left Ingleside at eighteen, Nana returned to Tewksbury and her grandmother Henrietta's boarding house on Rogers Street. Vulnerability had done nothing for Henrietta's character. In poor health and nearly blind, she had fired every housekeeper Albra hired, and he had pleaded with his daughter to take over. With no place else to go and trained for such work, Nana bent her shoulder to the task, washing sheets under the kitchen sink pump and emptying bedpans in the outhouse. She did the grocery shopping, scrubbed the floors, and accompanied the grandmother who had abandoned her to her medical appointments. After a year or two, Nana's own health faltered and, following doctor's orders, she left Henrietta's care to others. She found a clerical job with the Grand Union Tea Company, where she met my grandfather, a sweet-tempered Norwegian whose family had emigrated to Lowell less than twenty years earlier.

Nana's happiest years of early adulthood were the four she spent living with her Norwegian in-laws after she and Bumpa married in 1925. Bumpa's extended family was everything Nana's was not: loving and supportive, full of good cheer, good food, and good music, hard workers in Lowell's tool and die factories. Nana learned Norwegian cuisine and eagerly attended the Norwegian Sick Benefit Society's monthly gatherings, where dances and smorgasbords raised money for struggling families in their tightknit community.

Shortly after the birth of Nana and Bumpa's second child, however, Albra begged them to leave their Norwegian cocoon and return to the blighted house on Rogers Street to care for Henrietta, whose vitriol had splintered interiors of every sort. Finally holding the better hand, Nana made a trade: they would return to care for Henrietta, but first they needed to install indoor bathrooms, running water, and electricity. I imagine it's at this point that Nana also insisted she inherit the house when her grandmother died—which she did, two disagreeable years later.

It's a credit to Nana's emotional fortitude that she could imagine living and raising a family within walls that had contained so much of her suffering, and more redemptively, that she could grow to love and care for those spaces. Then again, it was the Great Depression, and while Bumpa was steadily employed, his pay was modest, and owning a home would have been out of my grandparents' reach for years.

With the keys to Henrietta's house in hand, they set about reframing the dim, utilitarian ark as a light-filled home. One of the first improvements was to tear down the walls of Henrietta's bedroom, the former "birthing room," opening up the first floor while erasing the architectural lines of Nana's servitude.

The changes they wrought, however, went beyond the structural. Remembrance of the past nipping at her heels, Nana not only raised her own brood of three in the house on Rogers Street, but over the course of twenty-five years also took in seventeen foster girls, many of them "unplaceable."

Once again, Nana has taken me by surprise. I was aware that she and Bumpa had taken in a child or two, even considered adopting one, but *seventeen*?

"I was always very sympathetic with children," Nana says, in the same voice she might have used if mentioning her shoe size.

Still at the kitchen table in Jacksonville, her deep red nail polish glossing over the early years of drudgery at Henrietta's beck and call, Nana begins to list all the children she cared for, from the dark-haired Greek infant who came straight from the hospital and stayed for four years to the rebellious teenager she sent back to Children's Aid after six months. It takes her an hour to account for all seventeen, but during that time Nana lets drop other tidbits, such as her visits to Miss Forbes at Ingleside with Mom and their Easter ritual of bringing dozens of decorated baskets filled with treats to the orphanage that had been Nana's shame. I don't say it, but I imagine my grandmother must have found a measure of healing, if not vindication, in these acts of charity and in taking shunted children into her care, though Mom once snapped at me that as a foster parent, Nana was earning a buck the best way she knew how.

These interviews with Nana are not the kind of spontaneous family storytelling over the supper table that nourishes what the psychologist Kate McLean would describe as a rich "narrative ecology" at home, one that gives children a sense of belonging and perspective. But it's a powerful second-best, an intentional filling in of a past that for most of my life had not existed.

Because I found Nana's stories so compelling, so vividly drawn, it's tempting to say that her memories feel like my own. Indeed, some aspects of them—especially how hard it is to be poor—are cuttingly familiar. While perhaps vicarious, Nana's memories do not create in me what William James calls the "warmth and intimacy" of episodic recall, the feeling of re-entering a lived scene. I do, however, value Nana's memories almost as much as my own, and some of them even feel more immediate, because I am not relying on recall but on imagination. This is why, of course, others' stories so often captivate us: we enter them more like an explorer to be entertained than a self-doubting conjurer.

There's a difference between secrets and untold stories—and Nana's early experiences were the latter, just waiting for the right questions to be asked, for a granddaughter to show some interest in her grandmother's earlier self. Shared stories can have startling explanatory power, and while we tend to believe that secrets offer the surest key—as if what is most hidden were most true— stories unearthed by empathic, or even just intentional, listening can reconfigure the map we've sketched of another person's life, carving rivers of meaning that flow into our own lives, perhaps even mitigating our disappointed hopes for a closer, more accepting, family.

It's easy to be distracted by the quotidian and to lapse into unimaginative expectations of others. But the stories Nana shared with me, just because I sat down with her at a kitchen table and started asking, allowed me to understand and better accept her practical way of showing love, shorn of compliments or physical affection and too often tinged with disapproval, because I could now see before me not only the self-preserving octogenarian with a trim physique, but the lonely adolescent drowning in a shapeless black coat bought at a cheap sidewalk sale—her sole Christmas present one year—or the reed-thin girl no one in her family wanted until they could use her as domestic help.

The sharing of stories also creates vulnerabilities, of course, allowing us to wound each other in unkind ways, whether intended or not. During the first summer of that year I lived at home before starting graduate school in Atlanta, Nana arrived on another three-month stay. Mom, aware of how intolerable Nana found our messy house and loose rules, was baffled by these visits and every May posted signs around the house to ward off criticism ("I know we have ants!" read one that appeared in the time it took me to collect Nana at the bus station; "don't tell me about them!"). The truth was, Nana finally confessed, Florida's seasonal thunderstorms terrified her, especially now that Bumpa had passed away. She also loved how easy it was, even for someone in her mid-eighties, to find paying jobs on the Cape after Memorial Day, and Nana was nothing if not eager to earn an extra dollar.

From June on that summer, small aggravations between Nana and me had been building, culminating one early evening when I walked into the kitchen den to discover that my grandmother had set the supper table for everyone but me. I looked up at her, confused. Nana, slightly flustered, said, "I thought you were going out."

It was a lie. Ever since my arrival home from Berkeley, Nana had made clear just how reprehensible my life was. For starters, I crowded her limp Lipton tea bag with my soggy Constant Comment bag in the porcelain dish next to the stove. "That fancy tea makes mine taste funny," she complained. "*I'm* not fussy." She enunciated each word, as if a virtue: "I like *plain, black* tea."

*But you are fussy!* I thought to myself. *You like only Lipton tea!* But I knew her complaint had more to do with me than with strong aromatic spices. Like my offensive teabag, I was a contaminating force who wasted the birthday money she gave me on expensive skin products, ate weird foods like tofu, and was undoubtedly, disgustingly loose.

This last charge followed my quick romantic involvement with Mom's new tenant, Bill, a graduate student at Harvard and summer bartender at the Gristmill in Eastham. He was renting my old bedroom in the main house, while I slept in the room above the garage. My second night at home, Bill stood below my window, hands on hips, and shouted up an invitation to dinner. We sped off to the Lighthouse Restaurant in his red Alfa Romeo and were together until he returned to Boston in the fall.

Bill was sensual, needy, and laissez-faire when it came to my relaxed bathroom etiquette. One morning Nana walked by the half-open door while I was taking a quick pee and Bill was brushing his teeth. I heard about it for the rest of the summer.

Staring at the place settings, I knew my grandmother did not want to share her home-cooked meal with an unsavory granddaughter. I was too hurt and proud to ask for a seat at the table. Banging the screen door, I grabbed the rusting Raleigh ten-speed Dad had given me just before the divorce and pointed it toward the beach. Reaching the sandy parking lot at the end of Lecount Hollow, I made a quick left onto Ocean View Drive and pumped hard up the steep hill toward my favorite views of the sea.

Past a carpet of bayberry, beach plums, and goldenrod shimmered open, endless water. Somewhere, invisible on the bright rim of the horizon, lay Portugal and Spain. How many childhood hours had I sat on the beach and imagined their shores? I sometimes convinced myself I could spot bits of land on the far side, proof of other worlds.

The evening air grew chill, stinging my arms and neck. I wanted to cry, but it seemed childish. Why should I care whether Nana included me? Why should I feel so wounded by her rejection? Taking a left off Ocean View Drive down Long Pond Road, I dared cars to hit me as I sailed through wide, leafy curves. I passed my beloved elementary school on the right before dead-ending at Main Street, then turned left and skidded to a halt at the Oyster

House, a fine-dining restaurant housed in an eighteenth-century sea captain's home where I was waitressing that summer. Propping my bike against the clapboard, I walked inside and hoped the bartender would slip me a drink.

Nursing a Madras, my stomach churning, I wanted to ask for a cup of clam chowder, but I didn't have any money on me. Waitresses loaded with trays popped jokes about me loving my job too much, while the sometimes irresistible, curly-haired sous-chef shot me a quick, questioning glance. Embarrassed to be among well-heeled diners in my shorts and tank top, I finished my drink, slid off the barstool, and biked down Main Street to a tiny cottage on Whit's Lane, as narrow as its name sounds. Milton Cohen, one of Mom's artist filmmaker friends, lived there in an ancient, hobbit-like cottage crammed with plants, books, and puppet props for his multimedia montages. He had given me my first car that summer, a beat-up Honda Civic he was about to trade in. When I told him I'd like to take him out to dinner in thanks, he said, "That would be lovely, but I refuse to let you pay."

Opening his door, Milton took one look at my face and, asking no questions, threw another handful of spaghetti into a pot of roiling water and opened a bottle of red wine. Above his two-burner stove sat a white, melted kitchen timer, his "clitoral clock," while one of Mom's patchwork quilts adorned the bed near our seats at the nicked wooden table, attached to the ceiling with a pole. As the evening eddied into night, Milton's innate courtliness guided our conversation down soothing, nonintrusive paths, and it was well past dark when we loaded my bike on the back of his new car and he drove me home.

I walked in to find my grandmother knitting, watching her beloved Red Sox. I had been gone for hours. She glanced up between stitches, asking no questions.

The next morning we had a fierce argument out by the hollyhocks. "You treat me just like your grandmother Henrietta treated you!" I cried, scrabbling to make her understand my pain while using hers against her.

Nana's face collapsed. "That's the meanest thing you could ever say to me," she sobbed, leaning miserably against the low garden wall.

"Acceptance is not Nana's forté," Mom said the next day. "I made myself sick for many years trying to please her." The only time I heard Nana compliment Mom was an afternoon when she came home from raspberry picking loaded with berries.

"You done good, Shirls!" cried Nana, so excited she started talking recipes before we made it to the kitchen counter.

More often Mom heard comments like, "You know, you've got a gold mine in your sewing shop if you'd only work harder." Mom wasted too much time having coffee with friends trying as hard as she was to stay sober. And who wouldn't hanker for a fifth of Jack Daniel's given a no-nonsense mother who said, "I can't honestly say I've ever felt tired"?

Though she was in her mid-eighties that summer, Nana and I worked side-by-side at the Oyster House, where Mom served as the hostess, my two sisters waitressed, and my brother filled in at the bar. I balanced trays of paella and prime rib while Nana dished up the desserts. I was paid; she was not. She loved to work and wanted to belong. One night, determined to reach the ice cream at the bottom of the deep freezer, she fell in head-first, with just her fanny and legs visible until she could leverage her way back out. She and I also cleaned summer cottages together on Saturday mornings, both of us paid, and both of us thrilled with the jars of condiments, the unfinished loaves of Pepperidge Farm, and the milk, juice, and butter that tourists inexplicably left behind when they loaded their Volvos and Subarus for trips home to Cambridge or Manhattan. Relieved to lower Mom's next grocery bill, we carted home bulging grocery bags, crowding our shelves with luxury's leftovers.

Six months after Nana's return to Florida for the winter that year, I had a dream about her, about us. In the dream, Mom and I are discussing some ambiguities about my age. She runs off to check my birth certificate and returns to say, "You know, you were born in 1903. You are eighty-four years old inside." I look at her with my twenty-eight-year-old body and eighty-four-year-old insides in amazement.

When I woke, I understood: *Nana is in me, and I am in her.*

After my interviews with my grandmother, I began to seek out the stories of other family members—cousins, uncles, and aunts—as well as those of friends of the family. Listening to Nana had made me realize how much color and depth oral histories can add to a family portrait. Although I prepared questions ahead of time for these sessions, I didn't always understand what I was after. And I had no idea what I didn't know about others, even people I had lived with or next-door to for years. While I never, of course, heard "the whole story" (does such a thing exist?), these oral histories with my grandmother and others did more than enrich my understanding of and compassion for my family; they also affected the way I think about autobiographical memory, underscoring how partial my version of an event, of a person, of a relationship could be, helping me to relax the taut narratives and judgments I had constructed over the years.

Personal memories are inextricably bound to our sense of self, to our identity, which is why we so often go to the mat to defend our version of a past event. Accuracy feels paramount. Autobiographical memories allow us to make sense of what we see in the mirror each morning: who we are today, who we were on all the days preceding this moment, and who we imagine ourselves to be in the future. But in collecting family stories, I have been struck by the unavoidable variability of memory and of our interpretations of the past.

It's hard to appreciate the degree to which even those closest to us can inhabit other worlds. Rather than attempt to adjudicate who is right and who is wrong, it's perhaps most honest to embrace a multiplicity of perceptions, the fluidity at the core of personal stories, the "maybe" that introduces uncertainty and openness, and perhaps even more kindness, in our relations with each other and with ourselves.

I felt this most particularly while interviewing relatives about my father, who died suddenly when I was fifteen, just a few months after Mom divorced him. As a teenager I could have sentimentalized him, and I did in my journal, but only slightly. His early death—he was fifty-six—allowed me instead to develop a hard-and-fast narrative that spotlighted his unpredictable temper, my fear of him, and the tyranny of his needs and preferences over our household. Doing so enabled me to exert control over the storyline of his personality and our relationship. By the time I was in my twenties, the narrative took less than a few minutes to perform.

There was no end in sight, on the other hand, to the story of my very-much-alive mother. I could and did talk about her for hours, but crucial elements remained a mystery, one I didn't feel I could question or probe. At the heart of that mystery, I came to suspect, lay a roped-off crime scene, where Mom was both victim and lawbreaker. It wasn't until I was in my thirties that I mustered the courage to begin circling that scene, straining to get a better view, poking through the debris, interrogating witnesses, not sure if I was a frustrated detective in search of one more clue or, worse, a guilty offender compelled to return.

# 3
# The Memory Keep

~

When I was a child, I sensed the existence of Mom's secrets, her hidden stories, but their content eluded me, and I knew better than to ask for details. I wasn't afraid of Mom—I adored her—but I feared posing questions whose answers came in a flash of anguish or irritation. Rather than the shape of words, Mom's well-guarded thoughts took the form of energy: her naturally merry and mischievous spirit counterweighted by the ruminating focus of her artistic projects, her back curved like a question mark while she smocked a blouse or sanded a pine dresser, as if still interrogating the choices she had made twenty or thirty years earlier.

Most afternoons after we tumbled off our mutinous school bus, I'd find Mom busy with her furniture refinishing, paper cutting, or sewing. She sent us off to school with decoupaged clipboards and lunch boxes—tin workman's pails covered with roses and birds—and sewed all our best outfits, as well as her own most flattering dresses, cut on the bias. Our secondhand furniture ("Early Attic," she called it) found new life under her upholstery needle and mallet, while her drapes adorned the windows of our house and separated our beds in the pine room I shared with Thelma and Beth. Later, after Dad died during my sophomore year of high school, Mom supplemented her summer waitressing tips with year-round tailoring, making wedding dresses and suits, altering women's clothes for male cross-dressers, and hemming hundreds of trousers, many of them for the short, fastidious Congregational minister, whose three extra inches of fine woolen clippings she fashioned into the quilt for her beloved friend Milton.

The rhythmic hammer of Mom's Singer atop a scuffed mahogany desk, which I could hear long after I climbed the narrow staircase to bed, helped her, I think, to pace her thoughts, to pin them in place along with the sleeves and collars and hems. She once told me that noise kept her company, and my guess is she was drawn to background sounds not because she did not want to think, but because she did not want to be alone with the images inking the screen between her and whatever sewing project was spread out on the dining room table.

Though Mom perhaps wanted to protect us from hearing stories we were too young to understand, her past traumas spooled into my psychic landscape like a finely spun web glimpsed only at a slant or missed altogether, an undulation in the air that snagged me in a confusion of sticky tendrils while I looked in another direction. I knew my mother experienced bouts of depression, but I didn't know why, and whatever secrets lay at the heart of that melancholy felt like a haunting.

This sense of an invisible presence spilled out of our house and into the woods and houses of Wellfleet's back roads. When we were young, my Aunt Judy would stuff a half-dozen of us into her white Volkswagen Beetle on popsicle-hot days and drive the back way along Ocean View Drive to a spot on Long Pond Road where we could cut through the woods and enjoy a secluded freshwater dip. Off the road, set back among the pitch pines, stood a small brown house that looked like something Hansel and Gretel might have passed on their way to gingerbread treachery. I was sure this was the bogeyman's house, and it made me shiver. Gazing out of the cranked-down window as we zipped past the lonely structure, barely brushed by sunlight, I used to wonder what went on inside, imagining the bogeyman lurching from room to room like a drunken Bigfoot, all hair and muscle and cunning. Could he see us from the window? Would he recognize and come for us?

As I think back to my fantasies about this modest house, which surely deserved none of my projections (I recently learned that one of my cousins thought it was Bullwinkle's house, while another called it Wee Willie Winkie's), I realize now that sharing a home with Mom's secrets felt like living with such a creature, one that only gathered a sort of vengeful power from the effort to silence it.

Although I couldn't "know" Mom's stories, absence has a way of taking up space, and I keenly felt her losses, whatever they were and however they had come about. The most obvious conundrum was why we had a brother and a sister we had met only once or twice, half-siblings who disappeared shortly after my birth. But that loss was just one element in an even more complicated narrative, a fortress I circled for years, finding doors with locked handles, windows with bars, ladders with the lower rungs removed.

Undeterred, I pried free any loose stone I could find, because while there were other stories, other secrets, this was the one I wanted, feeling that if I understood this history, the one connected to our absent siblings and Mom's life with another man before she married my father, I'd understand her long mental flights away from us, her drinking and pills, the generosity and easy forgiveness that came naturally to her, as if our misdoings were as inevitable as stray threads on a newly altered jacket and just as inconsequential.

We three girls had our chores at home, earning us each a dime a week. One night when I was eight or nine, I was washing the supper dishes at our deep, cast-iron sink when our crystal butter dish—a remnant, no doubt, from the house on Rogers Street—slipped out of my soapy hands and shattered as it caught the edge of the sink and crashed to the floor. I jerked my head up in terror, knowing I had broken a precious thing. "You didn't mean to," Mom sighed as she bent to pick up the shards, adding, "mistakes happen."

Love and gratefulness flooded me as I joined her on the brown-and-tan checkerboard linoleum, its decades-old pocks dimpling my bare knees as we gathered the glass. I thought to myself, *this is what goodness looks like*, convinced that if my father had walked into the kitchen at that moment, my punishment would have been swift, a slap across the face, perhaps, or a backside reckoning with the yardstick. "Mistakes happen," I would later come to understand, was one of Mom's mantras, an incantation in her life-long quest to ward off regret, her bleating response to the rod of Nana's judgment.

The censored story it took me years to uncover begins at Ingleside, the charity school in Revere where Nana spent four of her teenage years. Despite the stigma attached, the home for at-risk girls had been the making of her, rescuing my grandmother from hard-bitten relatives while offering structure and discipline, a reassuring moral sensibility coupled with useful skills. While at Ingleside, however, my grandmother formed a lasting friendship with another shuffled child nicknamed Kimi, who ten years later bore a son, the raven-haired, blue-eyed charmer who would be my mother's undoing.

Though forty miles separated their homes, Nana and Kimi saw each other often after leaving the girls' home, and Kimi's son Ben grew up visiting, then adoring, Mom. He persuaded her to date him when they were both still teenagers and then chased her down a wedding aisle just shy of her twentieth birthday.

"Ben Harrow had me on some kind of pedestal," Mom remembers, her lips wandering into a wry smile. "What a mistake."

Hers was giving in to his obsessive pursuit, though she had tried to dodge him and never got over the regret of having failed. Throughout her adult life, Mom often conjured one of her lost possible selves, those parallel lives that pull at our imagination with the force of a novel bearing our name. The projection is compelling, the storyline fiction, of course. What would any of us have become had we made different hard choices, or had chance moments—turning to talk to a stranger in the grocery line, sitting in that seat on a train, leaving behind a letter or scarf or book—not shifted the course of our lives in positive or detrimental, subtle or disruptive, ways?

For Mom, her most salient alternate self took the form of a career girl in Washington, DC, where she imagined herself an organizing marvel for important men during the day and the life of the party for drunk ones at night. Shortly after graduating from high school in 1944, Mom, who had excelled in her stenography classes, passed the federal civil service exam and received three consecutive job offers in the nation's capital, then swarming with young women supporting the war effort as secretaries, mathematicians, and code breakers. Her beloved and brilliant Norwegian aunt worked in the Department of State and would have welcomed Mom into her home and circle of connections. But Ben Harrow pleaded with her not to go, warning that "no one else would ever, ever" marry her, because she'd lost her virginity to him.

"I didn't doubt his word for a minute," snorts Mom. "Certainly, I wouldn't ask my mother!"

In her last serious bid for independence, Mom ran away to Boston after high school without telling anyone and moved into a rooming house in Brookline's knockabout Coolidge Corner. Once there, she carried on an affair with a world heavyweight wrestling champion in his thirties who sported the ring name "Texas Tumbler." Refusing to be thrown, Ben helped my grandparents to track her down and bring her home to Tewksbury. Mom then found a secretarial job with a lawyer in Lowell, but Ben parked himself in a chair outside the lawyer's office for long stretches every day, keeping guard, until she was fired for it. By then Ben had ducked into a tattoo parlor and had an anchor pricked onto his forearm, with "Shirley" lovingly, and forebodingly, entwined with rope.

"I finally gave in," Mom sighs. "My mother was terrified I'd get pregnant and humiliate her, and I told myself Ben would loosen his grip if I agreed to marry him." Eyes clouding, she says, "It was just the opposite . . . he only curled his fist tighter around me." Then, looking somewhere beyond me, somewhere into the still-erupting past, she shakes her head: "What a stupid girl."

On her wedding day in 1946, Mom panicked at the entrance to the sanctuary of the Tewksbury Congregational Church. As the wedding march sounded and her bridesmaids began processing down the aisle, she whispered, "I can't do this!" to her maid of honor. "Of course you can!" her best friend hissed back.

Mom caught a glimpse of the sanctuary, filled with expectant faces, with her friends and her parents' friends—from church, their Masonic Lodge and Eastern Star chapters, the Needlecraft Club, and the Norwegian Sick Society. Nana had seen to every detail: Mom's full-length, white-satin dress with a sweetheart neckline; the reception hall festooned with apple blossoms, the buffet table cheerfully laden with dishes prepared by Nana and her friends. Mom, caught in the rigging and props of not only the wedding but also the two people who most wanted to control her—her mother and Ben Harrow—avoided her father's kind, gentle eyes and took his arm. He would have understood her backing out, would have defended her choice, this she knew, but in Mom's world inconveniencing a man didn't come easily, be it asking him to shift a newspaper off the table or himself out of her life. Unable to face her mother's reproaches or Ben's fury, she stepped in time toward the altar, shaking so much she feared her white calla lilies would fall off their stems. Soon afterwards she moved out of the Victorian house on Rogers Street and into a knot-hole trailer that Ben had bought, shifting from one military base to another and having a child every two or three years.

Did the physical abuse start before or after the wedding? I don't know. But like a malign octopus curling and flexing in every direction, Ben Harrow passionately adored and equally passionately assaulted his young wife. He played both a short and a long game, combining impulsive blows with stratagem. In one neat trick, he gave Mom money for groceries and then beat her when it disappeared before she did the shopping.

"I racked my brains," Mom says, "trying to figure out how I had lost the money. Was I spending it without realizing it? Were the boys stealing it? Was I going crazy?"

Then she had a hunch: what if *Ben* were stealing it? On his next pay day, Mom marked the bills he handed her with a tiny red circle in the upper right corner before tucking them into her purse. Sure enough, the money vanished. That night as her husband snored, Mom eased open the top drawer of their dresser and, quietly rustling his wallet, pulled out the marked bills.

But from the way she tells me this story, it's not fury Mom felt at the discovery so much as relief—that her sons were not thieves, that she hadn't lost her mind.

"I didn't know where I was," Mom says of those years. "My father was devoted to my mother—I never heard a cross word between them—and I couldn't make sense of what was happening to me."

That very background, of course, was part of Mom's appeal. "Ben hated his father," she says. "He wanted a family like mine, but he didn't know how to be in it."

In the house on Rogers Street, Nana, inventively clever and schooled by her early years of penury, had kept the family humming on Bumpa's modest salary while also throwing cocktail parties, taking no prisoners at the card table, and organizing dinners for the Eastern Star, the Girl Scouts, the Congregational Church— activities that often splashed her smiling face onto the pages of local newspapers. But I wonder if it was Mom's loving relationship with her father that had not only appealed to Ben Harrow but also made her vulnerable to his manipulations. Against common expectation, some women who end up battered have had positive relationships with their fathers, and my grandfather's humble and mild ways, nurtured by affectionate Old World parents who reveled in music, food, and family, may have made it hard for Mom—especially at nineteen—to imagine what Ben was capable of. What she *could* imagine was others' suffering, and this empathy helped ensnare her.

"Men like Ben look for women like me," she says with hindsight. "Ones who will not only listen to a sob story but enter into it, ones who are too nice for their own good. He would have never married a mean person."

Fairly early in their marriage—it was 1949, and just two of Mom's seven children had been born at this point—she and Ben were living in Pine Acres, a wooded trailer park outside the Coast Guard base in South Portland, Maine, where Ben was stationed. Deciding she'd had enough, Mom told Ben for the first time that she was leaving.

"Like hell you are," he growled as he stormed out the door, leaving her alone, again, for several days with their two sons and no car.

I imagine her announcement was less a plan of action and more a cry for change. While Mom was desperate to escape, she had no money and no way to get herself and two children out of that trailer or out of Maine. She was not going to call her parents. Although she adored her father, she could not face her mother's sure reproof at her marital failures, or Nana's alarm at the social disgrace she seemed to fear even more than her daughter's pain.

As Mom starts, haltingly, to tell me this story, as I pull it out of her, I think back to my interviews with Nana and a story she told me of the night in the early 1950s when Mom unexpectedly appeared on her doorstep in Tewksbury. Mom and her now three children were living with Ben in Mississippi after his transfer there from Maine's Pine Acres.

"Ben beat your mother up something terrible," Nana told me, her voice unnervingly matter-of-fact, "and she took a train all the way up from Biloxi. He must have just got a pay, so she had money and took off." The train journey north lasted three days. "She was a mess," Nana says, "and had packed no food for the kids, so they went over to people eating their meals, asking for food. Shirley said it was awful."

Nana was hosting her church group that night, and the last car was just leaving the large Rogers Street yard when the yellow cab pulled in with the children and Mom, her fine-boned face swollen and bruised. My grandmother's relief as she recalls the scene stretches across the decades: "Thank God no one from my group saw her!" She then snorts something like a laugh and shakes her head in disbelief, as if the drama lay not in her daughter's battering but in the near-disastrous timing of her arrival. Nana locks eyes with me, her fine eyebrows arched and her lips flexed as if to say, *that girl nearly humiliated me.*

The day after Mom and the children's arrival, Nana and Bumpa brought her over to her in-laws' house so they could see the bruises and swelling, the miserable state of this ill-conceived marriage.

"We knew they wouldn't believe it until they saw it," Nana says. "But it wasn't a day before Ben Harrow was at our door. He'd gotten two weeks' leave and wanted her back. Promised not to touch her. He finally wrote up this big, long letter saying he would never hurt her again." Then, as if in a three-fingered count toward the obvious, Nana says, "He signed it, his folks signed it, and Shirley went back with him."

I wonder what Mom felt as she repacked her bags in Tewksbury, her blue-black splotches fading to yellow. Did she have any hope that her husband would change once they returned to Mississippi? That the beatings would stop, or that she would one day escape him?

Ben, Mom says, seemed sincere at apologies and remorse, telling her that the reason he hit her was that he idolized her and couldn't understand when she wasn't perfect. ("Obviously married the wrong woman!" she scoffs. "I leave perfection to the gods.") Given his unrelenting pursuit, Mom might have felt a divorce would have been meaningless—that Ben would not leave her alone whether they were married or not. She also had three children under the age of five and no way to support them. Or did she allow Ben to drag her back to Mississippi because of what had happened after she had announced her decision to leave him in Maine two years earlier?

Back in Maine's woodsy Pine Acres, Mom had not fully grasped the risk she was taking the first time she told Ben she wanted a divorce, because she didn't know that the most dangerous move for an abused woman is to tell her partner that it's over. For the abuser, it's never over, so once it is, there's nothing more to lose. In threatening to leave, Mom might as well have told Ben that she was planning to saw off one of his body parts, because I doubt he had any ability to distinguish between where he ended and she began—or between his delusions about himself and his fantasies about her.

I imagine Mom felt both anxious and resigned as Ben returned from his Portland bender and pushed his way into their mobile home, the musky scent of beer melding with the autumn-straw tint of the paneled walls. Rummaging in the tiny bedroom, Ben emerged with his shotgun and ordered Mom out the door. Following her, Ben locked the trailer, leaving their toddler and baby inside. "Walk," he said, prodding her in the small of her back. She walked. They marched deep into the woods surrounding the trailer park, Ben on the search for a suitable tree. He found it. Ramming his young wife against the pine, he burrowed metal into the soft flesh under her chin and hissed, "You'll never leave me. I'll kill you first."

When I first hear this story, all I can see is Mom pinned to the tree by the barrel of Ben Harrow's shotgun, her eyes darting between clouds, her slender body trembling like a bird trapped in a hand that could squeeze it to death in an impulsive instant. Only later do I try to guess what Ben Harrow might have been feeling as he threatened to kill my mother. I imagine a potent mix of fear and rage, but Mom says he was driven by jealousy and the need for control, by the pleasure of bending her to his will, of forcing her to be one way when she was quite obviously another.

Pressed against that rough and sticky bark, her husband's rancid breath on her lips, Mom did what any sane person with a gun to her head would do: she told Ben that she didn't know what she was thinking, that she loved him, that of course she would never leave him.

Lowering his gun, Ben shoved her back toward the trailer and unlocked the door. Stumbling past the crying boys, he fell onto the bed and into a rank slumber. Mom didn't dare touch the shotgun, still lying at Ben's side, but she spotted the box of deer shells on the floor and decided to hide it, "in case he was still in the mood" when he woke up. Scanning the cramped quarters, her eyes paused on the oven—the perfect place to hide something from a man who never cooked. She grabbed the handle and slid the box in.

The next day, still rattled, Mom decided to make one of her favorite comfort dishes, a tuna noodle casserole. Moving on autopilot, she pulled cans of tuna fish and cream of mushroom soup from the tiny cabinets and preheated the oven to 350 degrees. Within seconds an acrid smell split the air. Memory firing, Mom lurched toward the oven and raked the smoking box of shells onto a cookie sheet before gliding out the door and gingerly setting her unintentional bomb on the ground. She then scooped up her two kids and headed to a neighbor's trailer for a chat over coffee, ear cocked for explosions.

Although Mom laughs when she tells me the last part of this story—her toasting the deer shells and nearly detonating the trailer—the next morning she rails against me for pushing her into stories she prefers to leave untold.

"Damn you," she says. "I had an awful night. I just can't talk about Ben Harrow anymore, Cynthia, I just can't."

Feeling guilty, I of course promise I'll quit asking, but I also know that with the box now open, all it takes is a cue, a photo, a key word, for another story of Ben Harrow to pop up like a leering clown on a swaying coiled spring. It's as if Mom can't help herself from mashing the button, and neither can I.

The most buried family secrets are almost always the ones most mired in shame and social stigma, and Mom's were no different. Though she castigated herself for marrying Ben Harrow and for staying married to him for more than a decade, though she was not proud of her many years of drinking before sobering up when I was in high school, though she never got over her sense of failure in her mother's eyes, it was her arrest, public trial, and conviction in 1958 that shamed her the most, and it was the revelation of this trial, the aftermath of Ben's birthday visit when she was seven months pregnant with me, that took me most by surprise, that finally cracked open the fortress.

Many family secrets are badly kept—they leak out in asides or drift into consciousness through allusions in passing remarks or arguments. Some secrets might assume physical form in gestures or aversions, causing children to search for patterns in the static of a parent's inexplicable moves. Or they might be partially kept, with details intentionally omitted, the story edited to accord with a more conventional, perhaps idealized, family narrative. But I had known absolutely nothing of Mom's arrest and her three-month sentence to the Barnstable County House of Correction, had no inkling of its connection to the loss of two of my half-siblings, had no idea that her pregnancy with me was at the heart of it.

Several years before my birth, in one of the last of her many attempts to escape from Ben Harrow, Mom had braved Nana's longsuffering reproaches and moved into her parents' house on Rogers Street with her (now four) children. Having switched from the Coast Guard to the Air Force, Ben was assigned in the early 1950s to the state-of-the-art radar station at Truro Air Force Base, set up by the US Department of Defense as an early warning system against Soviet attacks. Scanning the empty horizon, he begged Mom to come back to him.

"Ben Harrow was the greatest convincer in the world," Mom says. "Things were always going to be different. And I was so stupid, I believed him every single time, just about. We'd just had another baby and he said, 'We'll move to Cape Cod and start all over.' Of course it didn't take long for him to start up again. Girlfriends, drinking, beatings." She rubs her left temple, her eyes anywhere but on mine. Her voice edged with self-disgust and wonder, she says, "I can't believe I put up with it."

Mom then stares into her coffee mug, her head lightly bobbing as a scene takes shape in the vanilla-scented steam. "I used to dream Ben Harrow was dead," she says. "He would be in a plane, it would crash, and he'd die. I'd get a call, or a telegram. In the dream, I'd be both delighted and ashamed I was delighted."

"How would you feel when you woke up?" I ask.

Bursting into ragged, asthmatic laughter, Mom says, "Miserable, because I knew he hadn't died!"

After Mom left her parents' home and rejoined Ben on the Cape, they rented a cottage on a narrow lane near the center of town and quickly became part of the village's tiny year-round community, making friends, joining the Congregational Church, and enrolling their two oldest children in Wellfleet Elementary School. A year or two later, in 1955, they bought the nineteenth-century saltbox on Lecount Hollow Road that I would grow up in. But not long after the sale went through Ben was transferred again, this time to Sembach Air Base near Kaiserslautern, built on hayfields wrested from resentful German farmers. Tasting a bit of freedom on Wellfleet's salt-scented flats and co-owning, for the first time, the house she lived in, Mom convinced Ben it would be better if she and the kids followed him to Germany later.

It was not an easy sell. Ben didn't like to see her head to the South Wellfleet General Store on her own, though it was just around the corner, much less put an ocean between them.

"He would measure the time it took me to get to the store and back and give me hell if I was ten minutes late," Mom says. "Then he'd cross-examine me: 'Where were you? Who'd you see?'" Shaking her head, she says, "Since then I've figured out that people who do bad things think other people do, too. That's their punishment—they can never trust anyone."

While Ben settled into life abroad and fell in love with a German woman named Freya, Mom tended her four children and got to know her neighbors on Lecount Hollow, including the tall, quiet man nine years older who had just been discharged from the service and was living next door.

"Your father was so different from Ben Harrow," she says, now sitting at her reclaimed pine harvest kitchen table, a gift from us children, and fiddling with a sterling silver scarf ring. The live ivy that once curled along the den's rough walls has been replaced with flowered wallpaper on Sheetrock. Gone, too, are the cast iron sink, the antique stove, and the enamel-topped table where we rolled pie crusts. Behind where I sit, instead of the pine dresser with a record player on top, a built-in bookcase stretches the length of the wall, crammed with cookbooks, novels, old textbooks, and photo albums.

"Your father never bothered or questioned me," Mom continues. "And I didn't bother him, didn't dig into his head. I was too inexperienced and too emotionally sick from all the hell I went through with Ben Harrow."

"And you had a bunch of children to look after," I say, imagining the daily diaper count might have distracted her from analyzing Dad.

"Yeah, that really set him on fire!" laughs Mom, her eyes catching the afternoon light through the window. The lilac bush in the side yard, which I can see from the table, is in full bloom, as is the ornamental cherry my younger sister, a professional gardener, planted for Mom. Their blossoms, soft purple triangles and pale pink circles, bob toward each other in colorful conversation.

Then, voice lowered, Mom says, "Honestly, I don't know why your father fell in love with me. Why does anyone fall in love? But he was kind to me. I thought I was so fortunate that somebody cared about me as much as he did."

While her husband enjoyed homemade strudels in Kaiserslautern, Mom and Dad started a life together in Wellfleet. Ben, perhaps suspecting objects off his radar screen, kept writing to insist that Mom and their four children join him in Germany.

Exhaustion sweeping her face, Mom looks down and says, "I finally decided, 'Well, I'll go. I'll go.' I was brought up that when you got married, you stayed married, come hell or high water. That's the way things were, so I decided to see if Ben and I could make a go of it."

Mom folds, flattens, and refolds a paper napkin, a coffee stain on one edge billowing like a brown cloud about to release a sullying rain. She loves straight lines but can't get this one right.

"I was so upset, I couldn't say what my emotions were, or why I did anything," she says, flipping the napkin again, her thumb compulsively creasing the edge. Looking up, she says, "Like most people who make bad decisions, I was trying to make a good one."

When she boarded the plane to Frankfurt in August 1955, Mom had no idea she was one month pregnant with my older sister Thelma. She and Dad had shared a romantic interlude on a woodsy back road near the end of our street, conceiving their first child while parked on what, ironically, is now the driveway to Thelma's home.

"If I had known I was pregnant, I would have never returned to Ben Harrow," says Mom. "Never. And I was so sick on the plane— I vomited, and vomited, and vomited. The kids were going crazy. When I wasn't vomiting, I was crying, because I was miserable over leaving Robert.

"When we landed in Frankfurt, there was no sign of Ben. Right there I knew I had made a mistake. I had five bucks, four kids, and didn't know what in the hell I was going to do."

Ben eventually showed up, his neck traced with the proverbial pink. "He was always a womanizer," sighs Mom. "Things just went from bad to worse."

She says that one of her beatings that year landed her in the military hospital, where no questions were asked. Mom knew that Thelma, who was born in Germany eight months to the day after their arrival, was not Ben's, and eventually Ben figured this out as well. When Thelma, still an infant, was admitted to the hospital for dehydration, he refused to pick Mom and her up, forcing Mom to find another way back to the base. Once again afraid that she—and now Thelma—might not survive her marriage, Mom obsessed over a permanent escape but couldn't imagine how she'd pull it off.

Then one Friday afternoon a trap door sprang open, an unexpected, serendipitous portal to a different future. Ben typically cashed Mom's military allotment check and meted out household funds with a reluctant hand, shorting the kitchen in favor of the beer hall. On that Friday, though, she got the check before he did. "My period had come the day before, so I knew I wasn't pregnant," Mom says. "I told myself, *this is your chance.*"

Throwing together a few suitcases and rounding up her family—Ben's four children and Thelma—Mom, barely twenty-nine years old, walked out the apartment door. She bought bus fares to Frankfurt and was on the next military plane to New York. This time, Ben could not get leave to chase her down.

Nana, resolute in her role as mother, met her daughter and grandchildren in New York. She and Bumpa drove the lot of them back to Wellfleet. Mom resettled in the house on Lecount Hollow, relieved to have an ocean between her and Ben. Though she was broke, she still had a sewing machine, a garden, and decent neighbors, one of whom was still in love with her.

She immediately filed for divorce. It was late summer 1956. Ben contested, citing a law passed during the Second World War that prohibited civil suits against military personnel serving overseas. Divorce was impossible as long as Ben stayed in Europe and refused to agree.

A year and a half later, Mom became pregnant with me.

Desperate, she wrote to Ben and told him, "Look, you *have* to give me a divorce. I'm pregnant." She made it easy, demanding nothing. "I was with all the kids in Wellfleet, and he was happy living in Germany with Freya," says Mom. "Your father did not want Ben to do anything. We didn't even ask that Ben support his own children. I mean, no terms, just a divorce.

"And what do you think that idiot did?" asks Mom, shot back through time to the devastating summer of 1958. "Instead of doing the easy thing, giving me a divorce, he flew to the States and went straight to the Wellfleet police station. He and the chief of police—Frank Davenport, a friend of mine—arrived on my doorstep, and Frank arrested me for adultery!"

My mother shakes her head in wonderment. "My God, nobody had ever heard of such a thing."

Images of Hester Prynne flash in my head. "But Ben was with Freya all that time," I say, indignation washing over me. "I can't believe he didn't just give you a divorce and marry her!"

"That's because you don't know Ben Harrow," spits Mom. "Ben Harrow never gave up anything. He only added to. He was never going to let me divorce him; he was going to divorce me and make damn sure it hurt. And after he got Charlie Frazier on his side, I knew I was in trouble."

Charlie Frazier was Wellfleet's longstanding town counsel, chair of the selectmen, and tax assessor. Known as "the Boss," Charlie had built his local fiefdom through stratagems of every sort, including trolling the tax records to see which summer residents were behind on their property bills and then paying the taxes until he could claim ownership. The year I was born, Charlie was waging a vitriolic battle against the proposed Cape Cod National Seashore, which would derail his plans for the thousands of acres of prime waterfront property he had snatched along Ocean View Drive, Gull Pond, and Griffin Island. But he still found time to accept Ben's case, dragging Mom—belly stretched eight months wide, with five children under the age of twelve at home—through a public trial for adultery inside Provincetown's Victorian-era courtroom in the town hall on Commercial Street.

Ben Harrow had irrefutable proof, the letter Mom had written saying she was pregnant by my father. Playing his part, Charlie badgered and insulted Mom before a room packed with curious onlookers. My grandparents, who had lent Mom the money to pay the outfoxed defense attorney, sat among them in the courtroom's wood-and-cast-iron folding chairs, anchored by row and bolted into dark oak floorboards.

Judge Robert Welsh, who had succeeded his father to the second district bench and who would, forty years later, be replaced by his son in a hundred-year Outer Cape judicial dynasty, heard the case. The Welsh family was devoutly Irish Catholic; Judge Welsh's father was a founder and grand knight of Provincetown's council of the Knights of Columbus, a conservative Catholic fraternal organization, and Judge Welsh himself was a fourth-degree knight, a "Sir Knight." Locals referred to the Provincetown Knights of

Columbus as "the Judge's Council," a hub in the Catholic power structure that dominated the town in the 1950s.

At the end of Mom's trial, Judge Welsh saw it morally fit—or felt legally bound—to sentence the pregnant wife of a philanderer to three months in the county jailhouse for having sex outside her abusive marriage. Her husband's enthusiastic infidelities failed to affect the trial's outcome, though they perhaps gave the family-loving judge pause.

My mother's humiliation was complete. I imagine her glancing, terrified, from Judge Welsh, who with his slicked-back hair and stout physique looked as much like a gangster as a jurist, to Charlie Frazier ("Mr. Wellfleet") and the spidery red blood vessels already creeping across his nose and cheeks, to her bantam husband and the cold flash of victory in his eyes. Or perhaps she simply stared dumbfounded at the dozens of Massachusetts case law books standing erect in the barrister bookcases behind the judge's raised desk, a battalion of the Commonwealth's edicts. The room's rich brown woodwork, its painted beadboard ceiling, and its antique brass hardware must have only added to the sense of having traveled back in time, of the uselessness of pleading a woman's case before men. The verdict was unambiguous. The century less so.

Later, on appeal, Mom's conviction was dismissed—"*nol prossed*"—by the district attorney, and she never served her jail sentence. Nor did the probation officer assigned to her ever pay a visit, sparing them both the embarrassment. But Charlie Frazier and Ben Harrow had gotten what they wanted: a conviction they could, and would, use against her.

Four months after my birth, twelve years after tattooing her name on his forearm and slipping a ring on her reluctant finger, Ben Harrow divorced Mom on grounds of adultery and "acts of a cruel and abusive nature." By this time his lover Freya had joined him in the States. While awaiting her arrival, Ben gave himself a skin infection blotting out Mom's name on his arm ("Served him right," Mom says). During the divorce proceedings, Ben played his trump card. With his childless lover sitting at the back of the wainscoted courtroom, he leveraged Mom's adultery conviction into gaining custody of two of their four children.

Never mind that Ben Harrow was a violent man and that Mom had her own damning letter, the one Ben had written after beating her in Biloxi, the panicked promise he would never again strike her. After reading the letter during the divorce proceedings, Judge Welsh ruled it inadmissible because too much time had passed and Mom had returned to him. Lowering the gavel, he awarded full custody of Drew and Maggie, still too young to start school, to a father who took them to make his future wife happy and his ex-one miserable.

Ben Harrow turned his car one last time toward the saltbox on Lecount Hollow Road before he, Freya, and two of Mom's children headed for the Sagamore Bridge and life off-Cape as a newly constituted family. Perhaps he wanted to pick up some of Drew's and Maggie's clothes, a toy or two, or to say goodbye to the two sons he hadn't chosen. I don't know. The what's, not the why's, animate the scene Mom reluctantly reconjures, Ben Harrow's parting gift of havoc.

Wired to strike and seemingly unable to stop himself, Ben slinked in the low front door of the house, through the drafty kitchen den, past the living room's amber paneling, and down the dim cellar stairs. Landing in front of the washing machine, he reached in and yanked out the agitator, whipping it against the cement walls until its hard plastic fins splintered. He then cut and stoppered the gas line, so Mom couldn't cook meals. Crossing to the other side of the cellar, he slid into the tiny, windowless pump room lined with wooden shelves holding the vegetables she had canned the previous summer. Kneeling, Ben popped the cap off the pipe to the well and poured laundry detergent into Mom's—and his other children's—drinking water.

Where was I, just a few months old? My two-year-old sister Thelma, my eldest brothers Geoff and Ted? Mom leaves these details out of the telling. Where was she? Hiding? Next door with my father and his family? Or was she in the house, pressed against a wall, relieved Ben was taking out his fury on objects instead of her? She knew the feel of bruised things, of broken things.

In his final gesture, Ben Harrow climbed out of the cellar, slung my mother's pocketbook over his shoulder, grabbed her sewing machine, and strode out the door.

"I will never believe what that judge did," says Mom, her face flushing, then collapsing, the details of this scene seemingly incidental, just another in a long string of invasions: "to give two children to me and two to Ben! If I was an unfit mother, take all of my children away from me!"

Fury and disbelief mingle with forty-five years of regret. "I didn't have a leg to stand on," she stammers. "But if I had been smarter, I would have argued about the kids."

Pausing between each word, her voice choked with remorse, she says, "I mean, I couldn't tell the judge which two children could go."

How could she, how could any mother, make a choice between one pair of children and another? Though often separated from their father for long stretches, my four older half-siblings had never been away from Mom. She had gathered them around her in every escape, carrying what she could onto train, bus, plane, car. To choose between loss and loss was impossible; it would have destroyed not just Mom's emotional self but her moral one.

Ben had no such qualms. He asked the judge for his two youngest, a girl and a boy. Perhaps he sensed my two oldest brothers' fear and ambivalence. They'd seen too much. Or perhaps it was a question of money: he'd have fewer years of paying child support this way. In the end, though, neither love nor legal obligation separated him from more than one or two token payments in support of the sons he left behind.

"Better to be dead than to lose two children like that," said Mom, who slumped into an emotional hangover for weeks after unearthing these memories. I felt as if I had yanked her off the wagon and forced a bottle to her lips. Seesawing between guilt and astonishment, I inwardly railed against Ben's brutality, against the calcified hypocrisy of the Commonwealth's adultery laws—still on the books—and against the cleaving of my mother in a Provincetown courtroom, the judge's gavel an unctuous blade. One thing was certain: we had reached the end of this story. I could never ask Mom for more.

It took me many months before I could discuss the adultery trial with anyone else in the family—I needed time to absorb this underwater blast in our shared history. I also felt the old, familiar need to protect my mother, so it was with trepidation that I eventually approached my two Wellfleet aunts to ask what they remembered. They claimed no knowledge of the trial, and for a moment, I'm ashamed to admit, doubts flashed in my mind (*Who forgets such an outrageous thing? Could it really have happened?*).

I couldn't bring myself to question Ted and Geoff, who were old enough at the time of the trial to remember it, so I turned to my grandmother, because in Mom's telling, she was part of the story.

I couldn't tell if Nana was relieved to share her memories, or if her natural frankness once again disinclined her to subterfuge. Fixing me with her pale Puritan eyes, she readily filled in details, including the letter signed by Ben after the Biloxi beating and the irony of Freya's presence among the courtroom spectators while Ben cashed in Mom's adultery conviction for the custody arrangement he preferred. Nana neglected, however, to mention a remark she had made that added to Mom's misery. Horrified by the trial, by the kind of sexual shame the Ingleside School had helped its pupils dodge, Nana had warned, "You'll lose all your friends now"—a tone-deaf, useless prediction that said more about Nana's fears than Mom's future.

Mom's partner Charles also admitted to knowing about the trial. Davey Curran, a fixture in Wellfleet's year-round drinking crowd, had told Charles about it when he and Mom started their affair in the late 1960s. Charles, a muscled and tattooed fisherman seven years younger than Mom, was aware of her reputation and wanted to know what he was getting into. But what I lacked was written proof, evidence of the adultery trial, of the legal choke-holds that had taken the place of physical ones. I didn't feel I could ever write about this without some kind of documentation, and it wasn't easy to find.

Although the trial had been held in Provincetown, the Outer Cape's district court seat at the time, the courthouse and its archives moved to Orleans around 1970. But the walls of the Orleans courthouse, whether intentionally or not, loomed as high as those thrown up by my aunts, and I left my first visit there emp-tyhanded. I floated some questions to a couple of lawyer friends from high school and called the Provincetown town clerk, to no avail. I finally spoke with the head of archives for Massachusetts court records, a competent, kind-sounding woman who ended up the most able to help. She told me that any trial transcript was likely destroyed but gave me the vocabulary to use at the Orleans courthouse to open the books.

On my second visit, I employed my most professional voice and requested the docket sheet for 1958 for documentation of a criminal trial. A clerk disappeared underground, emerging fifteen minutes later with a heavy volume. Relieved and apprehensive, I placed it on a large table and started to flip through its yellowed pages, trailing my eyes down row upon row of Cape Cod's petty crimes and misdemeanors, familiar names bobbing among the unknown.

Not far from where I sat hung a gilt-framed double portrait in which a world-weary man, awash in black robes, reclines in a red leather chair, his unnaturally large hands splayed on his thighs. On the wall behind him hangs the portrait of another judge, a painting within a painting, an echoing square of gold. The two judges wear the same necktie, the same white collared shirt tucked beneath identical robes, but the seated figure dominates, his elongated body stretching along the diagonal line of the canvas. The frame of the elder judge's portrait nudges the right shoulder of the seated one, like a good advisor against any gremlins on the shadowed left.

As I combed the docket sheet for traces of my mother, I had no idea that the unflinching eyes of the central judge in the painting were those my mother searched as she grew nauseous behind the defendant's table, hoping to find mercy there. I had no idea that the exemplar looming over his shoulder was his father, or that their namesake was at that moment adjudicating pasts and altering futures in the adjoining courtroom. I also had no idea of the true extent of Charlie Frazier's former power. Within weeks of his triumphant prosecution of my pregnant mother for adultery, Charlie won the sly prize he'd worked toward for years: appointment as an assistant attorney general of the Commonwealth of Massachusetts. Only later do I figure all this out.

Sitting at that courthouse table, it doesn't take me long to find the one line I am looking for. Seeing the legal details inked across the page, though, makes me lightheaded. Within the space of three weeks in the summer of 1958, Mom was arrested, brought to trial, found guilty of adultery, and sentenced to three months in the Barnstable House of Correction. Her appeal of the conviction was successful, and in October, shortly after my birth, the case was dismissed.

Then my eye wanders down one more line in the ledger book, and a phantom lurches off the page: Ben Harrow, arrested for assault and battery against Mom on the day of her own arrest, after he showed up unannounced at the kitchen door. No one—not Mom, not Nana—had mentioned this part of the story when describing the birthday visit, the blows conjured by these dutifully inscribed entries. Fixing my eyes on the red-brick walls of the Orleans courthouse, I imagine the scene: Ben and the chief of police at our front door; Ben enraged at the sight of Mom's fruitful body carrying me, another man's baby; Ben rushing past the chief, pounding or kicking Mom's belly as he had in Portland and Biloxi and Kaiserslautern; Ben yanked off Mom by the chief of police, who then had to arrest the both of them.

While unexpected and disconcerting, this evidence of Ben's violence is also oddly welcome, undeniable proof of what Mom had told me about her dangerous first marriage. Injustice, however, still floods the page: Mom got jail time for loving another man and carrying his child, while Ben Harrow was fined $10 for beating her for it.

Though Mom got the divorce she'd sought for years, though she married my father and kept her ark-like house in South Wellfleet with her parents' help, her losses were immeasurable. Nor was Ben through exacting revenge. After crossing the Sagamore Bridge with Drew and Maggie, who had never been separated from Mom, Ben and his lover disappeared into a web of military bases, rarely sending a forwarding address. He and Freya eventually married and moved back to Germany with the children, out of touch and out of reach.

For years Mom had no idea where Maggie and Drew were, how they were faring, or even if they were alive. She wrote to school districts where she thought they might be enrolled, pleaded with the military for an address. To no avail. Four years after the divorce, someone—I don't know who—brought Drew and Maggie for an afternoon's visit. Then they vanished again, to whichever military base or country they were living in. In two photos from that day, we children are standing in a line between the lilac bush and the privet hedge. Someone has arranged us from shortest to tallest, a shy smile on my half-sister Maggie's face, a stranger to us and us to her. At the back of the line stands Mom, smiling but with her eyes closed, as if she can't face the photographer, can't figure out how she feels or how to show it. She twists her slender neck away, her head tilted with joy or unhinged by grief. I can't tell which.

In the years that followed, Mom, willing herself through days without two of her children, folded mounds of laundry, canned summer vegetables, and drank to distraction on a circuit of cocktail parties and cook-outs. "No amount of booze could fill me up," she says. "I was in such despair I didn't care about anything. Your father kept you alive, really."

Growing up, we seldom spoke about our lost brother and sister, but when I mentioned them to friends, the story sounded simple. "They live with their father."

We children knew nothing about the divorce proceedings, and I didn't know how to talk about a brother and sister who were strangers. Invisible, they made their presence felt not in stories, visits, or letters, but in my mother's dreams of losing babies, forgetting babies, misplacing babies, then bolting up in terror and realizing her children are gone. The rest of us watched, uncomprehending, from the waking sidelines. We had little understanding of the forces behind Mom's drinking, of the despair that oddly heightened kindness and tolerance. Ambivalent about living, she didn't care about broken dishes, clean rooms, or school detentions. Mom forgave and shared. She drank, flirted, tried to forget.

Evenings, she often slipped out with friends to Al Graham's, a low-slung piano and dance bar on the harbor filled nightly by local workers and fishermen, or to the Chart Room overlooking the marsh at Duck Creek ("a party every nite!" blasted the summer flyers), other men buying the drinks while Dad snored on our couch. Weekends, my parents' friends arrived for dancing and whiskey sours in our kitchen den, the Formica table pushed into a corner, the record player blasting from the top of a dresser Mom had refinished and wedged into a corner. My sisters and I, camped in the attic, spied on the unleashed grown-ups through a trapdoor in the ceiling, their laughter foreign, reassuring. Many nights though, Mom sat past midnight at her cluttered sewing desk, ripping seams and basting hems, her eyes focused on some other world than the one around her.

Maggie and Drew began to get to know Mom and us again in their late teens, when they had a bit more independence. But what they didn't want to hear, ever, were negative comments about their father, whose heart, Maggie said, had been broken by the divorce. Mom had been the love of her father's life, Maggie would say, and Mom's infidelity had crushed him. "Dad loved her until the day he died," she told me, shaking her head in wistful empathy.

But the story I lived with had a different cast, one in which obsession had been mistaken for love, violence for care. During one family visit I unguardedly made a short, critical remark about

Ben Harrow (I may have called him a bastard) in Maggie's presence, a slip-up she never forgave.

"My father was a very fine man," she retorted before turning her back on me in disgust.

It was only in that moment that I realized the depth to which Maggie was herself invested in a legacy of secret-keeping, of avoiding anything that might bring stigma or shame on the family, or more precisely, on the Harrow name.

The need to hide such stigmas is what sociologists call a "slow violence," one that undercuts the very family life that the secret is meant to preserve, even when cultural changes may have softened its consequences. I had unwittingly wounded Maggie's pride, threatened her version of family history. Though her quick-fire remark struck me as protectiveness, it also betrayed an underlying discomfort with my digging into family history, an uneasiness that grew over the years to full-blown fury. My sister stopped talking to me, and Mom and I had a meeting with a lawyer during which Mom signed each page of a detailed summary of her marriage to Ben Harrow I had written, based on my interview transcripts and notes, Mom's unhesitating hand attesting to its truthfulness and to her refusal to have that history erased.

Seen in another light, Maggie might have also resented me for appropriating Ben Harrow's story, in part because like all stories, mine is but one version of the truth and unavoidably fragmented. We are such complex creatures, it's hard to fix our *own*, ever-evolving stories in a cohesive, consistent version, much less those of others, whose minds we can enter only through imagination, a medium ripe not only for empathy but also for projection and misinterpretation. This narrative about Ben Harrow is inescapably limited to what I have been able to glean about the role he played in my mother's unhappiness. Despite my asking family members for positive memories they might have of him, opening the door to countervailing views, none have offered anecdotes of his better moments, though Mom told me more than once that "Ben could be charming when he wasn't drunk." A sort of backhanded compliment, this remark says as much about Mom as it does about him. Her failings and generosity have allowed her to see gradations of character in others, streaks of white zinc under a dusky portrait.

Mom wonders if Ben improved with age, telling me, "He had very bad male genes, you know. Not long after our divorce, he had to stop drinking because of a heart condition." Perhaps becoming sober improved Ben's temper, making him less likely to lash out and his marriage to Freya a relative success. If so, Maggie and Drew had a different father than their older brothers did. Even when children grow up in the same household, though, they can experience the word or the rod in vastly different ways, often to each other's bewilderment. "If I had been big enough," said my brother Geoff, a rough Adonis who labored on California oil rigs for nearly twenty years, "I would have killed Dad for what he was doing to Mom." Maggie, too young to remember the early years of her parents' marriage, may not have seen such violence up close and was freer to choose a different story to listen to, a different one to tell.

Two questions dogged me through all this searching and interviewing: who owns a memory, and who is keeper of a secret? Or is the very notion of ownership a ruse, one that obscures the ways our histories and experiences bleed into those of others?

Maggie perhaps thought that because I never lived with her father, was a stranger to him, it was her story to tell, not mine. If so, that's like arguing that carbon monoxide, because it's invisible, won't poison you. Throughout my childhood, the aftereffects of Mom's marriage to Ben Harrow rose from some invisible, noxious pile in the cellar of our house, seeping through the fir floorboards and settling like oily kerosene on our couches, cabinets, and brass headboards. Nothing in that house felt clean. Maggie grew up with a doting German stepmother grateful for the two children she had been given to raise, not with a mother whose emotional being suffered a chronic internal bleed.

I met Ben Harrow only once, during the summer after tenth grade, sixth months after my father died. My brother Drew and

his young wife, perhaps hoping to strengthen our family connection, or just to get me out of the house, picked me up in Wellfleet
and drove me to their house outside Boston for a weeklong visit.
While there, Drew gave me my first tennis racket, taught me how
to waterski, and took me clothes shopping. But he also dragged me
to a small family party hosted by Ben and Freya, who had moved
back to the United States by then. I realize now that Ben might
have put my brother up to this, wanting to get a good look at the
child who, in his calculus, had cost him a wife.

I didn't feel I could say no to my brother, who had been so
kind to me, but I wasn't about to greet that man. Although at
that point I still knew next to nothing of my mother's history
with Ben Harrow, I had collected a handful of odd, unmatched
puzzle pieces and, overidentifying as I did with Mom, I instinctively disliked him. After guiltily, warily, slipping into the house
behind my brother, I watched Ben out of the corner of my eye as
he sank into a La-Z-Boy, where he cooed over two dachshunds
on his lap. They gazed up at him with the brown-eyed soulful-
ness of creatures bred to adore their master—or to anxiously
await his next gesture.

Ben then slid his eyes in my direction and hoisted himself out
of his chair. Making a beeline for me, he cornered me near a table
covered with a brown vinyl tablecloth and laden with mayonnaise-
drenched chicken salad in white hot dog buns, a bowl of potato
chips, a heavily frosted cake, and oversized bottles of Coca-Cola,
all of it as poisonous to me as the house.

Leaning close, his crystalline eyes drooping with bags, he cut
straight to the chase: "You know, I've never stopped loving your
mother."

I could have jammed the cake knife into his belly. And perhaps
I would have, had I known then about the card he'd sent Mom
a few months earlier, telling her that the happiest day of his life
was when he heard the news of my father's death.

Ben began telling me about the divorce from Mom, how he had
never wanted it, and I learned for the first time that it had taken

place in 1959. "But I was born in 1958," I said, my voice trailing with uncertainty, another puzzle piece wedged into my hand.

"That's right," he said with a conspiratorial nod, a satisfied grin, before lapsing into strategic silence.

He couldn't land a physical punch, but the psychological blow fell true. Perhaps he hoped I would run home and pelt Mom with questions that would hurt her, that would force her to a confession, but that's not how it worked with Mom and me, not then. Nor did I ask him more questions, as he might have wished, because I both believed and distrusted him. Though I neither took the bait nor encouraged the story he wanted to tell, Ben had won, like he always won. An easily flustered fifteen-year-old, I was outmatched by this man's cunning sentimentality. And as he no doubt intended, I edged away wondering if he was my biological father.

It was not a hard sell, after all: there were no wedding photos of my parents, no anniversary celebrations over the years, no stories around the table of how they had met. When I was a child, my parents' origin as a couple was a mystery: dateless, timeless, another absence with a worrying presence. This lack of a marriage story also felt like a secret, but what was there to hide? No one needs to justify a convention that society tells us to expect. Weddings are one of those pivotal life events captured in photographs on the mantelpiece, alongside images of graduations, children, and grandchildren. But when such events are wrapped in silence, in an active hiding of particulars, these milestones can become millstones, and this one bent my neck in an uneasy suspicion I could neither acknowledge nor articulate. This is above all what I felt about my parents' marriage: that it was not like those of my friends' parents, not like that of my grandparents' (whose fiftieth wedding anniversary was fêted with a huge party, a cruise to Hawaii, and a write-up in the local newspaper), not like the romances I dreamed of—and I carried that difference, that absence, as another form of shame.

It wasn't until ten years later, when I was living in Berkeley, California, that I finally had the courage to ask Mom who, exactly, was my biological father. It was my twenty-fifth birthday, and Mom, calling from Lecount Hollow, described for the first time the day I was born: how her water broke in the afternoon and how she waited in the autumn garden with her small suitcase for the trip to Hyannis. I saw my opening and asked, "Who took you to the hospital?"

A bit startled, Mom said, "Your father."

"So Dad was my father?"

A long pause. "Of course he was your father!"

Still unsure, not wanting to accuse Mom of anything but desperate to know the truth, I told her about the exchange with Ben Harrow when I was in high school, his claim that Mom and he were still married when I was born, the implication that I was his.

"Oh honey, have you been worrying about that all these years?"

Mom then related how she had gotten pregnant with Thelma and me when she was separated from Ben and how hard it had been to get a divorce from him. Nothing of the adultery trial or why she had lost two of her children—that information would come much later and after far more prodding—just how "impossible" Ben was.

I was mostly persuaded, but I also knew that in her eagerness to make others feel better, or to make unpleasant things go away, Mom sometimes offered me what she thought I wanted to hear, or what she wished were true. Maybe she wasn't sure which of her husbands had fathered me; I didn't yet know that Ben had been an ocean away when Mom became pregnant with me. So I pretended to believe her and hoped it was true.

A few years after that telephone call, when I was working as a legal secretary in an Orleans law firm during my gap year between graduate degrees, I serendipitously came across evidence that filled in Mom's story. One afternoon my boss, a real estate lawyer, asked me to search the dead files in the law office's basement for papers related to a disputed land-ownership case. The dim, cavernous room housed row after row of filing cabinets, gray metal pilings rising from a cement sea. The folder I was looking for happened to be in the "B" drawer. As I flipped through the dog-eared tabs, I started at the sight of my father's name, followed by the word "adoption."

*What the hell?* I thought, glancing around as if I'd stumbled upon contraband. The basement was empty.

I pulled out the yellowed folder and tilted its pages toward the fluorescent ceiling light, transfixed. It was one of Charlie Frazier's old files. Wellfleet's legendary lawyer had died less than two years earlier and bequeathed his legal files to a fellow selectman's law firm, which happened to be the one where I was working. Flipping through a dozen or so carbon-copied letters, I learned that Dad had needed to adopt Thelma and me, his biological children, because we had been born during Mom's first marriage and were legally Ben Harrow's. Perhaps in keeping with his attitude toward wives—not wanting to give up anything, even children he knew weren't his—Ben ignored Charlie Frazier's good-natured reminders for months, dragged his heels, and refused to sign affidavits, stretching what should have been a quick, pro forma process to two years. He only yielded when Charlie warned he could be held liable for child support for Thelma and me. By then I was kindergarten age, and though I had received all my medical inoculations, I was short a social one: my last name was not my mother and father's, but that of Mom's abuser.

Suddenly aware I had lingered too long among the dead files, I stuffed the folder back into the file drawer and climbed the stairs to my cubicle on the second floor. Crossing through the reception area, I passed the kind of wide-aperture beach photos and seashell pastels that adorn office walls from Provincetown to Sandwich. Beach grass and blue horizons, sailboats and sun. Just outside my cubicle I ran into my boss, a short, brilliant, vulnerable man whose lopsided and slightly stained tie matched the rest of him. I told him what I had discovered.

"Can I copy the file?" I asked.

"Jesus Christ," he said, massaging his forehead with a pudgy hand and starting to sweat. He glanced left and right, then lowered his head toward the low-pile carpet. Like the good lawyer he was, he muttered, "Ask me tomorrow."

I took it to mean, *yes, just don't tell me about it.*

More than two decades later, toward the end of her life, Mom turned the tables on family history one last time. Unbeknownst to any of us, she had another stunning secret, one she had kept astonishingly close for over sixty years. Driven by some internal imperative, by a sense of guilt, perhaps, she logged on to her computer and shot Maggie an all-caps email. Then, in a fit of regret, she forwarded it to me, calling and asking if she had done the right thing.

"MAGGIE, I AM SUCH A COWARD," her message begins. 'IT HAS BOTHERED MY SLEEP FOR YEARS. I HAVE TO FACE IT. YOU KNOW ABOUT ROY, DON'T YOU."

Few things capture Mom's impulsivity more than this unprefaced barrage, which exploded on delivery, vomiting undigested history all over my sister's neatly organized desktop.

Like many confessors, Mom seems to have been motivated more by feelings she couldn't tolerate than by those she was bound to create in Maggie. She was eighty-five years old and had something she needed to say, but did her daughter need to hear it? Too much childhood suffering lies in the difference between what parents need to say ("you should lose weight" or "stop walking with a swish") and what children need to hear.

No, Maggie responded, she did not know about Roy.

In the back-and-forth of emails and conversations that followed, Mom limped through the story, many details of which she'd forgotten. A few, however, remained clear. Back when Mom and Ben were living with their children in the woodsy trailer park in Maine, Mom noticed an announcement of an upcoming wrestling match in Portland's Exposition Building, a cavernous red-brick arena that hosted agricultural shows, sporting events, concerts, and rallies. The name on that announcement jolted the memory of happier, more adventuresome days.

Ever since his dalliance with her five years earlier in Boston, Roy—also known as the Texas Tumbler—had held on to his AWA World Heavyweight Champion title, and as a regular on the Bowser circuit he occasionally performed at Portland's Expo. A big, handsome rancher's son from Jack County, Texas, he toured not only in the US but also in Europe, South America, and Africa, earning features in wrestling magazines in which he taunted other wrestlers, boasting that he would take on any opponent, at any moment, in any ring.

The Texas Tumbler had no idea Mom was living in Maine. He had not pursued her after Ben dragged her back to Tewksbury and down a church aisle several years earlier, and he himself had long been married, with children of his own. He was also at the height of his career, traveling the globe in an era when embarking on a ship or international flight meant landing out of reach. I imagine Mom doing a double take at the sight of Roy's ring name in bold letters on a poster in downtown Portland, or maybe it was the excited brief in a local morning paper that caught her eye, announcing that the wrestling wunderkind would be competing in a best-of-three falls duel. The Texas Tumbler, the notice declared, had already defeated a long string of challengers to his title. His signature moves included the flying scissors, in which he'd trap and flip his rival between his boa-constrictor thighs, and the giant swing, in which he'd levitate and twirl his opponent by the feet in dizzying circles before dropping him to the mat and pouncing on his chest.

Mom, alone in the cramped trailer with her young children (Ben once again AWOL), made what would become a signature move of her own. With a ready band of friends in the trailer park, she had no trouble rustling up a last-minute babysitter. Making her way to the Expo, she arrived sometime during the middle of the fight. She could not afford a ticket to the match, but she wrote a note and slipped it to an usher, who delivered it to her former lover after the crowd-pleasing toss of his opponent in the ring.

I picture Mom as she waits, leaning her back against the cool, red brick of the sporting arena and flicking an Old Gold between her fingers, her exhaled stream of smoke the beam of a projector lighting up the brief season of freedom in Boston five years earlier when she had laughed and drunk and danced with wrestlers and their handlers, with salesmen, and with her tribe of young and single pink-collar workers still in the first celebratory flush of independent youth.

One victory secured and another imminent, Roy met Mom outside the Expo, and together they went up to his rooms. Within a week or two he was across the ocean on a four-month tour in Europe. Mom and he never communicated again, but she knew from the moment Maggie was born nine months later that she was not Ben Harrow's child. In a quirk of DNA fate, Maggie not only looked nothing like Ben, but hardly like Mom, either. Photos of her once-famous biological father in his prime look uncannily like a male version of Maggie in wrestling attire. The effect is surreal, with my sister's features—her high forehead, proud gaze, and prominent cheekbones—transposed onto a trading card picturing a bare-chested hunk with a belt buckle the size of a brick.

Because Maggie died just a few years after this revelation, before I worked up the courage to ask her about it, I don't know how Mom's confession affected her. What happens to your identity, I wonder, or to your feeling of continuity with the past, when the family you thought you had turns out to be only part of the story? Whether deservedly or not, the biological imaginary has extraordinary pull, and surprise twists like the one Mom sprang on my sister can fundamentally restructure one's self-narrative or notions of a "true self." But DNA is just one element, of course, in the constellation of events, relationships, decisions, luck, proclivities, and genetic inheritances that plot our lives. The stories these elements frame are both true and function like fiction, marked by leaps and elaborations and multiple interpretations. This pliancy of stories, affecting even which details are remembered, underscores the primacy of *understanding* over faultless recall when it comes to autobiographical memory, and it opens the door to personal growth as we experience, observe, and learn over time.

It is facile, perhaps, to suggest that discoveries like Maggie's effect a seismic shift in our sense of self, though they do point to identity's malleable aspects. I wonder if this revelation caused my sister to reinterpret some of her earlier experiences, changing her narration of them in ways that admitted, in part, what for her had been unspeakable. At a family event not long before she died, I heard her refer to the man she once fiercely defended not as "Dad" but as "Ben Harrow." Learning that she had been torn from her mother to be raised by adults with whom she shared no biological connection must have brought her a measure of grief. Did she continue to think of the man who had battered and vilified our mother as "a very fine person"? I can't know any of this, because our disagreement over how to handle family secrets fractured our already tenuous relationship. Without a story to share, or at least to partially agree on, we lost what little common ground we had.

Oddly enough, I think the notion of honor was at play for us both: Maggie wanted to preserve her father's honor, while I want to protect my mother's by turning the stigma of her abusive first marriage and the bad choices surrounding it into something else: an homage, perhaps, to Mom's survival in the crosshairs of a violent man and retrogressive state statutes, her disregard for convention, her emotional generosity—and most of all, to her ability, despite the weight of regrets she could never shake, to pour herself into generous relationships and creative projects. Mom sewed all our best clothing and warmed us under home-made quilts. She tackled our flower beds with her wood-and-iron rake and silver-spoon trowel, splashing color across the yard. She filled our messy house with redeemed, half-broken objects whose beauty she could still appreciate. Chips and cracks and worn spots never bothered Mom, and perhaps this is one of the reasons she not only survived her unhappiest moments but, especially in the last few decades of her life, thrived.

By unearthing and writing down parts of her story, by bolding the lines of her secrets, I realize that, at least in part, I am still taking on the dramas of my mother's life as my own, but I hope it's to a better end. I want to change the haunting of my earliest years to a hallowing and to stick up for my mother in a way I never could as a child.

Mom's secrets once dragged me under with the force of a hook snared in the belly, but her translation of those secrets into shared stories helped me to wiggle the hook free, to loosen my overidentification with her. Our differentiation, however, came at a price: my unintended bruising of my mother as I pushed her toward a mirror she would have preferred to pass by. Gazing into that mirror painfully framed her in her past and, indirectly, me in my own. But doing so made it possible to picture a very different future.

# 4

# Memory's Angles

My father got his hair cut on Saturdays at the barbershop around the corner, one of several businesses—the South Wellfleet General Store, the post office, the bait shop, and the liquor store—that filled the hollow off Route 6 nestled between the swampy ground bordering our backyard and Blackfish Creek. This salt marsh inlet was once the center of a thriving trade in mackerel and cod, as well as the stranding place of disoriented pilot whales—intelligent, social creatures that occasionally fling themselves ashore, returning to perish on the sand with other members of their pod even after pushed back to sea by human hands. Marine biologists still don't understand why most rescued blackfish fail to return to open waters, why their navigation systems go haywire, their bonding instincts overriding even self-preservation.

When Wellfleet was still a whaling town, residents would rush to the inlet after spotting the bounty, stripping the dead whales of blubber and boiling it for hours to render oil, the air thickened with a rancid, dead-fish stench. Dad, however, sought a different kind of harvest from the marsh. Each spring he raked up thick windrows of drift—winter's dead grasses peppered with broken shells—to mulch our vegetable gardens, while my sisters and I bent the green marsh reeds into fragrant beds, our pale faces turned toward the sky to watch gulls scan the mud for unsuspecting crabs.

This tiny commercial strip, South Wellfleet's crossroads of business and gossip (the town offered no home mail delivery, so everyone had a post office box), felt like an extension of our backyard. During the summer we made daily trips past my father's rows of carrots, tomatoes, and beans, through the scratchy privet hedge to our cousins' yard, past my uncle's yelping beagles, then down the root-stepped footpath to the back of the post office and general store—called "Blakeley's General Store" during the years my Uncle Waldo owned it. But biking down the paved street was quicker and often more fun. The hill descending from the intersection of Route 6 and Lecount Hollow Road was a thrill to take at full speed, my arms outstretched, the wind tangling my long curls, my scrawny frame all power and balance and daring.

A tall, elderly man named Willy had owned the barbershop for years, and he cut the hair of half the town, though it was children he liked best. He offered candy to any kid who wandered in, with a parent or not. After my grandfather, he was perhaps the friendliest man I knew. If one of his barber chairs was empty, he'd let me sit in it, where I'd twirl left and right, left and right, catching the snap of my brown ponytail in the mirror as it whipped the air. Willy would glance at me with encouraging amusement, his wet-lipped smile urging me to take a lollipop as he trimmed my father's prematurely graying head.

One summer morning between third and fourth grade, I sailed into the hollow on my red bike and took a wide turn at the end of the strip near Willy's shop, doubling-back toward the post office on my daily run to pick up the mail for Mom. Dodging treacherous patches of sand that could wipe me out in a second, I heard a sharp whistle and saw Willy gesturing to me from his doorway. I don't recall any words, only his head pivoting left and right and the commanding turn of his hand, whisking me urgently his way. Curious, I swung my bike into the small parking area beside the shop, leaning it against the building's white clapboard and under the red, white, and blue swirls of the barber pole.

The barbershop is empty.

"I have a treat for you," Willy says in heavily accented English, which makes me think he is French. Although I know a few

Norwegian words—the ones my grandparents use for Christmas treats, like *julekake* and *spritz*—French is the non-English language I hear most at home, because Mom, who waitresses on summer nights in a gourmet French restaurant, is forever trying to learn it from a boxed record set she has ordered.

"Sit here," Willy says, pointing to the row of grubby plastic chairs where customers flip through that week's *Cape Codder* as they wait their turns. I hesitate before scooting onto one. The seats radiate the smell of sweat, of grease, of baggy-panted men tooting gas.

Digging my hand into the candy jar Willy offers me, I wonder why I am there without my father, where all the customers have gone.

The barber then steps toward the door, flips the "Open" sign to "Closed," and slides the lock into place. A large plate-glass window to the left of the door bathes the shop with the Outer Cape's sharp summer light. Stretching out a pasty arm, he lowers the blinds. My heart begins to pound, and my world shrinks to the scuffed walls of the barbershop, my thin back curling as I wrap my arms around my knees.

With a reassuring nod as he hurries by, the scar on his right eye twitching a froggy wink, Willy steps into the open washroom to my left. I hear him whistling through his teeth—tuneless notes of nervousness and excitement—as his hands splash in running water. *Why in the world*, I wonder, *is he washing his hands?*

The barber is suddenly next to me, slipping onto a seat in a hungry rush. "Here, sit in my lap," he says, laying a thick hand on my shoulder.

I never sit in my own father's lap, unsure of his temper, and Willy's is even less appealing. But he is big, and I am small.

The barber pulls me up on himself and jiggles his knee as he hisses his whistle into my right ear. His sour breath and tangy armpits mix with the cloying scent of aftershave as he squeezes my flat chest with one hand and slides the other over my stomach. Loosening the button on my blue shorts is a matter of seconds.

Fat, insistent fingers plunge down and up, probing smooth, fleshy furrows until they find my modest opening. I hold back cries and tears as the barber pushes me past all stretching points, past all that is familiar and allowed. Unable to understand what is happening, I stare straight ahead, fixating on objects as my body becomes one. I see the chairs I have twirled in and the counter strewn with Willy's tools: brushes, hand mirrors, razors, and a large jar of barbicide eating the grease and dandruff off combs. They look like fish skeletons dangling in blue acid.

In the next moment I can remember, I am standing, facing him, my eyes on the door. Willy is bent at the waist, his sagging ass pointing to the plate glass window, but no one can see the obscene sight, the old man about to pay the nine-year-old for sex. His chin rolls toward me, his skin speckled with liver spots and his eyes filled with uncertain power as he hands me a five-dollar bill.

"Don't tell anyone."

To this day I wonder why I did not fight this man. If you were to ask my sisters and cousins, they'd say I was half feral, especially compared to my kind and shy sister Thelma. I drew blood in games of spoons and trapped my younger sister Beth under chairs so I could spit in her face and punish her for being Dad's favorite. But memory, especially of trauma, typically compresses and disorders time, so my fiercest fighting days may well have come after I tripped, unwitting and unprotected, into the barbershop.

I do know that after this, in fourth and fifth and sixth grades, I often ran next door before supper to challenge my cousin Richard to wrestling matches on the half-circle of grass in his front yard. Careful not to topple into Nana Lyda's prize flower beds, I'd wrangle him to the ground and sit on his belly, pinning his wrists and drooling on his face as he whipped his head back and forth to avoid my spit, the dark joy of domination coursing through me. But when I found myself captured in the barbershop, why did I not bite and scream and kick?

Re-entering that child's body as best I can across the decades, all I can feel is her paralysis and confusion. My father's temper was nerve-racking; did I fear angering Willy? Or did failing to understand, not having the language to name what Willy was doing, make knowing how to respond impossible? My guess is that, like many children unlucky enough to cross paths with a pedophile, I was immobilized by shock.

When I now picture myself in that man's lap, it is from the perspective of an adult who has just entered the shop, back to the door, happening upon the perverted scene. It's as if the little girl with unzipped shorts were waiting for someone to ignore the "Closed" sign and force the door, to growl *what the hell*, to lunge at Willy, just as I have imagined myself lunging and attacking a thousand times to protect my own daughter from imagined dangers. As my panties slid down, who was I hoping would walk through that door? My father? One of my uncles? A familiar local? Or was it a wiser incarnation of myself, there to urge my disoriented and dumbstruck self to claw my way out of that man's grasp, to run? Where had my fierceness gone? In that dim space between the locked door and the scooped out plastic chair, the seat of so much grief, wavers the ghost of my future self, straining to reach back through the years and failing.

So that little girl sits still, both stone and clay, in Willy's lap, vacantly trembling as she is invaded. A rogue current has flung her onto a merciless shore, like a stranded blackfish that can no longer breathe and no longer knows the safe way out.

Little does Willy realize how readily I'll obey his warning to keep silent. I don't tell my mother. I don't tell my father. I don't tell Thelma. I don't tell my friends. I don't have the words. Like any child, I have no vocabulary for an old man forcing his fingers—or more, but I will never know for sure, because what I remember most is the pain, not the assaulting body part—deep inside me, bouncing me against his secret place. I can't psychically organize it, and my staying silent means no one else can help me organize it either.

Just as my own secret place rebels against the excruciating stretch, so, too, does my mind. Unable to translate what happened inside that barbershop, I can't even confide in my favorite cousin, Holly, with whom I split the five dollars a day or two later, pointing to the place in the tick grass between the post office and General Store where I told her I had found it. This unkempt passageway, next to a phone booth we raided for the nickels and dimes that heedless tourists left in the change slot, was strewn with half-torn candy wrappers, cigarette butts, and concert flyers set loose by the wind. "Can you believe it?" I ask her, nearly squealing. "It was right there!" How else to explain a sum so far beyond my 10-cent weekly allowance that it feels unnatural, foreign, obscene, just like how I earned it?

Wandering down the gray, unfinished planks of the General Store's candy aisle, Holly and I pick out all our favorites—Sugar Babies and Charleston Chews, Mary Janes and Squirrels—before moving over to the magazine rack, where we snap up Archie comic books, Veronica's and Betty's bulging breasts a glorious sight, an inspiration. Topping off the shopping spree, we grab boxes of red cap gun rolls, which we smash between rocks in the sandy lot behind the store, breathing in the sulfur and tiny power of rapid-fire sound.

The last, but perhaps most lasting, image from this montage of memory clips is the ride up the hill toward home after Willy raises the blinds and reopens the door to his other business. Shaky, bewildered, wincing from pain each time my pelvis shifts to pedal, I know in my bones what is now foreclosed to me, what really did happen as an old man with a funny accent tore into me, whistling through his teeth. I even have the words for it. "I'll never be able to have children," I tell myself miserably. "He has ruined my insides."

These memories are among the clearest of my life, but I recalled them for what felt like the first time only many years later, when I was pursuing my master's in Berkeley, California. It was the fall of 1982, and the recovered memory / false memory debates—which pitted those who believe in the possibility of delayed, unexpected recall of "forgotten" sexual abuse against those who dismiss such "memories" as fantasy or stratagem—had yet to hit the public stage. I had never seen a therapist, and no one had ever suggested to me that I might have been sexually abused as a child. The return of memory came instead in a moment of prayer after an embarrassing exchange over dinner at the community house I had recently moved into.

"Dwight House" served as the student residence for New College Berkeley, a politically progressive graduate school of lay theology. I had met the dean at a dinner party in Bordeaux, France, several months earlier, and he had persuaded me to pull up my stakes in Europe and New England to join his band of leftist evangelicals in the Bay Area.

Though I had been raised in the Congregational Church, I was "born again" as an evangelical at sixteen, converted by my high school algebra teacher. Until I met New College's dean, however, I had never considered studying theology. But my heart had been broken in France, and grief found places within that God had never touched. So I gave up a scholarship to study international relations at Johns Hopkins and bought a one-way ticket to Berkeley, hoping that theology would help me sort out the experiences and questions rattling my faith.

In Berkeley, *everything* flourished: the gardens spilling vibrant, massy blossoms between stones and wrought iron rails; the Hare Krishnas who hopped, jingled, and chanted outside the window of my Biblical studies classroom; the seekers and healers and artists; the bars and coffeehouses and late-night movie theaters. I discovered lattes and salsa dancing, used bookstores and organic markets, hidden staircases in the Berkeley hills and heart-stopping views across the bay to the Golden Gate Bridge.

When I lucked into an unexpectedly vacant room in Dwight House, I joined a disparate gaggle of fellow theology students—male and female, African American, White, Asian American, Hispanic, straight, and undeclared—who were eager to forge a common life of shared meals, spirituality, and social activism. Although our trajectories varied, as did even our politics, we all thrilled to the drama of being single, in our twenties, and three blocks north of Telegraph Avenue.

On All Saints Day that first fall in California, I woke from a dream of rushing across a huge, arched, beautiful bridge. The moment I reached the other side, the bridge rose into the air and floated away. A change was on the way. That evening, my nine housemates and I cooked a dinner for New College's dean, who brought along his ten-year-old son. A brainy, charismatic gourmand, the dean took a pause from his lasagna and asked about my job at the county Blood Bank, where I registered blood donors for 30 hours a week to support my part-time master's.

"I just got a raise to $4.90 an hour," I said, delighted to be making more than minimum wage—at the time $3.35 in California—as well as to have medical and dental insurance, a godsend for a devoted flosser like myself. The dean's son, apparently unimpressed by my good fortune, asked, "But how do you live on so little pay?"

Dipping my head and giving him a knowing look, I said in a sultry tone, "I have my ways."

The boy reddened in surprise as his father laughed uncomfortably and my housemates looked confusedly at me. I was mortified.

After dinner, in the privacy of my room, I threw myself to my knees. Since childhood—since Willy, but I had never made the connection—I had been convinced I was, at heart, a whore and would have ended up selling myself in the streets had I not found Christ. It was absurd, a child's logic, a terrifying thought I kept strictly to myself, not even examining it in my own meditations. I think I believed it had something to do with my mother, her warm sexiness, the expert makeup she applied before sailing out in the evenings, the string of men she had dalliances with over the years. Charles, her French fisherman lover, had kept our family afloat after my father died when I was fifteen. That same year a short businessman with a second home in Wellfleet handed me a fifty-dollar bill for earning straight A's in tenth grade. Another unimaginable sum. My head had swiveled to my mother in the kitchen, where she stood making a boeuf bourguignon, knowing the gesture was made in pursuit of her.

Kneeling at my single bed in Berkeley, I dropped my head and asked, with maddened tears, "God, how can I think of myself as a prostitute, when I'm still a virgin? How?"

As if I had uttered an incantation, uncorked the genie of memory, barbershop scenes flooded me, ticking away like a 16-millimeter technicolor film, its razored images slicing through the intervening years of amnesia: the plastic chairs, Willy's whistle, the sound of splashing water as he prepped himself, the five-dollar bill, my painful bicycle ride up the hill.

*How could I have forgotten?* I asked myself, over and over. The work of repression astonished me. I had never taken a psychology course, had never been in therapy, had never even heard of such a phenomenon—the sudden return of lucid memory fifteen years later? How was that even possible?

What I didn't understand until much later was that consciously, audibly, voicing the word "prostitute" in relation to myself—probably for the first time since I was a child—must have served as a powerful retrieval cue, one that lit up the memory circuit for this experience, vividly reassembling the scene's visual elements, its smells, the spoken words, the pain, the overwhelming feelings.

Like much recovered memory, mine had the qualities of a flashback: involuntary, full of sensory detail, emotionally disruptive. Instead of recalling scenes from a conscious distance, I felt in that moment of prayer as if I were both viewer and viewed, transported onto my bike, into the parking lot, over the threshold, onto Willy's lap, the intervening years extinguished.

Though traumatizing all over again, this paroxysm of memory came also, oddly, as a relief. For years I had feared where my sexual hungers and economic insecurity might lead me, and I rose from my knees dizzy with the realization that in paying for the use of my body, Willy had treated me like a prostitute—I had not been born one.

I first believed the repression of this memory had been iron-clad from the morning I pedaled up the hill from the barbershop until the evening I fell to my knees in my room in Berkeley, but like many adults who recover genuine memories of early sexual abuse, I soon realized I had never completely forgotten it. Related memories began to surface, bobbing like buoys in the harbor, connected under the surface in an undulating line that still held fast.

The first such memory involved an exchange between my parents one late August evening at our Formica supper table, two months after my graduation from sixth grade at Wellfleet Elementary School.

"Did you hear Willy died?" asked my mother, passing a cracked Blue Willow platter piled high with summer corn from Dad's garden.

I went still, not wanting to reveal any interest, anxious to hear all.

"Yeah," said my father. "He had gangrene. Doctors had to amputate his leg, and then he had a heart attack."

"How awful," Mom murmured.

I sat transfixed, immobilized once again, but this time instead of combs and brushes I saw Willy's blackened stump, the surgeon's handsaw, the sweat dripping from his forehead as he shredded muscle and splintered bone.

*Serves him right*, I thought, jabbing yellow plastic corn holders into the ends of my cob.

A few months after this, I wrote a string of poems about forgotten memories, helpless children, and undecided minds. No names or details, just abstractions:

*Nothing came and took my mind*
*To a far-off forgotten memory.*
*It came and took my heart and soul*
*And left me in a trance.*

All radio transmissions from this sinking raft then went silent until my senior year in college, a decade later. From middle school on, as far as I can remember, I never brought Willy to mind, and I never thought of myself as someone who had been sexually abused. I did, however, make a vow to stay a virgin until I was married, though as hormones lay their inevitable siege, I only technically—Jesuitically—kept it (as one partner said, "If you think we're not making love, Cynthia, you're fooling yourself"). But it wasn't until I kissed Gary for the first time on the night before my college graduation that the memory of Willy flickered back on, like a stuttering filmstrip that had sat too long in a cellar corner.

Gary and I had been in love for months, but he wasn't free, and as far as my intentions went, I wasn't either. Our emotional intimacy, however, lassoed us both, and that first kiss, so long ached for, flooded me like none other had. It was as if every joint were a lifted dam, tenderness and desire and joy rivering through the channels of my body. As we lay spellbound on my old chenille bedspread from home, its raised mazes turning in worn, golden fuzz, I heard myself say, as if someone else were pulling my vocal chords, "I think I may have been molested when I was a child."

The thought was spontaneous, unexpected, the outlines unclear, no names or specifics. I might have even smiled in bewilderment, as if mentioning a girl I neither was nor knew. But I sensed her shadow just across the threshold, caught the swish of her skirt as she disappeared around a corner.

Gary, radiant in our embrace, said, "Your eyes are so expressive . . . I see in them exactly what I feel."

*He didn't hear me*, I thought, stunned. I could not repeat myself, could not swim against the currents and leave the halcyon harbor of his arms. The next day, according to my journal, I told my roommate what had fleetingly risen to the surface, but I wrote nothing about how she responded. I imagine she advised me to turn it all over to Jesus. She would have assured me that I was washed in his blood, that Christ had taken that wounded child and made her whole. Summoning the evangelical script that had carved deep grooves in our ways of thinking and speaking, she may have even urged me to forgive Willy.

While I don't recall my roommate's words, I do recall my feelings: against all odds I was graduating from college, I was in love, and I was heading to France on a Fulbright teaching assistantship. Why in the world would I distract myself by chasing memory's fugitive form?

This disinterest in remembering has been called a number of related names by social psychologists—directed forgetting, thought suppression, inhibited retrieval, dissociative amnesia—and the variety of terms speaks to researchers' efforts to make sense of the conjoined twins of remembering and forgetting. It also speaks to the rancor of the controversies in psychology and law over the possibility of accurately recalling long-forgotten instances of childhood sexual abuse. But is the practice of not remembering—that is, temporarily forgetting, even over long periods of time—the same as being unable to remember? I had not, it turned out, fully repressed this memory, but on the cusp of a major life transition—graduating from college and moving abroad—neither did I want to fully unearth it. Digging for treasure is one thing; dredging the mud another, and I probably asked myself what good would come of clouding the waters. One of my mother's mantras was "the past is a cancelled check," and at twenty-two, I wanted nothing more than to bet on the future.

The last scene in this constellation of abuse-related memories took place the following spring on a street in Bordeaux, where I had been teaching English at a lycée since the fall. I was walking past the stately but sooty eighteenth-century buildings on Cours Victor Hugo, snatching another peek at the medieval Grosse Cloche, one of France's oldest belfries, and dodging curls of bourgeois dog poop as I wended my way home to my tiny room above a mechanics garage. I never saw him, but I heard him: a cheerful man a few steps behind me half-whistling, half-hissing through his teeth in a blade of sound that sliced down my back, making me want to jump out of my skin. I had no idea why I loathed that man's whistle, why it created a desperate impulse to run, why it

sounded obscene, why it depressed me for days—and not knowing made me feel crazy.

As I stitched together these episodes in my thoughts and journal
over the months following the flashbacks in Berkeley, connecting
the dots and beginning to make sense of my baffling reactions to
seemingly random cues—that first kiss with Gary, that whistle
in Bordeaux—the complexity of the psyche awed me, its power
slightly alarming me. The return of memory, which I experienced
as an astonishing mental phenomenon, exerted an epistemologi-
cal force that humbled me, rattling the comforting certainties of
my evangelical faith and its tidy paradigms for what passed as
emotional honesty.

Unlike some women who have suffered sexual abuse, I never
doubted my long-delayed recall, never asked myself, "Did that
really happen?" Perhaps this is because I had no need to protect
anyone; the man who assaulted me was neither parent nor trusted
teacher, and while I had appreciated his kindness before the abuse,
hating him after it created no disjuncture in my world. I had no
one telling me that what I experienced was imagined, and I had no
doubt that what Willy had done was wrong. The five-dollar bill was
his confession, his acknowledgment of a crime he couldn't resist.

In the kind of triangulation many researchers seek when assessing the reliability of recovered memories, my experience was also
corroborated. A few weeks after the revival of memory in Berkeley,
I told my mother for the first time about the assault, and she told
one of my aunts, who told one of my cousins, who wrote me
to say: *Me, too.* Willy had lured her into his shop a year or two
before me, and though she had confided in her mother, they had
not—my aunt now regrets—gone to the police. Wellfleet, after
all, was a village, and I imagine more than a few of my friends
at Wellfleet Elementary suffered in Willy's hands because adults
feared exposing or further harming their children. I have no idea
what my mother would have done, but she was sure of my father's
reaction: "It's a good thing he never found out," she said in her

first rush of fury, "because he would have killed Willy." Whether true or not, it was what I needed to hear.

Later, after I finished my master's and moved back to the Cape for a year, I shared the story with my best friend from high school. Diane had grown up in Orleans, and her house—filled with sailing trophies, a ping pong table, and a miraculous array of vitamin jars—was my safe harbor during high school. Her parents added a photo of me to their mantel, next to those of their three girls, calling me "daughter number four." Diane had that marvel of a father, one who would hold thoughtful conversations with you, who understood minds nearly as well as he did the motors he fixed in his car dealership across from Town Cove. Her mother cooked healthy dinners (too healthy, her husband might say) every night, gave us milk to coat our stomachs before we went out partying, and drove me back and forth between Wellfleet and Orleans more times than I could count. Little had I realized, however, that Diane's family lived just a street or two over from Willy's house. In a low voice she said, "My mother used to warn me about him. We were never supposed to play over there."

I wondered if others in Orleans had known of his reputation and if this was the reason the barber had decided to hang his shingle two towns over in South Wellfleet, in the heart of a small community swarming with kids, a dozen of them with my last name.

I was to be a bridesmaid in Diane's wedding that year, and a few weeks after this conversation I attended her wedding shower in Boston. I took the Plymouth and Brockton bus there, and she arranged for me catch a ride back to Wellfleet with one of her summer friends.

"Do you know who her grandfather was?" asked Diane.

I had heard her name a few times in conversation but didn't know her family.

"He was Willy."

My stomach flipped. "You're sure?"

"Yeah. She said her grandfather owned a barbershop in Wellfleet. People used to say he was a dirty old man, so I knew it must be him."

My anxiety about spending two hours enclosed in a car with Willy's granddaughter—what would I say? What would I learn?—has erased most details of the bridal shower, but images and feelings from the ride home feel indelibly inscribed.

I was first struck by how chatty this young woman was, how quick to laugh. Her long, lemon-streaked hair swept tanned shoulders whenever she turned to talk with me, her hands resting easily on the steering wheel. She seemed so *happy*. We bantered for the first hour or so while I edged my way into asking about her grandfather. Finally, stomach tight, voice as casual as I could make it, I said,

"You know, I think it was your grandfather who owned the barbershop near my house."

"You knew my grandfather?"

"Wasn't his name Willy?

"Yeah, it was!"

"He was French or something, right?

"German, actually."

"I remember his accent."

"I can't believe you remember him! He died a long time ago."

"He had gangrene, didn't he?"

"Yeah, that was awful. He was a diabetic, gangrene set in, and they had to amputate."

I couldn't force myself to say I was sorry, but I could stay silent for a moment, dog-paddling in the honest waters of hesitation. Then I spit out the question I'd been contemplating for days, the one I'd been circling since the moment we left Boston, the one I was praying she'd honestly answer.

"So, what was he like as a grandfather?"

Had she been abused, would she tell me? I was desperate for a moment of commiseration, a history I could understand, maybe even an explanation.

She turned to me with a wide, toothy smile, her sun-kissed face glowing, and said, "He was the best grandfather a little girl could ever want."

I stared straight ahead as Route 6 streamed beneath us, wanting to strangle this beach girl. I forced myself to hold my hands still, to stay quiet, to resist poisoning her with the words *child molester, criminal, pervert!* I hated that man and his granddaughter's bubbly, childish love for him. My thoughts pinging, I wondered—had Willy spared her and her siblings, reeling in his supply of children on our stretch of the sandbar instead of his? Or had she been abused and suppressed the memory, as I once did? Regardless, I knew I had no right to shove her face against the window of my pain or of her potential past.

A half hour later, she pulled up to the privet hedge in front of Mom's house, crunching sand and stray oyster shells under her tires, and cheerfully chirped goodbye. Nauseous from the roiling desire to know, I stumbled, miraculously intact, out of the car and into the salty tang of Wellfleet's air.

Nearly twenty years later, I finally had the will to go looking for details. On a May visit home, lilacs and lily-of-the-valleys spilling from chipped crystal vases in every room, I sat at Mom's messy pinewood dinner table and began dialing. I called my sister, my aunts, my cousins. Did anyone remember the old barber's last name? I needed a name to find a death certificate, a death certificate to know the age of whatever was forced into my young body.

"Try Glen Rockwell," suggested my sister Thelma. Glen had grown up across the street from us and for years managed the General Store. "He knows everyone."

"Nope" said Glen. "Can't remember his last name. But I know who would."

I jotted down the number of a man who had trained under Willy and owned a barbershop up-Cape.

"What's it about?" he snapped when I asked for Willy's last name. Was it suspicion in his voice? Protectiveness?

"I'm trying to date something that happened around the time Willy died." I didn't tell him it was my private celebration at the supper table, my relief.

"Oh." His voice lost a hint of its defensive edge. "Celms, his name was Celms. He's buried in the Orleans cemetery."

*So close?* I thought. *Time for a reckoning.* I asked Mom for her car keys. "Don't make yourself sick," she said as I headed out, the brown leather strap of sleigh bells on the door clanging a jangly goodbye.

Twenty minutes later I pulled into the parking lot of the Orleans Town Hall, an ambling, white clapboard building bordered by a picket fence under maples and oaks. Inside, a clerk fetched an oversized, dusty book of deaths from the vault for me. Flipping it open and trailing my finger down the list of C's, I found Willy's information and inwardly gasped when I realized just how old this rapist had been. Seventy-nine. Eighty-two when he died. *My god*, I thought. *You'd think he'd have given it up by then.*

"Is there a map of cemetery plots I could look at?" I asked, hoping my troubled eyes wouldn't give me away.

The clerk fished in a drawer, then said, "Doesn't look like I have one, but the keeper of the cemetery should." She showed me a name and number handwritten in the top margin of a computer print-out and slid the phone toward me.

"Celms, Celms," said the friendly voice.

How often did strangers call, I wondered, searching for the markers of ancestors, distant cousins, predators?

"Looks like he's in the American Legion lot," said the voice. "Turn right off Tonset Road, 'til you hit a fork. That's the beginning of the American Legion section. Shaped like a teardrop. Drive around to the widest part and look around the center. You'll find his grave there."

*How fitting*, I thought. Willy in the swollen end of an earthy teardrop. I parked Mom's gold Saturn at the curve and wandered under spruce and cedars, Town Cove twinkling to my right in the undiluted spring light, sailboats scattered like white petals on the water. I missed Willy's grave my first time around, as I was looking for a tombstone, not a small plaque in the ground. The taller, granite headstones read Nickerson, Snow, Hopkins, old Cape Cod names that crowd my family tree.

Retracing my steps along a row of markers flush with the ground, I caught sight of a "C." There it was. Wilfred Celms. I scuffed the slab with my right foot, clearing off dead leaves and creeping grass to read the five-line inscription. Though raised metal letters marched across the surface, no epitaph, no words of relation or endearment or loss—"devoted father," "beloved husband," "forever in our hearts"—joined their ranks, just dates and the notation of military service and rank. An American flag stood at the head of his marker, tilting, off-balance, in a jagged parade of red, white, and blue, the colors of his barber pole.

This smear of stone, hardly bigger than a shoebox, somehow felt as if it were holding the weight of Willy's chest against my narrow back, his chin on my head, his hand on my life, all within the hard angles of a five-dollar bill. I wanted to spit on the marker but instinctively drew back, because doing so would have sealed something venomous between us when what I yearned for was less fettering than vengeance.

Memorials can work in this way, like lightning rods inviting the strike to spare the spot where one reads and creates and loves. But this stinting tribute in the ground, on a level with worms and ants and ticks, was also as prosaic and as devastating as the smudged assemblage of linoleum and plastic chairs where for years Willy spiffed up men and forced children, where one sparkling summer day he bent my 55-pound body and child's mind into shapes that, despite future healing interventions of every sort, would never regain the lines of an unviolated self.

Trying to organize my feelings in that graveyard, to channel them into some kind of action, I imagined posting a sign reading "Child Molester—Deserved Prison" next to the Stars and Stripes. Was it against the law? How many children would have been spared, I wondered, had Willy not been free to scout the playing fields with a candy jar and a clutch of bills? He should have been locked away years before it was my turn to sit in his lap. He may have been a prisoner of his own perversions, but it wasn't jail enough.

Standing irresolutely before Willy's grave, I shifted my gaze from the green cache of bones to the open sky, looking, I suppose, for an answer from above since none rose from the ground. To my surprise, I sensed Willy's disembodied spirit drifting among the whitecap clouds, freed from his body's obsessions, and it spoke to me. "I'm sorry," it said. "Sorry for the life I led, for the sorrows I caused."

*How could I still hear, still feel a connection to, this man?* I wondered, shaking with disbelief. I was stunned by this sudden presence, by the barberian molecules dispersed across the sky, tingeing it not with color but with a weightless, uneasy searching.

*I'm sorry, too*, I thought bitterly, the lichened stones my witnesses, the spring grass my anchor. *Sorry for the twisted life you led, sorry I ever met you.*

Maddeningly, against my will, I also felt the rise of something like compassion within. Someone who caused so much pain in others, I reluctantly conceded, must have suffered in debilitating ways when young. Willy, I knew, could well have been remorseless, considering me just more fodder for his pleasure, but what I imagined in that moment was a life pocked with self-hatred and self-recrimination, and it blurred my will to condemn, blunted my intellectual refusal to let this man off the hook.

*That's the way life is*, I thought, taking a step away from the memorial and, though I hadn't anticipated it, from the fight that had already cost me so much. *Can't force justice at every turn.* Our paths had crossed and there was nothing I could do about it. Regret it, that's all—regret it deep inside and one day tell the story that my memory, unbidden, had told to me.

# 5
# Dreams of Memory

~

Fear of my father thrummed through me whenever I found myself in the same room with him. Old before his time—he went gray in his thirties, pot-bellied in his forties, to his grave in his fifties—he was the chill to my mother's warmth, the killjoy to her party mood, the maker, not the breaker, of rules. One of three boys but the father of three girls, he was more at home with guns and dogs than with dolls and kittens. When I was in elementary school, he tried to rid the house of our orange tabby Rusty, tossing him into a sack and driving seven miles to Truro to release him into the woods. Two weeks later Rusty showed up at the front door, skinny for once and stickered with burrs. Dad, perhaps appreciating his guts but more likely never hearing the end of it from Mom, allowed him to stay.

In my early thirties I had a dream of Dad driving our old Coupe de Ville through the center of Wellfleet, heading back toward our house on Lecount Hollow. In the dream, Mom and I are on the trunk of the car, my sister Thelma on the roof, all three of us hanging on for dear life. I find the danger thrilling at first, but when Dad turns the corner from Main Street to Route 6 and I slide toward the edge of the car, I'm terrified by how easily I could fall off. The three of us, I realize, need to be hypersensitive to his movement and speed, compensating for every step on the gas pedal or brakes, the slightest change of direction.

Once I learned to approach dreams as visual metaphors and puns, images such as these went from bizarre to astonishingly incisive. In an elegant economy, this dream encapsulates the dynamics of our family life, my feelings toward my father, and the relative relation of other family members to each other and to him. My alertness on that car trunk, my response to every twitch of the steering wheel, mirrored the way I navigated our home, aligned with my mother and constantly aware of my father's coordinates.

If he was reading the *Cape Cod Times* in his chair by the kitchen stove, I moved to the living room. When he sank onto the couch to watch the news, I chose to play in the dining room or upstairs. If he was snoring, we tiptoed. I had a bag of tricks for winning fights with my sisters, and the most reliable was a one-word incantation, shouted into the next room: "Dad?" Terror flashed on my sisters' faces, and I tamped down my own by adding, "What time is it?" Because even I did not dare to enlist my father as a referee. He cared more for peace and quiet than small injustices, and his arbitrary belt could as easily hit me as a guilty sister.

Given my identification with my mother, it makes sense for me to be on the trunk of the car with her while my unassuming older sister Thelma is on her own. My youngest sister, Beth, is not in the dream, but if she had been, she would have been in the car, safe with her ally. Blond and freckled, the only of Dad's three living children to be born during his marriage to Mom, Beth was his anointed favorite. Their regard was mutual. She toddled after him when he visited his imperious mother next door, helped him pull weeds, and played with the rope as he strung up deer carcasses from pine limbs during hunting season.

Perhaps they also recognized each other. Beth and Dad held their cards close to the chest, noncommunicative stoics with temper flares. On the rare occasions we've talked about Dad, Beth—who hates these conversations—mutters, "I can't believe you were ever afraid of him." Thelma and I shake our heads in wonder at how differently our little sister experienced him.

As does our half-brother Geoff. "He wouldn't say nothing," Geoff says. "He'd just start swinging." While Geoff called my father

"Dad" (or "Bobcat" behind his back, because of the naps he loved),
Dad called my brothers "those boys of yours, Shirley." One day
Geoff and Ted decided to surprise him by polishing the hubcaps
on the Coupe de Ville. The sound of popping metal woke Dad,
and without a word he stormed outdoors and started knocking
the hell out of my brothers. Geoff cried out, 'We're just cleaning
your hubcaps, Dad! We ain't stealin' 'em!'"

On another evening, Mom asked Geoff to empty the trash,
which we burned in an oil drum down by the one-room summerhouse near the edge of the swampy marsh. Geoff brought along
his .22 rifle to shoot at the crows hovering over the blackened can.
No need. With the first glint of polished metal, the birds scattered.

Walking back into the house, Geoff heard the *Wagon Train*
theme song rumble through the living room, where Dad was
stretched out on his favorite ride, the couch. As Dad woke to another
hour of winning the West, Geoff crept noiselessly across the carpet,
gun in hand, and crouched behind the couch's bulwark. When
Ward Bond began galloping across the screen, Geoff popped up
and trained his rifle on the fleeing band of Indians, remembering
a split-second too late that his gun was still loaded.

Shards of glass shot back and the prairie went dark. Dad
exploded in fury, belting Geoff and yanking the rifle out of his
hands. Stomping into the garage, Dad fixed the barrel in a vise,
bending the shaft into an unlucky horseshoe that aimed the gun
directly at the person pulling the trigger.

The writing was on the wall. A year or two later, Geoff followed
Ted and volunteered to serve in Vietnam, though he was but a
seventeen-year-old junior at the vocational tech school. Promising
Mom he'd one day get his GED, Geoff got her to sign a permission slip for his enlistment, trading the books his dyslexia made
it impossible to read for the guns his hands felt made for.

Though I can't recall anything from my brother Ted's departure
for Vietnam a few months earlier, I have a mental image, much
like a photograph, of the day Geoff shipped out. He is standing
in our low kitchen doorway, one hand on his right hip, the other

cradling the plain pine trim just above his head. Snug Levi's, ten dollars in the pocket, hug his muscular frame. Light bounces off the white clapboard of the garage, flooding him from behind and shadowing his uncertain smile.

Mom is pacing the kitchen, her face strained, hands restless. She has argued bitterly with Dad, because he refuses to take time from work to drive my brother to Hyannis, where he will catch the bus to Boston and from there the plane to boot camp in Great Lakes, Illinois. Mom is too anxious to drive, so my brother hugs us goodbye, walks to the end of Lecount Hollow, and hitchhikes the first leg of his ride to Southeast Asia.

Tucked in his jacket pocket is something Geoff will carry during two hellish tours in Nam, two marriages, and eighteen years drilling crude in California: a delicate, half-empty bottle of Shalimar perfume.

It was the scent of the willowy, dirty-blond summer girl he loved. Her father, an off-Cape bank president with a summer home near us, had told Geoff he wasn't good enough to date his daughter. Offering a career warning, he said, "No one who stays on Cape Cod amounts to anything. All they do is fish, push brooms, or hammer nails. To make money, you have to leave."

"I loved her more than life itself," says Geoff, transported back to a brief season of Southern Comfort and sex among the pines. But for her, my brother was a hot diversion from a boyfriend back home itching for Labor Day. By September, Geoff had carved her initials into his forearm and poured in ink.

"I decided to prove I wasn't a zero and to get the hell off Cape Cod," he says. "So I went to fight for the good ol' U. S. of A."

With Geoff and Ted in Vietnam and my missing half-sister and half-brother with Ben Harrow in parts unknown, life in our house, with his wife and three daughters, became more agreeable to Dad. Cold after his days outdoors surveying land parcels for the Commonwealth, he warmed himself every evening in the tan, molded, plastic chair squeezed between our cast-iron stove and the kitchen counter. Directly behind the chair stood our makeshift pantry, an old army locker salvaged from Camp Wellfleet, the military installation on the bluffs at Marconi. Camp Wellfleet had been dismantled in the early 1960s to become part of the Cape Cod National Seashore, and one of my uncles had snagged the locker for us (and plenty of other stuff for himself). Mom painted it beige, wedged it behind Dad's chair, and filled it with breakfast cereal, sugar, flour, and canned goods.

Dad's evening ritual was as predictable as his outbursts were not: he'd pour himself the first of two bourbon-and-waters, sink into his chair, rub the deep indentations from his heavy glasses on the bridge of his nose, and read the *Cape Cod Times* as he waited for supper. We knew better than to interrupt. Only Mom dared annoy him, chiding, "Robert, no!" when he stuck his fingers into whatever was simmering on the flat iron stovetop.

I liked the way Mom—otherwise allergic to rules of any kind—refused to let any of us begin eating before she took her place at our small table. My sisters and I jockeyed to light bayberry candles from the Wellfleet Candle Factory, rushing to touch three wicks with one match before burning our fingers. In the way that some families kept lightbulbs or batteries on hand (nearly impossible to find in our house, aggravating me to no end), Mom stockpiled candles and an assortment of candlesticks, including a set fashioned from the dark oak spindles of the old Congregational Church banister. Her favorite was the ornate silver candelabra she'd had to buy back from the thrift shop in the center of town after my aunt cathartically dumped it there following Nana Lyda's death. I loved to pass my finger through the candelabra's three flames, to play with the fire and not be burned while waiting for supper to begin.

I don't know why Mom insisted we eat by candlelight every night, an incongruous flicker of elegance, but I think it must have had something to do with her artistic sensibilities, some need to refract our messy life with a glow. The ambience required a soundtrack, so just before taking her place, Mom would fish out an LP from the top drawer of an antique pine dresser she had wedged into a corner and put on Julie Andrews or Roger Miller for a spin. In place of conversation, cream colored ponies and crisp apple strudels, the rain in Spain, and trailers for sale or rent filled the spaces between us.

One Saturday during sixth grade, my friend Sheila Adams came for a sleepover. Earlier that day, I'd had my first trip to Betty's Beauty Salon in downtown Wellfleet, losing my long, tangled curls to what Mom reassured me was a "fashionable" pixie cut. Emerging from Betty's, I giggled and shuddered in embarrassment, pulling a First National grocery bag over my head as I walked down Main Street toward our old Cadillac, itself a rusty embarrassment we called the "Super Pig."

That evening at supper, my father turned to me with undisguised disapproval and said, "Cindy, you don't look like a little girl anymore, but like a little boy."

In a bolt of insanity, I blurted, "Well, Dad, you don't look like a man, but like an ape."

It was equally stupid to duck his first blow, as the second fell all the harder. Blood spurted from my nose, leaving me stunned and breathless. I let my mother lead me into the next room, where she cradled me on our hard green divan and held a facecloth to my nose. *I love you*, I thought, as my tears mixed with blood, *and I hate him*.

I then remembered with a horror worse than any physical pain that Sheila Adams was still at our supper table. A second later, I heard fast steps on the stairs and knew she had run to the safety of the bedroom I shared with Beth. I like to think I joined her there, but I don't remember. All I can recall is Sheila's fear, and my shame and fury.

After dinner my father, as was his custom, retreated to the living room couch, where he lay until bedtime, taking in the news and watching another round of Bob Hogan outsmarting Colonel Klink in Stalag 13, the Nazi POW camp pitched in the eucalyptus groves of southern California.

Fear of my father made it nearly impossible for me to speak with him, much less ask him for anything—money, a ride, help. Mom didn't drive, so friends' parents would have to pick me up whenever I was invited over. Our beloved PE teacher, Mrs. White, ferried me to my softball practices and games. I'd slide onto the scuffed seat of her brown and tan Ford station wagon as she puffed a cigarette and welcomed me aboard. Her discolored, horse-like teeth fascinated me as she asked friendly questions or told me to take my pick of the gloves and bats cluttering the back of the wagon. By the time I was in high school, though, my thumb was my surest ride up and down Route 6. I'd stand on the highway shoulder across from the entrance to Lecount Hollow Road and seldom had to wait long before a friend or teacher—or sometimes a stranger—swerved into the sandy embankment to pick me up.

Although my father never drove us anywhere he wasn't already going, he owned a turquoise, 1965 step-side Chevrolet truck that was, I now realize, his preferred vehicle for showing us love. He piled us in back—sisters, cousins, friends, whoever was around—and bounced us down Wellfleet's dirt roads, through woods filled with elephants, giraffes, and rhinos we "shot" on safari. He took us to the Brewster herring runs every May, when thousands of silvery alewives and bluebacks, catching the scent of their natal rivers, leap against tumbling streams to spawn in quiet, familiar ponds. We skipped along the stone gateways of the runs, climbed the boulders at the Gut down by Duck Harbor, and hopped the rocky length of the Indian Neck jetty, which my Uncle Kenny had helped to build.

A die-hard golfer, Dad often hauled us with him to the Eastham driving range, where we whacked our way through buckets of balls and he perfected his drive. We'd make a Poit's pitstop on the way home, licking cold softserve in the back of the truck as wind whipped our hair into sticky spikes. Back home, though, I stole Dad's golf balls and hid them in the backyard, driving in nails until green, compressed rubber squirted out like icing.

On weekend trips to the Wellfleet dump, my father would back the truck to the precipice of a gigantic, stinking pit, scaring my sisters and me witless. More fun, but almost as frightening, were the steep dunes Dad ploughed down to reach the beach at Duck

Harbor—a short-cut that is of course illegal now. The bed of Dad's Chevy would be filled with coolers, firewood, hibachis, and charcoal, along with an assortment of children, all of us sliding hard against the back window of the cab. Once Dad's truck reached level sand, we'd spread blankets, dig a bonfire pit, and head toward the water, picking our way across the prickly wrack line and a wide band of blue, green, gray, and purple stones. Friends of my parents might join us by boat, puttering toward shore and raising Budweiser cans in salute.

The water on the bayside is gentler, warmer, and saltier than the backshore's restless expanse. Just right for kids and older folks unwilling to tumble in the muscled waves at Maguire's Landing or Newcomb Hollow. At Duck Harbor, the adults drank, Hula-Hooped, and lounged in beach chairs beneath polka-dotted, floppy-brimmed hats. We kids turned over horseshoe crab moltings tossed off in a fit of growth, not knowing we held the casings of living fossils, creatures who were tracing flirtatious circles in the sand before the dinosaurs appeared. We dug holes for seaweed stews and combed the damp beach for vibrant stones, most of which disappointed when dry. Our most coveted finds were rocks with lucky rings, narrow bands of white streaking like a promise through fields of black.

I now wonder why it is that in my twenties and thirties, even my forties, I talked about my father only as a tyrant and not as a man who, unlike Mom, loved to organize outings and adventures for his kids. Though he made a modest salary as a surveyor, he arranged family vacations to the White Mountains, to Vermont's maple syrup farms, and to Expo '67 in Montreal, where I eagerly climbed atop an elephant for a ride. In the way of childhood memory, so imagistic and fragmentary, the only detail I remember from the world fair is a long, wiry hair rising from the cracked earth of the elephant's hide. The sounds and rides and curiosities from across the globe have vanished, but this astonishing strand of elephant hair remains.

The powerful link between emotion and memory might explain why I for so long privileged more painful memories when I told others the story of my father. Emotion is memory's jet fuel and landing gear. Affective intensity influences which of our memories are likely to be encoded and recalled, and which will reappear in vivid, well-defined images.

As others have pointed out, we might forget what a person has done, but not how they made us feel. For too long I remembered not the good my father did but the fear he instilled in me. On the beach, at the driving range, in the sailboat, I laughed and played, but never without care for where my father stood in relation to me. I knew the blow could come out of nowhere, and sometimes it did.

For many years my sporadic dreams of Dad tapped—and, it could be argued, amplified—these early childhood feelings. In most of these dreams, my father is trying to hurt me. In one, I am with Thelma, and Beth, and Dad at the beach. The three of them head off in one direction, but I choose another, wanting to escape my father's presence. Later, I am walking home alone when Dad, in his truck, spots me. He guns the Chevrolet in my direction, trying to run me over. I escape him, barely, by dodging between parked cars.

Like most nightmares (except, perhaps, some of those that arise from PTSD), this one doesn't replay a specific lived event, but it does capture the emotional gist of our relationship. Dad never, of course, tried to seriously harm me, but children are small and adults are big. When the adults in your life are angry with you and decide to act on it, no physical or moral boundary has the power to keep you safe, and this truth hurtles toward you like three tons of hot metal.

At forty, I had a brief conversation with my mother about Dad. She was on an early spring visit, trading Wellfleet's April bite for Atlanta's azalea warmth. We are sitting at my small kitchen table, covered with a cotton tablecloth from France, its black field popping with grapes, apples, cherries, and plums. Through the kitchen window we watch cardinals and goldfinches alight on a bird feeder near the blueberry bushes my husband has planted.

Looking up from her cup of tea, Mom says, "You know, your father was an easy man to get along with." She pauses, then adds,

"Mostly because he was totally uninterested in what the hell anyone else was doing. I could go out any evening I wanted, so long as I didn't ask him to go along."

How differently, I reflect silently, children and partners can feel about the same person. Or even siblings, as evidenced by Beth's warm attachment to Dad and Thelma's and my anxious one. Like many families, we children had different parents.

"Dad scared the shit out of me," I say.

My mother shakes her head in wonderment. "God, I wasn't afraid of him."

"Well," I point out, "he never hit you."

Her head stills for a moment as she scans the past. "No, he never did." Then a laugh. "That was a big plus, after Ben Harrow, with his flying hands and feet! But I never saw your father hitting you, either."

"Are you kidding me?" I ask, my anger rising. *Where in the world was she all those years?*

"I said, I never *saw* him hitting you kids. In fact, Ted told me your father used to kick him, Geoff too, with his boot!" After a long pause, and with genuine bewilderment she adds, "I couldn't believe it."

Did she not remember holding a facecloth to my bloodied face after Dad belted me at the supper table in front of my friend? Was she so grateful not to be hit herself that she failed to see the blows that landed on us children? How is it that I can still feel the bolt of weakening nerves that coursed through my thighs whenever Dad slid his leather belt out of his sagging pants and instructed me to pull down my own, so I could be whipped? I can still see the yardstick, Dad's other punishing rod, resting on the doorway trim between the dining room and the hall. My eyes flew there whenever we misbehaved or played too loudly for his comfort.

I can't, actually, recall the frequency of our spankings, which is no surprise. Our brains are better at remembering *what* rather than *when* or *how often* something happened. Maybe Dad didn't strike us often, and us girls only rarely. Maybe this is why Mom has no memory of our spankings. Or maybe the reels in her head, be they about Ben Harrow, her lost children, other men, sewing projects, Nana's criticisms, the next drink, were so distracting that she just didn't notice. Or, most plausibly, perhaps the spankings took place mainly while she was out and we were home with Dad, who wanted nothing more than a quiet evening watching television and was willing to strike to get it.

This I do know: the moment Dad walked in from work and hung up his orange surveyor's vest on one of the pegs near the door, fear of his anger caught me like a rogue wave, tumbling me over my head in anxiety until I swashed out the kitchen door the next morning and caught the bus to school.

Once inside our yellow bus, the best part of my day began. After a ride over the sandy crest of Ocean View Drive, where the vast, sparkling ocean promised a world beyond my own, I arrived at Wellfleet Elementary, joining the stream of kids jostling through the school's huge double doors. For the next several hours our teachers told us stories, guided our art projects, defined words, explained math problems, devised experiments with Wonder Bread and tin cans, and even played softball with us during recess. Despite the occasional reprimand, from 9 a.m. to 3:00 p.m., I was in heaven.

Though I was fifteen when my father died, to this day I remember only three things he ever said to me. The first was at the supper table when he told me my pixie cut made me look like a boy. The second also took place in elementary school, when he ordered me to bed early one evening when I played too roughly with Duke, our golden retriever. The third occurred a few weeks before he moved out of the house. I was in ninth grade, copying Rod McKuen poems into a spiral notebook at the old mahogany table in our dining room, its legs gnawed and shredded to pulp by Duke. Absorbed in my poetry project, I didn't hear Dad approach me from behind, but my neck prickled when I realized his balding head was by my right ear. Anger and anguish in his voice, he said, "It isn't me who wants this divorce, you know. It's your mother."

It was the most personal thing my father had ever said to me. I couldn't speak and stared unseeing at the papers in front of me, my pen paused mid-word. It was as if I had just walked into a bathroom and found Dad with his pants around his ankles.

*I'd divorce you, too*, I thought.

The morning after the papers were signed and Dad moved out—he held his ground until the last minute—I bounded into the kitchen and stopped short at the sight of him smiling, half-embarrassed, in his tan plastic chair by the stove, as if it were the only place he knew where to be.

*What the hell is he doing here?* I wondered, confused, even disappointed.

I failed to understand how the new liberty I relished—no more walking on eggshells! No more evening curfews!—had cost Dad his bearings. How attached, at heart, he was to the structure of our family. He had never lived alone. When Dad and Mom met, he was living next door with his family after years in the Air Force. Unflappably loyal to Mom and his children, anchored by daily routines, he was undone by the divorce, a single man set adrift at fifty-five.

He looked to us children, all teenagers now, as his raft, but we had already floated out of reach. He kept hoping my sisters and I would take to his freshly built, empty house off Indian Neck in Wellfleet. But the place felt foreign, and I dodged every invitation to spend a weekend there. What in the world would we do, what would we talk about? On the first and only, though we didn't know it then, Christmas after the divorce, Mom forced us to visit him. She knew Dad was alone and missed the ornaments and tinsel and homemade wreathes and gift-wrapped clothes and Norwegian cookies that filled our home every Christmas. We went, but nothing was familiar, little was said, and every minute felt more awkward than the last.

Again, in the way of childhood memory, I have a single visual fragment from the inside of Dad's house, and it's of an everyday item that the social scientist Sherry Turkle would call an "evocative object," one imbued with feelings and ideas and significance. Such objects are those which, regardless of their monetary value, we keep for decades, because they have absorbed our memories and connect us to stories that help scaffold the past.

On Dad's kitchen table sat a napkin holder he had bought at Snow's Hardware in Orleans. A modern confection of seeds and ferns embedded in acrylic, it was shockingly new, like everything in Dad's house—and like nothing in Mom's, where nearly every object pulsed with histories and accidents and associations. That napkin holder, which I loved and guiltily wished I could take home, encapsulated for me the twinned feelings of divorce and desire, the appealing novelty that even painful ruptures can bring. But it felt impossible to bridge the chasm between Dad's modern house, with its bare white walls and spare rooms on a bald patch of land, and Mom's creaky ark on a verdant swath at the edge of the marsh, with its bubbly windowpanes and hand-hewn rafters skirring with ghosts. I knew where I belonged.

Dad came over to our house after work nearly every day to check on us and on Mom, who was drinking heavily. He probably hated the emptiness of his own home and couldn't rid himself of the habit of silently caring for us whether we appreciated it or not. Thelma and I usually hid. One day when I heard the crunch of his tires on the sandy asphalt outside, I fled through the side yard and straight to the sandpit to wait out the visit. Did he see me run? How did he feel, I now wonder, when he saw Thelma and me squirm in his presence, embarrassed by his pain?

Once the divorce was final, Dad never forced us to spend time with him, never again yelled at us, never again hit us. He began leaving peace offerings, gestures of love that startled me into thinking differently about him. I grew to miss him more than I expected. On my fifteenth birthday, a few months after he moved out, I found a maroon knit hat and a box of chocolates on the chair outside my bedroom. The hat, with a small knit flower on one side, was perfect; how did he get it so right? Did he actually know something about me? He had already surprised me just before the divorce with a brand-new Raleigh ten-speed, gray and sleek and so much cooler than the handed-down one-speeds I had pedaled throughout my childhood. Dad bought ten-speeds for my sisters, as well, and I inwardly marveled that he could afford it. Was he trying to win us over? Perhaps, but that wasn't his style. I now imagine that Dad wanted to make sure we could reach his house, a place of safety, on the nights that Mom, as he no doubt predicted, didn't come home.

I began writing letters to him in my journal, trying out feelings I still too shy to express aloud: "I miss you . . . I know you were trying to do the best for me." I even admitted that I loved him, though I didn't dare say it to his face. One day, though, when I was finally an adult, he and I would talk, have an actual conversation, and I would set free the strangled words.

Nine months after the divorce, three weeks after his first Christmas without us, Dad was surveying land in Hyannis when he turned to a work buddy and said, "I feel dizzy." A second later, and Dad was on the ground.

Around six that evening I burst through the kitchen door crowing, "We won our basketball game against Harwich!"

Mom sat crying next to my brother Ted at the kitchen table. "Cindy, I have terrible news," she said.

"What, what's happened?" I asked.

Mom mumbled something—something, I thought, about money. *Oh my god,* I thought. *Am I going to have to give up my dance lessons?* I knew we could barely afford the portion not covered by my drama club scholarship.

"What, Mom?" I still hadn't moved from just inside the heavy door, too nervous to enter the scene. A wisp of January's chill slid across the threshold and swirled around my wet sneakers.

"Come closer," she said.

I took a few hesitant steps toward the table, strewn with papers and cut-glass ashtrays piled high with cigarette stubs and ashes. Night pressed against the single-pane windows behind Mom and Ted, the darkness and cold leaking in.

Mom couldn't lift her head. Was she drunk? She looked three times smaller than when I had left for school that morning.

"Your father had a heart attack today at work," she said. "He went very fast."

I burst into disbelieving tears. A few seconds later, I began a silent chant, *Get a hold of yourself, get a hold of yourself.*

Without a word, I yanked open the refrigerator, fished out a Macintosh apple, grabbed a steak knife from the drawer, and fled to the living room. My sister Beth sat motionless on the couch. I sank into our scratchy green armchair and stared unseeing at the console television set, where a talking head droned nonsense. I could not meet Beth's eye, could not utter a word to my little sister, who was thirteen years old and had just lost the one parent she adored.

After finishing the apple, I escaped to my room and scrawled a short, anguished entry in my journal. Flinging myself onto my bed, I sobbed and banged the peeling mahogany veneer of the headboard. "I wanted the divorce, not for you to die!" I moaned into my pillow. "Who will take care of us? How will I know you?"

Where I had often felt fear and something like hatred, I was now heartsick, ripped through with longing for a relationship unexpectedly lost. I felt like shouting into the void, *I didn't mean it, come back!*

"Are you all right?"

Mom, in a rare visit to my room, had come to check on me. She looked absolutely beaten.

"Yeah" I said, wiping my eyes. "I just want to go down to the liquor store and buy a pack of gum."

I was desperate to talk, but not with my mother, whose fragility and drunkenness only added to my despair and made her needs seem greater than mine. I slipped into the phone booth by the Black Duck and called my friend Karen, who'd seen her own share of family troubles. Though we raised hell at school, Karen and I traded poems and stories, secrets and philosophies, and I knew she would listen to me, would not need me to comfort her after the shock of my news. "You'll get through this," she told me, her voice already low and reassuring at fifteen.

"Crummy weather, huh?" said the liquor store clerk, when I walked in.

"Yeah," I said, looking down to hide my bloodshot eyes as I picked out a yellow pack of Juicy Fruit.

"I'm sorry."

Who was this person? And what was he talking about? Confused, still unable to lift my eyes, I slid a dime across the worn counter.

"I'm sorry to hear about your father."

I froze, stomach lurching. So even strangers knew. My blighted life instantly made public. As embarrassed for the clerk as for myself, I mumbled the inane response of teenagers and women everywhere—"that's okay"—and headed for the door.

The next morning I went to school, unable to bear the depression at home. Instead of banding together, my mother, sisters, and I scuttled to our corners. We had long before lost the art of talking with each other, each of us spiraling in separate universes, fractured by the stresses at home into jumbled collections of secrets we mistook for survival strategies. My father's passing, nine months after my parents' divorce and during the worst stretch of Mom's drinking, was just another in a string of crises that marked our family as doomed. I was terrified of being pinned under the weight of our relentless, destabilizing dramas. Desperate for an exit.

Friends handed me notes, ran interference with teachers, cried with me in the bathroom. They told me I was brave to come to school the day after, but it was fear, not courage, that drove me out of the house. I craved the structure and normalcy and warmhearted sympathy I would find at school, not the dark silence of my homelife. Though my geometry teacher poked fun at me for looking glum, my poetry teacher allowed me to leave class, no questions asked. After a classmate explained, he left class, too, and found me sitting on a stone wall between school buildings.

"Do you want someone to talk to, or do you want to be alone?" he asked.

Mr. Gray was my favorite English teacher and track coach, one of the few adults I could imagine crying in front of, confessing my pain. A brilliant, pot-smoking marathoner, he shepherded us through literature, poetry, and song lyrics during class time and then onto the playing fields after school. I ran for him, wrote poems with his voice in mind, and stayed scorchingly, at times daringly, honest in the journals he assigned us to keep and I knew he would read, not skim.

"Yes," I said.

"Which one?"

"Alone," I answered.

He kindly walked away.

We had an open casket at the wake. I did not want to see my father dead, and when I did, I saw a stranger: hands frail, face plastic, paunch sunken, his body flattened and widened into a human-size brick. But was he really dead? Part of me feared he'd jump up and grab me if I stood too close.

My mother stood over him, fixing his collar, as if she were still his wife.

"Mom, how can you touch him?" I asked.

"Why not?" she said. "He's not in there anymore; his life and soul are gone."

Horrified and curious, I mustered the courage to touch Dad's dark suit. I felt the thick arm underneath and jerked my hand away. After a long moment, I fingered the dark sleeve again. Then, as if in a trance, I slid my hand to my father's shoulder, cheeks, forehead, lips. His flesh was cold and tight under the pressing warmth of my fingertips. It was the most physical contact I'd had with my father in years, and I couldn't stop myself. Before I could wrap my hands around his cheeks, lean closer in, my brother Ted, sitting in the first row, hissed, "He's not Play-Doh, Cindy!"

Chastened, I sat down and shivered, staring at my father's profile. I was miserable, not sure I had ever told him I loved him.

In the weeks that followed, I clung to my daily schedule as if to a lifeboat. I told myself there was nothing I could do about my father's death, that I had to keep living as if nothing had happened. But I felt as if each of us in the family had been marooned on shattered planks, swept in errant directions by a capricious riptide. None of us was headed toward shore.

Six weeks after Dad's death, I had a dream of partying in a bar with friends. My father walks in with some of his buddies, really drunk. He doesn't know me. I keep saying to my friend, "Look at that man. He's an exact replica of my father!" He walks right by me without any sign of recognition.

But in a second dream that same night, my father arrives at the living room door and knocks. Opening the door, I see him through the screen and shout, "Daddy! You've come back! But how could you? You're dead!"

"My corpse was only a dummy," he says.

I am beside myself with joy, kissing and hugging him as I wake up in my chilly room. The house is dark and silent, not yet stirring in daybreak's streaked light.

Propping myself on my pillow, I stare into the shadows and know I have to try, again, for one more day, to live without a father.

To my own astonishment, I felt lost without Dad, desperate to know him. For a short while, I strung together the signs of his love—the sandy bonfires, the golfing, the truck rides and ice creams, the press of his hand on my forehead every evening in from work—that had been overshadowed by my fears and resentments. The divorce had made Dad less a tyrant and more human. Although his pain embarrassed me, it was something I recognized, and a vulnerable space had begun to take shape between us, a sandbar where a slack tide might have allowed us to meet.

I knew now I had lost my chance. My grief, so acute in the days following his sudden death, was treacherously aligned with love, sliding me toward quicksand that might swallow me whole. I needed thick branches, firm ground, and a horizon, and the only way I could find them was through hardening the story.

As the months and years passed, what I told myself and others about my father and our relationship became more negative and more fixed. I boxed up the letters I had written to him but never sent, preferring the drama of a father I feared to the loss of a father I might have loved. By the time I was in my twenties, the script went like this: "I was afraid of my father, he never talked to me, he's the reason I'm a feminist." Instead of romanticizing our relationship by ignoring its failings, I used a different sleight of hand, one that obscured nearly everything good about him, giving me something hard to push against as I tried to move forward.

I don't know if I was protecting myself from having lost him or from questions of "what if?" but I do know it would take too many years for me to appreciate a man who had chosen to marry a penniless woman with six children. The toddler and infant—Thelma and me—were his own, but we were born while my mother was still married to Ben Harrow. Dad could have dodged responsibilities few people recognized as his, something his mother had badgered him to do. I failed to see what this had meant for my father and took for granted his defiance of her, not to mention his struggle to fashion a family with half a dozen children bearing another man's name and a woman hounded by loss.

I was no less blind when it came to smaller, day-to-day kindnesses. Although Dad made us breakfast and got us off to school every morning while Mom slept in, what I remembered was butter-drenched toast turning my stomach and heaps of eggs I slipped to Duke under the table. Dad loved beach parties and barbecues and digging for clams with us, but as I told it, he never talked with us and I couldn't ask him for anything.

When I was a junior in college and still understood little about Dad's role in holding our family together, I dreamed of his cold face and threatening form chasing me through a series of events. In one of the first scenes, we are on a bus on his and Mom's wedding day, and he is—once again—trying to kill me.

At this point I still had no idea that Mom had stood trial for and was convicted of adultery, a public humiliation that shadowed her pregnancy with me and her relationship with Dad. I did not know they had been unable to marry until five months after my birth, or that Nana Lyda never forgave Dad for choosing Mom. It's tempting to think that my dream "remembered" something from my infancy, when I had no consciousness or words to organize the emotions or conversations filtering through or around me, but this is unlikely. That said, I do believe that dreams sometimes know before knowing occurs, which is one of the sources of their revelatory power.

While it was impossible to infer from this dream the circumstances of my parents' marriage, which for most of my life were utterly opaque, the dream's dynamics cut to the bone. Only now do I wonder if Dad resented the way Mom's scandalous pregnancy with me had boxed him into a corner. He could get away with being Thelma's unacknowledged father, since she was born eight months after Mom left him behind in Wellfleet to attempt, yet again, a reconciliation with Ben Harrow. But me, born two years after the last time Mom had seen her husband? The game was up. When my father looked at me, did he see the trouble I had caused, the way my birth had forced his hand? Is it possible that the dangers and the angers of those months before and after my birth carved pathways in my brain that imagination, in the form of dreams, later filled?

The murderous dream continues, with variations on the theme of me trying to escape my father's fury. In the last scene, I am throwing books at Dad, running around the library stacks, terrified and trying to get away from him. I aim for his forehead, hoping to knock him out. He's carrying a huge stack of books and is hurtling them at me, too. Just before waking, I am trapped in the well of a librarian's desk as my father rushes toward me in a deadly rage.

"What a horrible dream," I wrote after waking in my Trinity College dorm room. "I haven't dreamt about my father for years. I wonder why now."

Though I failed to understand it then, the imagery of the library and books couldn't have been more telling: analysis and nimble explanations had become my modus operandi, the avoidance of pain dressed up as wisdom trapped under her own desk. And in the multivalenced ways of dreams, that librarian's desk was also a womb. I curled myself in the hollow space between its legs, desperate to protect myself with books and failing.

During three years of therapy while doing my master's in Berkeley, I seldom spoke about my father. Whether with my therapist or my friends, I preferred the drama of my charismatic, recovering mother, who was very much alive. Hard and fast narratives, like those that framed my father, have a way of ending conversations, especially when a person is dead and can't mess with the storyline.

How do memories, or more importantly, our interpretation of them, change? Much of this transformation can take place in therapy and in conversations with friends, of course, or in reading, journaling, and even selective forgetting. I'd like to suggest, however, that it can also take place in dreams.

Starting in my twenties—and especially in my thirties and forties—I began dreaming about Dad more often, as if some internal clock had decided it was time to catch up on our relationship, or at the very least to add a few light brushstrokes to the rayless portrait of him I had drawn.

In Berkeley, just before returning to Wellfleet for a year, I dreamed of coming across our old sailboat at the harbor. In the dream, I want to re-enact a moment from my childhood, so I step aboard and sit on a pew-like seat. The sailboat, I quickly realize, is unmoored, and it starts to float away. Thelma, watching from the dock, is afraid for me, but I am calm, and the boat starts drifting back toward shore on its own. I decide to jump in the water to swim the remaining distance to the dock. To my astonishment,

I see my father in the water, rushing to save me. I don't need to be rescued, but the gesture is wonderful.

This dream, so unlike those that had long preceded it, was the beginning, though I didn't understand it as such at the time, of a tentative change in my relationship with my father. It became the first in an archipelago of remembered dreams that would lead me into more open waters, where other ways of seeing him and our relationship became possible.

My father's silence and temper had scared me, and his rules had maddened me, but during the years that followed this dream, I began to admit that his unyielding demands—dinner at five-thirty, quiet after six in the evening, a full breakfast whether hungry or not—contained the disorder of my mother's life, staving off the chaos that swept over us after the divorce.

How can a dream, or a series of dreams, change your relationship with another person, even if that person has been dead for over twenty years? The answer comes, in part, from how profoundly experiential dreams can be, combining perception, memory, and imagination in ways that feel very much like our engagement with the "real" world.

In dreams I *feel* my body flying through the air, falling from a great height, and swimming under water. I *see* extraordinary buildings, lush or scary landscapes, odd creatures, and people from my past, their faces more finely and accurately detailed than anything I can conjure in waking life. I *hear* words, crashes, footsteps, and songs. Although taste, pain, and smell are less common, they, too, can find their way into our dreamscape. Dreaming is its own world, and the images we recall upon awakening comprise our memory of that place. When a dream scene, or oddly juxtaposed elements, or even a single image, jolts us from sleep to wakefulness, we often begin to fashion a story of the dream, much as we narrativize the events of our waking lives to make sense of them.

But the congruences between the events in our dreams and those in our waking lives might be even closer than this. Similar neural structures light up when we *imagine* an event and when we *experience* it, meaning waking imagination can be described as a weak form of perception. If waking imagination can be characterized as a form of perception, and if waking mental imagery can modulate both our response to past events and our anticipation of and engagement with future ones, how much more so dreams, which are far more vivid and realistic than most waking imagery?

This question is important, because perception is intrinsically linked to long-term autobiographical memory. We don't, of course, remember everything we experience, perceive, or imagine; quite the contrary. But perception is essential to the formation of retrievable memories, those we can incorporate in our self-narratives as we grow and change over time.

What, we might ask, enables us to pluck an experience or sequence of events from the continuous stream of sensory information flowing toward us and to create a memory of it? Attention plays a critical role, of course, which is why two friends attending the same event might have different stories to tell about it. Sensory salience, such as vivid color, bright light, loud sound, and extreme temperature, contributes as well. Stress often enhances memory, though it can also impair it, especially if the stress is chronic. But one of the most significant contributors to the formation of long-term, retrievable memories is something we experience every day in both waking and sleeping states: emotion.

Mental imagery and varying types and degrees of emotion have long been linked. Is it therefore of any surprise that emotion is a cardinal characteristic of our most memorable dreams? I have felt paralyzed by fear, enraptured by love, and riven by grief in the scenes my brain creates while I sleep. Further down the scale, dream images and experiences have amused, confused, and frustrated me. Still others seem to contain no emotion at all, utterly unremarkable or simply nonsensical.

Dreams, in other words, have as much variation in significance and emotional valence as do waking experiences. The banality or seeming insignificance of many dreams does not render them meaningless, any more than the banality of many aspects of waking life renders *it* meaningless.

The point is not that dreams are inherently dramatic or pedestrian, comprehensible or bizarre, meaningful or meaningless, but that they can be any, or simultaneously several, of these things. Like waking experiences, dream experiences range from the inconsequential to the intriguing to the disruptive. We forget most of them, or don't bother to try to recall them, while now and again a dream might so affect or frighten or move us that it lodges in our consciousness for years.

Like an emotional waking experience, a powerful dream is much more likely to be remembered and to cause us to wonder. We might write it down, mull it over, tell it to a friend, or analyze it in therapy. This is the way, I believe, that such a dream takes on the quality of, even becomes, an episodic memory, one that recreates the feeling of an experience and its mental imagery.

To be honest, I no longer know if I remember this dream of my father swimming toward me to save me, or if I simply recall having had it. The externalizing power of narrative began to exert itself the moment I set this dream to paper, and I may be remembering what I remembered.

But like the memory of an event relived in the telling, recalling this dream affects me in the present: I see my father in the water, the concern on his face, his arms slicing through the salty ripples as he rushes to reach me, and my eyes begin to sting. I am not afraid, and this is a new feeling in relation to my father. Though I am re-imagining his attempt to rescue me as I write about this scene, in my dream I *experienced* his show of love, and this pushes the visual re-creation another degree into the real.

Is this dream less authentic than my memories of my father? Yes and no. It may have even replayed a forgotten waking experience. Throughout our childhood summers, Dad often took us sailing on the light blue boat that his former woman friend, the one with land overlooking Wellfleet Harbor, had given to him. Dad and my cousin Brian rebuilt the boat, which Mom rechristened the "Lucky Lady." Dad taught us to swim by tossing us over the side of the boat when we were close to shore and telling us to dog-paddle until our toes could touch the sandy bottom. Did he have to jump in after me a time or two? Maybe. Yet a plausible waking experience I have forgotten is less relevant and affective for me than this vivid dream experience. Though the father in my dream is a figure my mind has created rather than one with agency and his own internal reality, my sleeping consciousness experienced him as a live, active person, not a figment of my imagination or an extension of myself. That counts for something, and that something feels very much like a memory.

In the years following this sailboat dream, my father visited me, or I revisited him, in dreams that departed from the worn nocturnal scripts of my teens and twenties. I was not "working" on my relationship with my father in therapy or in my journal, in part because I was still in the throes of disentangling myself from my mother—an intense, messy affair. While some insights and admissions—like those concerning Mom—ambushed me, those about Dad more often edged in when my attention was focused elsewhere.

In one such artful dream, Mom is in the kitchen, and Thelma is with me in the adjoining den, furnished as it was when we were children. Dad has returned after a long, long time away. I am delighted and ask him all sorts of questions about his past, first in the kitchen den, then later on his favorite berth, the couch. He describes to me at length the many places he has visited and the various jobs he has held. He mentions teaching several times, and I realize, with astonishment, that my father has gone to college.

"I am a teacher," he says, as if I should have known it.

"A teacher of what?" I ask.

"Of history."

The irony hit me before I even lifted my head from the pillow. My father had not, of course, attended college, but my dream suggested he had much to teach me about the past.

I was launching my own teaching career at this moment, offering an undergraduate course on dream theories and interpretation, the subject of my dissertation. Little did I realize, even at this juncture, how much I still had to learn about the ways we not only remember people from our earlier years but also recreate them through selective recall and interpretation. It was as if Dad were subtly defending himself from my biased curation of our shared past, suggesting that the archives, both internal and external, might add other angles to the story.

Freud characterized dreams as disguised wish fulfillments, and while it takes mental acrobatics to make most dreams fit this description, this one wonderfully fulfilled two of mine: to have a long conversation with my father and to learn about his past, of which I knew, and still know, so little.

Dreams of my father were neither frequent nor uniformly positive during these years, but the balance was shifting. I now wonder if the oral histories I had begun to conduct—including with Dad's brother and an old friend of his—were "working" on me, albeit in the background, suggesting counter-narratives and more positive associations than those I had foregrounded since childhood. Through hearing others' stories, I found that my father, though still dead, was no longer pinioned in my memories like a beetle on a spreading board but had life and movement breathed into him. My interior representations of him were changing, which meant our relationship was changing. I did not understand this then, but my dreams evidently did.

Several years after casting my father as a teacher, I dreamed again of being in Wellfleet, in a large room with many others, including relatives. One of the walls is filled with old black-and-white family photographs, many from the 1940s and 1950s. I walk along the wall of photos, looking at them, and toward the end spot a close-up of my father, his face filling the frame. His expression is an admixture of anger and amusement, even more. There are so many emotions in the portrait that it scares me, and I burst into tears.

In the next scene, I am standing, clothed, in the bathtub of my childhood, sorting through a motley assortment of old objects as the bathroom undergoes renovation and yet oddly stays the same. Some of the stuff is my father's, and it's garbage. I box it up and toss it out the bathroom window. My husband, outside, works to dismantle a rotten porch attached to the house until it falls away in a heap.

Other details—boring, seemingly irrelevant—clutter this dream, and I've left them out of this retelling, despite Freud's assertion that "the most trivial elements of a dream are indispensable to its interpretation." While psychoanalysts and Jungians might mine such details for added meaning, they are, I believe, often the trees that obscure the forest.

I imagine that free association to each of this dream's details would lead *somewhere*, as most free association will, or that amplification might connect some elements to mythic or cultural parallels. But dreams, at least in my experience of them, are more illuminating when treated as visual metaphors than as a collection of disguised clues to repressed thoughts or a proscenium for the archetypes.

In order to discern the visual metaphors, we sometimes need to ignore extraneous details, fascinating and perplexing as they might be. Though this might sound like a dodge, it has its corollary in waking life, where the ability to generalize from myriad details is necessary to engage flexibly with the world. My dreams are sometimes elaborate, and when I wake from a vivid one, I can fill pages recording it—or bore to tears the unlucky soul who first crosses paths with me in the kitchen. But once I step back to consider the dream's architecture, the visual metaphors and incisive puns emerge from the patchwork of bizarre elements and shifts, often giving me that "aha" moment that so many dream psychologists privilege in ranking the competing interpretations that most dreams can absorb.

Though black and white, the portrait of my father on the wall in my dream was complex, even more than I could handle, offering a fitting metaphor for my evolving attitude toward him. When I first attempted to write about my relationship with Dad, fear of him had driven the story. I had made it the beginning and the end point, adding memories and details I had been nurturing for decades: his yelling at us for being too noisy, disciplining us with a belt, refusing to drive us to playdates, bossing us but not talking with us. The "aha" moment in mulling over this dream came in realizing that my portrait of my father was morphing from a single image to a mosaic. Like many changes, even positive ones, this one was not entirely comfortable.

While I have oral histories and dreams to thank for moving me toward more complexity, I also have my cousin Richard. A ruggedly handsome shellfisherman who still lives in the eighteenth-century colonial next to Mom's old saltbox, Richard agreed to read an early draft of this chapter. I was eager to hear his impressions and waited expectantly on his sitting room couch. Sand and dog hair stuck to the back of my legs while Uncle Kenny's hand-carved duck decoys stared beadily down at me from a high shelf running the length of the dark plank wall. Richard lumbered uneasily into the room, ran a calloused hand through his wild and salty curls, and handed back my pages. "This is not the man I remember," he rumbled. "You've written about a stranger."

I was stunned. Growing up, Richard was as much a brother to us as a cousin, as were so many of my Wellfleet cousins. He had *been* there. What was he talking about?

"Don't you remember the beach parties?" he asked. "The rides through the woods? That Chevrolet truck is one of the best memories of my childhood. Uncle Bob always let us join you guys wherever you were going. You've got this ass-backwards, Cindy."

I walked back to Mom's house with my deficient pages in hand, mystified and chastened. Though I don't remember the year this conversation took place, it was a turning point. I would not depreciate my own experience, but I couldn't ignore Richard's, either. And with that obligation to allow competing narratives to co-exist, I began to question the partiality of my adolescent memories, re-examining my journals to see what I might have ignored and mentally traveling back in time with a bit more honesty. Richard's construction didn't make my memories untrue, but it did make them less totalizing. In pushing back, my cousin offered me a window out of the claustrophobic room where I had lived with petrified memories of my father for too long.

As the second half of my dream suggested, I had a lot of garbage to throw out that window. It might have looked as if nothing was changing, but a renovation was underway. My husband, so unlike my father, was part of that, helping to tear down a rotten appendage to the haunted stage set of my childhood.

Two years after this dream, I had one of those rare, numinous experiences that shifts one into another register altogether. Love and transporting harmony suffused this dream, which ended with words from my father that melded solace and prophecy.

The dream arrived on the weekend that Dad's one remaining brother, my Uncle Kenny and Richard's father, was dying from a rapid series of strokes. I had seen him, healthy and smiling broadly at the sight of me, just a few weeks earlier during a summer visit to Wellfleet.

Though I was thinking about my uncle that weekend, grieving his impending loss, my father's words in the dream spoke to existential doubts I have felt since childhood. These doubts, these preoccupations, concern the worth, or in darker phrasing, the cost, of living. Too often, the world's problems—pollution, racism, war, misogyny, injustice, and sexual violence—have caused me to rank life as overrated. It took me a long time to recognize that this ambivalence was rooted not so much in the world's objective ills as in something far closer to home: my fear of physical pain and loss of control over my body. While the kindness of others, beauty in nature, and promises of science feel every bit as real as any negative counterparts, the unpredictability of suffering has sometimes threatened to trump all.

While studying World War II in my tenth-grade European history class, I was amazed by the drive to live on the part of concentration camp inmates. Had I landed in that hellscape, I knew exactly what I would do: hurl myself against the electrified wire, hopefully taking a sadistic guard with me. Any other response perplexed me. Well into my twenties I had recurring dreams that I was a Jew chased by Nazis, their accents, unsurprisingly, echoing the one I first heard in the barbershop but didn't remember. I knew I was prey and instinctively understood the value of a cyanide ampoule disguised as a coat button or tucked inside the mouth. Suffering has frightened me far more than death, which tempts with the guarantee of an escape hatch, a strategic maneuver outflanking cruelty or pain. How confounding, though, that taking control of one's life could well mean ending it.

In my Sunday morning dream, I am standing under a large, open tent in the yard of our home in South Wellfleet, by the living room my father added to the house a couple of years after my birth. It is pouring rain. Suddenly Dad joins my husband and me, and I silently introduce them with a gesture. Dad is the age when he died, fifty-six. I understand that the veil between our worlds has torn, that Dad is dead and this is a visit from the other side.

My father is emanating love, quietly overjoyed to be with me, as I am with him. We do not speak but hold each other's gaze, currents of loving kindness flowing between and around us. I know Mom won't join us because of the rain, but Thelma walks quickly toward us under the tarp. She stays at the edge in her tan raincoat, smiling widely, goodness personified.

The scene shifts, and now Dad and I are sitting on the edge of a small rise in the yard that borders what used to be his vegetable garden, near the summerhouse and Mom's irises. The rain has stopped. I ask my father about my future. A radiant smile on his face, he grasps my hands in his and looks me in the eyes. "There will be moments you will want to kill yourself," he says, "but you will live a long life."

The air still tingles with his promise when I wake.

Experienced as intensely real, even transcendent, this dream brought tears as I remembered it, wrote it, and shared it. And it helped to order all the other dreams that had come before, revealing them for the steppingstones they were. If I hadn't acknowledged it already, I now knew without a doubt that a boundary had been crossed, both inside the dream and outside it. My relationship to Dad had changed.

But did this archipelago of dreams *reflect* my altered view of him, or help *create* it?

I hadn't, of course, willed myself into having positive dreams of Dad, nor had I attempted to "incubate" them by looking at a photo or focusing my thoughts on him before falling asleep. I didn't even realize I needed or wanted such dreams. Each of the dreams in this series—which continues to this day—arrived like a gift, unexpected, even bewildering. But these unanticipated visions did not just lead me to new understandings or admissions. They *happened* to me. They had the same being-there, from-the-inside quality of episodic memories, much like my "impossible" memories of the ghost.

The immersive, perceptual experience of these dreams, coupled with their intense emotion, caused them to exert enduring effects on the present. How like dreams, though, to have done so by predicting my future to my present self in the landscape of my past!

Gravity, according to Einstein, is caused by the warping of space and time, a fitting metaphor for most dreams, but especially this one. Such warping can be disorienting, but it also has the power to ground us. And the unrestrained choreography of tenses in our dreams is replicated in our waking lives, albeit more subtly. It is well established that we experience the present through the past, remember the past through the present, and use the present and past to picture the future. Indeed, functional brain imaging shows that recalling past experiences recruits the same network of brain regions as imagining future ones; this neural network also lights up when creatively solving problems in the present.

I would argue that dreams, however, take this temporal agility a step further, by enacting their often bizarre melding of tenses through characters and props and scenery that paint concepts into animated existence and thereby insist, without brokering dissent, on our presence.

I have come to think of this succession of dreams about my father as analogous to the stories I coaxed out of the living: events powerful enough to loosen the hold of fixed judgments, nudging our relationship along a narrative line that has allowed me to recognize love, both his and mine. These dreams, I believe, laid new neural connections and mental associations that have built on each other over time, allowing positive changes in our relationship. I now appreciate Dad in a way I couldn't when younger, blinded first by fear, then by ignorance of his history and adolescent preoccupation with my own dramas, not his. Now an adult and a parent, I have more compassion for him, a slightly better idea of what he might have been experiencing behind the wall of silence.

I wish I had found a way inside while Dad was still alive, but I am grateful for the avenues that conversations and interviews with others, historical documents, rereading my childhood journals, and, most significantly, my dreams, have offered in the last few decades. Despite the anxieties he provoked in me, despite his faults and limitations, my father was, and probably had always been, on my side. Perfect? Not even close. A failed father? No longer.

Although I still have a rare bad dream about my father, far more often it's a joy to meet him in the landscape of wakeful sleep. His death may have erased one kind of voice, but dreams have allowed another to emerge, taking a pencil to the script and revising the storyline.

# 6
# Found by Stories

~

"I know you," my mother would sometimes say to me as an adult (usually during an argument). Few things irritated me more, because "I know you" tossed me into a pen of her assessments and expectations, with no gate for escape. I could change my actions, but fix who I am? That was a taller order.

Depending on whatever we were fighting about, I was selfish, I was stubborn, I was wild, I was a problem.

I was also a prude. "What do you think you have that no other girl has?" she scoffed one morning as she breezed into the bathroom to apply her make-up before a waitressing shift. I was about to jump into the shower and reflexively clutched a towel to my chest. While I was used to sharing spaces, my fourteen-year-old body felt like a brush fire, melting and exploding into new shapes that astonished and, at times, pleased me. But its newness made me shy.

I had no answer for Mom, and even conceded her point, because at this stage I still desperately wanted her to be right, despite how risky, how wrong, her choices felt. From her first cigarette when she woke, her cocktails at noon, and her diversions at night, she was shredding herself, bit by bit, before my eyes. I couldn't afford to lose her and knew I might. So her scolding became my own, and I told myself that privacy was a luxury in a crowded house with two small bathrooms. I just needed to get with the program.

Mom's own riotous immodesty set the standard. My friends would come over and find her standing in the dining room in her bra and underwear, ironing her waitressing uniform as an Old Gold teetered on the edge of an iridescent abalone shell and a cup of Sanka stood, half drunk, on the nearest table. She'd simply wave to my pals with a cheery hello and welcome them in.

Mom's lack of embarrassment enveloped the house, which she artfully filled with cast-offs from neighbors, friends, and relatives. While Nana, with her self-playing piano and aluminum Christmas tree, thrilled to the modern, Mom never saw a piece of furniture she couldn't refinish or reupholster into something useful, if not beautiful. "I *like* old things in old houses," she snapped as she ripped off the sticky decorative paper an elementary school friend and I had used to spiff up the trusty, enamel-top baking table in our kitchen. Mom was heartbroken when the house on Rogers Street was torn down to make way for I-495 and discovered that Nana had consigned the attic—crammed with vintage clothing, antique trunks, dinged mahogany furniture, and turn-of-the century books—to the wrecking ball. Twenty years later, after my grandfather's death, Nana sold most of the best pieces she had kept in a dollar yard sale, her eagerness to earn a bit of cash overriding values of another sort.

The only new piece of furniture in our house might have been the Formica and aluminum dinette set in the kitchen den where we ate most of our meals. But that also could have been a hand-me-down. Everything—our living room couches, our bureaus and beds—had histories coded in burn marks, jammed drawers, loose knobs, and hollows where someone else had loved to sit.

Even our floor-to-ceiling bathroom shelves were crowded with lotions or pills that were years, and sometimes decades, past their expiration date, because throwing away anything Mom considered "perfectly good" was treason. Our pine cabinets in the kitchen were equally jumbled, filled with uneven stacks of Dresden porcelain, clunky supermarket give-aways, my great-grandparents' Blue Willow china, and Cunard Line crockery that had been tossed overboard by cruise ship revelers and dragged from the seafloor thirty miles off the coast of New York in Charles's iron and twine scallop dredges. "Matching," Mom says, "is for squares."

Though I longed for more order and less clutter (and more modernity, such as outlets near the baseboards instead of near the ceiling), my friends seemed to find our house relaxing. They didn't mind the faucet handle that turned on in both directions, or the seven clocks set at wildly different times, none of them right ("I never know what time it really is," one of my brothers grumbled. "Shows you how important time is," Mom said). If we tracked in mud or chunks of icy snow, she just threw more newspapers on the floor. And rules? They had been Mom's bête noire, so she went easy on us, as long as we conducted our pillow fights *inside* the house, not in the garden, and our squirt gun battles in the cellar, not the living room. She made batches of fudge on the cast-iron stovetop and left boxes of Whitman's chocolates open for raiding. "Have a rip in those jeans?" she'd ask my friends sleeping over. "I'll fix it tonight." If they were homesick, she'd rub their back until they fell asleep.

They adored her almost as much as I did.

What Mom didn't realize when she chided me in the bathroom was that the story I couldn't tell, the one I would do everything to forget, had lodged itself in my body, leaking out in choices that might have been read as the alarm signals they were but got lost in the household noise.

In one of the first Halloweens after my exchange with Willy in the barbershop—it must have been the fall of fifth or sixth grade, because by middle school I had swerved from collecting candy to throwing eggs—I knew instinctively what I wanted to dress up as.

I put a lot of thought into my costume, though I told everyone I chose it because it was so easy to pull off. Excessive jewelry seemed key. I fished inside my mother's silk-cushioned jewelry box and pulled out a strand of faux pearl beads long enough to hang around my neck and swing from my hand suggestively, my bony hip jutting into the air, my small, tousled head cocked to one side.

It wasn't, however, enough. Then I spotted it, the showstopper: Mom's multistrand, gold-plated necklace, its four chains weighted with two dozen coins in ascending sizes, each one struck with a high-relief image of "Empereur Napoleon" or "Queen Victoria." I lifted the necklace over my head and felt its heavy clasp against the back of my neck. Circles of gold coins cascaded down my flat chest and swept the band of my miniskirt. *Perfect.* Should I wear a scarf? Mom had dozens, most of them silk and scented with Chanel N°5, supplied on the sly by Charles, though I didn't know that then. I pulled on fishnet stockings and rummaged inside the messy closet I shared with my sister for shoes, knowing it was hopeless. We had nothing with spike heels, nothing pointy, nothing appropriate. I sighed and resigned myself to the least dowdy pair I could find among the handed-down sneakers, boots, and loafers strewn across the floor.

Part of me knew, even at ten or eleven, that dressing up as a prostitute for trick-or-treating was off-color, unseemly. But no adult questioned me or suggested a different costume, and in the divided state I would come to know intimately, I billed it as funny and original. I simply didn't know what I was about— I only knew what I was compelled to do, a marionette of veiled emotional memory. I imagine some part of me wanted to reveal to the world what I had become, to name the fear haunting me. With the scattershot, half-amnesiac mind of a child, I could do so only obliquely, through the topsy-turvy doings of Halloween.

In a black-and-white photo from sixth grade, a close-up taken by my aunt's photographer brother, I stare into the camera with a fight-me-if-you-dare look, freckles biting my nose and cheeks, uneven bangs fringing the scar above my left eye, the remnant of some accident or fight I've long since forgotten. Gone is any glance of childhood—just hard, weary, budding adolescence.

In middle school, I proved myself the troublemaker most teachers seemed to expect from our family. I whipped up a riot in French class, piling desks in a miserable barricade against monsieur, or "Mape the Ape," as we called him behind his back. Although he wasn't a bad teacher, his hairy fingers made it impossible to like him. That bit of insurrection landed me in detention, for "insolence and disrespect in French." I brought the detention slip home and pasted it into my scrap book, since finding a picture frame in our helter-skelter cupboards was hopeless.

In another class we locked a substitute teacher in the supply closet, only someone pushed me in at the last minute, leaving me to pound out my fury on the heavy wooden door as this benign, lumbering man looked down at me and shrugged his shoulders. One morning a friend and I, late for third period, delayed our moment of reckoning by dragging ourselves on our bellies through the school corridors and screaming for water until doors flung open and we ran for it. Then I was called to the principal's office to be grilled by the cops after a teacher tapped me, undeservedly, for pulling the fire alarm, which had begun ringing as I sauntered late, again, into class.

Even medical woes were chalked up to delinquent behavior, and it nearly killed me.

The summer before eighth grade, I started coughing up globs of grossities I couldn't bear to swallow. "You're such a show-off" scoffed my friend Samantha as I spit into the privet hedge. "*So cool.*"

I looked at her, bewildered. "Only *boys* like hocking loogies," I said.

Sam rolled her eyes and we continued our walk to the General Store to steal our daily candy fix.

During one of our first gym classes that year, the coach ordered us to run around the track outside the middle school, and I nearly collapsed before the quarter turn.

"I can't," I sputtered, bent over. "It hurts my lungs."

"Either get out there and run," said the coach, taking me for a faker, "or hike yourself to the nurse's office."

Settling into the hard chair next to the nurse's gray, metallic desk, I told her I didn't feel well enough to do gym. "Running hurts my lungs."

She arched a dubious eyebrow and pressed a stethoscope against my back. I coughed up more crap, and she sighed and wrote an excuse note.

When I asked Mom yet again to take me to the A.I.M. clinic in Wellfleet, she raised her hands in exasperation and said, "No one dies from a cough. You'll get over it." Lying on my twin bed after supper, I stared at my huge, black-and-white photo poster of Elsa, the regal lioness from *Born Free*, wishing I had her calmness, her power. I knew, in my bones, that I was sick in a different way, a scary way, but no one seemed to believe I needed to see a doctor, and I was twelve, too young to drive myself. Who could I persuade to help me? How would the bill get paid? I had been to the big hospital in Hyannis only once, when I was five, after an older cousin goaded me to jump off a high swing and my forearm fractured when I landed hard. But regular doctors? I wasn't even sure how they worked. Apart from my broken arm, I couldn't remember ever seeing one. With every breath a stretch, I feared I would simply die one night while no one noticed.

In a last attempt to rouse Mom to action, I crept up to her late one afternoon as she was stuffing cubes of beef into the cast iron grinder clamped to the kitchen counter. "Mom, you *have* to take me to the doctor's," I said to her back, an animal instinct for self-preservation kicking in. "I *can't* breathe right!"

She finished cranking the grinder, the last of the bloody hamburger curling into a bowl, and wiped her hands on her apron with a harassed sigh. A few days later, I had an appointment.

"We could take an x-ray," said the doctor after pressing a clean, shiny stethoscope to my hunched back. "You do have lung congestion."

An x-ray sounded like an excellent idea, and I would have run down the hall to the radiology closet if I could.

An hour after we arrived home from the appointment, the black rotary phone next to our kitchen table rang. Hanging up, Mom told me we were returning to the clinic. More x-rays were taken, and when the doctor held one against the light, Mom gasped. There, among the silvery gray shadows, lay a long, dark object in the deepest regions of my left lung. Mom recognized it instantly. One of my father's carpenter nails.

The doctor turned to me. "Do you ever remember inhaling a nail?"

"No!" I said, stunned.

"Putting one in your mouth?"

*What sort of idiot would do that?* I thought, shaking my head.

The doctor told us I needed surgery, as soon as possible, adding it was a miracle I hadn't yet collapsed running down the basketball court. The Hyannis hospital was out of the question, so he started dialing Boston.

Two weeks later a thoracic surgeon at New England Baptist Hospital plied a scalpel from the front of my rib cage to the back of my scapula, cracking me open like a lobster claw to extract Dad's nail from the swamp in my lung. He then inserted a tube to drain the festering pool over the next few days, bequeathing me two scars: an "X marks the spot" where the tube had been, and a thin, red, 11-inch seam that pleased me so much I'd hike up the side of my shirt in the middle school halls to show anyone with the slightest interest.

I brought the nail in a washed jelly jar to school and marched triumphantly into the school nurse's office. "Guess what!" I announced. "I had a *nail* in my lung!"

The nurse looked up, flummoxed. "What do you mean, a nail? A fingernail?"

"No, the pound-pound kind!" I crowed, holding up the jar and striding out the door.

In science class we debated the most plausible ways for something that sharp and long to skitter down a windpipe. Had I picked it off the floor as a toddler? Put it in my mouth on a dare? Been forced to swallow it by an older brother?

Our teacher had the last laugh. "Cindy," he said, "you probably inhaled that nail sniffing glue off the floor."

This is one true way to describe myself during the years immediately following elementary school. But there's another, and these contrasting stories speak to the pliable and selective nature of what we remember, and how we remember, not only our earliest years but also what happened yesterday.

In fifth grade, our English teacher at Wellfleet Elementary School, Mrs. Winslow, assigned us journals to write. Young, bug-eyed, and liberal, Mrs. Winslow believed children had something meaningful to say, and she organized a way for us to say it. She also believed we could, and would, appreciate literature, and she fed us readings by Emily Dickinson, Langston Hughes, e.e. cummings, Homer, Tolkien, and Robert Frost. She had confidence in us, and we adored her.

I imagine Mrs. Winslow provided us with our first journal, a composition notebook with wide-ruled pages covered by blue-gray paper stock and bound with black tape. I filled it with my poems and limericks, art and musings—even my political worries and rants. It was 1969, and though only ten years old, I couldn't help but be preoccupied with problems of war and racism, which I invariably paired with longings for peace and brotherhood. The civil rights movement, refracted in our classroom through the Indian rights movement, presented irresistible polarities of right and wrong, peopled with villains, heroes, and survivors. The South was a mythic place, ripe for our projections, but other injustices lay as close to the surface as the arrowheads on the harbor flats.

I don't recall any Black schoolchildren at Wellfleet Elementary when I was a pupil, but two Indian students lived with their mother in an isolated, unheated post-and-beam house off Route 6. I sensed they were poor by the way they climbed on the school bus, dressed haphazardly, unsure of where to sit. Their marginalization was contrasted, however, by the celebrity of the school district's brilliant band and orchestra teacher, a full-blood Aquinnah Wampanoag named Frank James who had been born into poverty on Martha's Vineyard, graduated from the New England Conservatory of Music, and raced down Route 6 in a red Corvette with a "Custer Had It Coming" bumper sticker.

A well-regarded orator, Mr. James was president of the Federated Eastern Indian League, and in 1970 the governor of Massachusetts asked him to deliver the traditional Thanksgiving Day speech at Plymouth Rock to commemorate the 350th anniversary of the Pilgrims' landing. When the event's planners received his speech, however, they backpedaled straight into revisionist history. Mr. James's white-hot indictment of the Pilgrims' food raids, grave robbing, and decimation of Native peoples through violence and disease was not the sort of patriotic puffery the governor had envisioned. Nor was Mr. James's advocacy for a "more Indian America" in the future, with Indians restored to their rightful place.

When our music teacher refused to perform the governor's revised script, he was dropped from the program. Keeping true to his own beat, Mr. James co-organized the first National Day of Mourning at Plymouth Rock, where he delivered his censored keynote before two hundred tribal representatives from across the country. They gathered under the bronze statue of Massasoit, sachem of the Wampanoags, at historic Cole's Hill, a stone's throw from Plymouth Rock, their drumming and cries boomeranging through the air over a crowd of white townspeople dressed in colonial breeches and doublets, smocks and aprons, black sugar-loaf hats and white cotton coifs. A throng of national tribal members, led by a Sioux, buried Plymouth Rock under several inches of sand while an Omaha Indian chanted a dirge. Two dozen Indians then scaled the ratlines of the Mayflower II and tore down the English flag of St. George, while others on deck tossed a Pilgrim dummy overboard, inciting the police to swarm and clear the ship.

I was taking clarinet lessons from Mr. James during this time, scaling lines of a different sort with an instrument borrowed from my aunt. I was hopeless at learning music, however, unable to imagine how it was done. I kept at it for a short while, but Mr. James's rigor and perfectionism finally got the best of us both, and I abandoned our lessons after he tapped me on the head with the clarinet for my lack of practice and off-key notes. I'd had enough of being hit at home, and I wasn't about to let a teacher strike me, even in jest.

Vietnam, of course, was a more pervasive drama than the Indian rights movement, streaming nightly into our living room through our RCA television console. My half-brothers Geoff and Ted had volunteered to fight at seventeen and eighteen, and I knew they were somewhere in the gray and black images behind Walter Cronkite's head, chasing Viet Cong instead of girls. They were also alive in the worry and strain on my mother's face as she circled our mailbox and packed up boxes of fudge, socks, and Marlboros to ship to Southeast Asia.

Though these social and political ills spilled onto the pages of my first journal, nearly every poem or paragraph moves from tragedy to hope, as if I were straddling two worlds: one in which evil threatens the world and the other in which goodness will prevail. A typical sixth-grade poem opens, "The war began with hating hearts / for then the families had to part," followed by several lines of battleground horror. By the third stanza, however, "New hearts were formed with love for each other / now everyone is a fellow brother." As a child who had fought her own small battles, I couldn't help but wound others at times; as a child of the 1960s, I hung my hopes on peace and love.

Once I ran out of space in that first journal, I started making my own out of loose filler paper and Mom's fabric scraps. For my second journal, I fashioned a cover out of rosebud flannel left over from a nightgown Mom had made for me, poked three holes along the folded edge, and threaded pink puffed yarn through the lined paper and cloth. For others, I glued fabric or felt on hard cardboard, using brass paper fasteners to secure them to the paper. In these eight journals from fifth and sixth grades, I drew and wrote with abandon—about friends, boys, my family, our cat, the ghost in my bedroom, love, tobogganing, peace, singing, happiness, grief, war, and, a bit prematurely, marriage.

"Nobody knows the true meaning of love, and for that reason I don't know if I want to get married," I wrote. Being married, I decided, was "kinda like being communist," with your husband as "your leader."

I might not have known the word *dictator*, but I knew I lived with one, and he was enthroned on his chair by the stove. Over the course of my two-page diatribe, I reassured myself that if I did mess up and marry, I could always undo it. The kids would have to split up, and I'd "lose my reputation as a happilly marraid woman," but there was "one good thing about divorce": I'd be an all-caps, no-regrets, "FREE WOMAN AGAIN!"

Though I was eleven years old and my parents' divorce was still years away, I couldn't help but notice the distracted bounce of my mother's knee on the evenings she sat at our kitchen table dressed to the nines, waiting for the honk that would free her from the house, from her husband asleep on the couch, from us. "Needlepoint meeting at the Congo," she'd say, conjuring one community but diving into another with Charles, the two of them speeding past our stately church on Main Street to join their crew of lively drinkers at Al Graham's bar on the harbor.

The archive corrects and instructs, reveals and surprises. Reading these elementary school journals now, as well as those I wrote in high school, I am reminded of the past's myriad angles, how the present tosses molecules into the light and refracts what we see. My intentional recall over these many years has perhaps focused too often on how strained our homelife felt: my mother's confusing grief, my father's unpredictable anger, my missing siblings, my older brothers' and older boy cousin's pranks, some of them malign.

The pages of my journals, however, also offer countervailing images, ones tingling with an existential joy. I wrote about the beauty of flames curling around the logs in our fireplace, of our bus ride to school along Ocean View Drive, and of snowflakes that "fall like dimounds from the sky." I loved my friends, my teachers, our cat Rusty, and our golden retriever Duke. Over and over again, my childhood writings celebrated life, even as they lamented racism, poverty, war, and Richard Nixon, who I wished "had never been born."

This embrace of life persisted throughout my adolescent and teenage years, though the move to middle school didn't make things easier. Located two towns away in Orleans, Nauset Regional brought together students from Wellfleet, Eastham, Orleans, and Brewster for the first time. It then promptly segregated us through its corrosively tracked system, which seemed to have as much to do with town and social class as intelligence.

Although Nauset's middle and high schools were ninety-nine percent white, class differences leapfrogged from outright poverty to conspicuous privilege. And more of the poor kids came from Wellfleet, shuttered-up all winter, waiting for the tourists to return to the beaches and art galleries so the grocery stores and restaurants would re-open. Fortunately for the adults, and many of the teenagers, two of the Wellfleet stores that kept year-round hours were the ones selling cheap bottles of Jim Beam and Strawberry Hill wine.

Stranded on a sandbar, we Wellfleetians lived just over the line from Truro's unmitigated desolation. Those Truro kids who chose Nauset over Provincetown High might as well have been commuting from Timbuktu. Truro's steep sand dunes, historic lighthouse, and emerald salt marshes were nothing compared to the social prestige of the Orleans Cinema, Army Navy store, and bowling alley. Even tourists intuitively understood this. Every summer I'd meet at least one summer kid at the beach who would ask, "You really live here year-round? You mean, there are schools?"

To my consternation I did not make the middle school cut for 7-1, reserved for the smart kids, but was funneled into 7-2 along with a few others from Wellfleet. God help those students consigned to 7-5 or 7-6. About them, the school system was wrong. Most of them were far smarter, of course, than given credit for, but the official segregation openly branded us all, for good or for ill. Embarrassed and mad, I slumped at my desk, tormented Mape the Ape, and hung out after school with friends who hid pot in their turntables and hitchhiked up and down Route 6 with me, since our parents were not the chauffeuring-kids kind.

In ninth grade, when my class moved to the brand new, open-campus high school in Eastham, I knew I had reached that fork in a yellow wood that Frost had met with. Peering down one road,

I saw skipped classes and stupid reasons for getting drunk or high, culminating in the mistake that would change everything: an unexpected pregnancy. The other was trod by the fresh-scrubbed, financially comfortable kids from Orleans, which had a year-round grocery store. I wanted to be one of those jocks and high achievers, not a sorry Wellfleetian who bought her clothes at the thrift shop on Main Street and stole her father's whiskey sour mixes or shared other kids' joints because she couldn't afford her own. But such a social leap, as I wrote in my journal, seemed improbable, if not impossible. "I feel really low to that group," I confessed, "like I'm striving to get up to their height." All I could do was try.

Stories find us, be they about Odysseus's long, diverted struggle to return home or Frost's snowy solstice evening. But we are also *found* by stories. We shape who we are by the memories we return to again and again, as well as by the intentional—and less intentional—choices we make in fashioning the stories we tell as we define, and subtly redefine, ourselves. Naming things can be the beginning of understanding, celebrating, and surviving them.

To figure out my story, to bring some order to it, I needed a private space. That summer after sixth grade, I talked my parents into letting me move out of the upstairs pine room I was sharing with Beth and into an L-shaped corner of our dank, cobwebbed cellar.

Mom helped me tie-dye old white sheets to cover the cement walls, which rose four or so feet before meeting the small windows that let in light at ground level. We bunched and twisted the sheets, wrapped rubber bands at intervals, and poured a box of blue dye into the washing machine. Coordinating the bright colors, we painted three wooden bureaus lime green, sunshine yellow, and rose-tinted red, daubing flowers on the wooden knobs. Mom hung yellow ruffled café curtains she made on the windows and indulged my vision for covering the rough-hewn crossbeams holding up the house. Shortly after I started sleeping in the cellar, she hauled home a huge, gray mound of rope stinking of fish and seaweed. "I got this from a fisherman friend," she said as I jumped up and down, ecstatic she had pulled it off. We tacked the net to the ceiling, where it billowed from steel hooks, and decorated it with a constellation of driftwood and shells from my walks on the beach. Decades later, I realized the net must have come from Charles, Mom's secret lover.

"Ah yes, I get it from Capitain Billy King," he told me in his intractable French accent and haphazard verb tenses. "'Ee was a portugais fisherman from Ptown 'oo is the first Americain I meet when I ahrive in 1954."

Charles and Billy fished for cod and haddock out of Provincetown together for three years, until Charles took a site in the New Bedford scalloping fleet. In 1976, the year I graduated from high school, Captain Billy King and seven crewmembers overloaded the deck of the *Patricia Marie* with a bonanza of sea scallops that slid portside during the night. The boat rolled and sank in the frigid Atlantic, dragging the sleeping crew with it. Billy had made a desperate scramble to survive and jumped into the dark waters, only to be found in a life jacket, facedown, half-a-mile off the Eastham coast.

But in 1970 Billy was still fishing, and one of his torn nets floated like a looped cloud above my bed and desk, lacing the cellar's kerosene odor with brine.

For the first year or so, my new room had no heat, just a Class-A fire hazard of a plug-in space heater whose bare coils glowed orange through the icy winter nights. My father—conceding I was unlikely to move back upstairs anytime soon—eventually installed fake wood paneling on the walls, baseboard radiators, a drop Celotex ceiling in place of the fishing net, and an aquamarine indoor-outdoor carpet, under which an earwig civilization soon flourished, its pincered, celluloid-brown troops emerging from loose corners on nocturnal raids.

Next to my poster of Elsa the lioness, I tacked up a parchment poster of Max Ehrmann's "Desiderata," which I read a thousand times. "Go placidly amid the noise and haste," it begins. While few would have described me as placid, I was eager to live up to its calligraphed conclusion: "Keep peace in your soul. With all its sham, drudgery and broken dreams, it is still a beautiful world."

Neighbors chipped in furniture, my favorite the mahogany twin bed Scotty Maguire dragged out of her attic for me. She also gave me a fraying, antique, yellow silk bedspread and matching Victorian bed lamp that hung from two wrapped hooks over the headboard. A childless, salty Yank with wiry gray curls, Scotty lived with her husband in a gingerbread-trimmed house as old and eccentric as ours, with strangely placed stairs and a beach-stone fireplace. She taught us how to heat maple syrup and pour it over snow for a teeth-chilling, ribboned treat. Watching our doings from over the split rail fence between our yards, cocktail in hand, Scotty perhaps understood why a girl on the cusp of adolescence might need a corner of her own.

Despite the damp and the spiders and the earwigs, I loved my room. A long, open-air bulkhead jutted from the cellar door into the backyard, offering both freedom (I could come and go as I pleased!) and danger, since we never locked any of our doors. In high school I installed a hook-and-eye latch, which one of my friends laughingly declared nearly useless, but it made me feel safer. And I could decorate my room as I wanted—no more negotiation with sisters. I filled empty wine bottles with dried grasses and fronds, pasted school photos of my friends along the rim of my oval mirror, and stacked my shelves with candles and porcelain figurines and books.

For my eighth-grade Christmas, Mom and Dad bought me an unfinished pine desk with three drawers—the first piece of furniture I ever owned—and Mom refinished it, leaving the pale wood unstained but applying a semigloss varnish that made the unscratched surface glow. For pencil holders, I peeled the labels off empty soup cans and glued on purple, blue, and yellow felt in the shape of the sun, moon, and stars. The wall behind my desk was perfect for taping up squares of construction paper I filled with quotes from Elizabeth Barrett Browning, Alexander Pope,

Mme. de Staël, Langston Hughes, and Benjamin Franklin, among many others. Their words and wit, though from other interiors or centuries, leapt across the chasm between us to encourage and inspire me as I bent my head over my schoolbooks. In the desk drawers (my own—no one else's!) I stored notes friends had passed me in class, scores from *The Music Man* and *Oklahoma*, images I tore from *Life* magazines or *National Geographic* to illustrate my poetry projects, and, of course, my growing stack of journals, in which I recounted my days, recorded dreams, copied favorite poems, confessed my crushes, wished someone would "report" adults to AA, made lists to keep myself organized, and philoso-phized endlessly, hopefully, about the meaning of life.

Psychologists tell us that the reason we sometimes forget why we have walked into a room (to find a book? fetch a sweater?) is that changing physical scenes alters mental ones. This is what happened every time I slid open the cast-iron bolt on the wooden door to the cellar, reached for the rough brown rope that served as banister, stepped past the torn portrait of my great-great-grandmother Henrietta in her gilt frame, and turned the corner at the bottom of the steps, where a friend and I painted a huge rainbow along the wall bordering my room. Descending into the cellar, I left one world—of siblings and cigarette smoke, of messy dogs and cats and parakeets, of a schmoozing Lawrence Welk and his bubbles—and entered another. It was dank, it was dusty, but it separated and sheltered me in ways that no other space in that house could.

Although forged in relation to others, stories need privacy to gain traction, the inner tumbler smoothing and polishing them into mirrors of interpreted experience. It's one of the reasons we seek out secluded spots: the sheltering crook of a tree, an empty stretch of beach, that path through the woods. In such places we can hear our own story and try to make sense of it.

My small cellar windows offered just a glimpse of eye-level weedy grass, but it was of no matter; the only view that counted in that half-submerged room was the internal one. I was trying to discover what I thought of my life and those around me by herding my thoughts onto the page, where I could sit and contemplate the scene. Like any teenager, I wanted to change some aspects of my life, move a few pieces around, switch out props. To do so, I needed a better sense of the landscape, its possibilities and its hurdles.

I didn't know at the time that adolescence and early adulthood are the years in which we are first able, and motivated, to forge what psychologists call an internalized "narrative identity," or a more conceptual sense of self. Younger children can of course recall past events but don't have the skills yet to create a nuanced, relatively coherent life story that links past, present, and future in a "grand narrative." Though a pliable and ever-changing construct, the fashioning of that life story, the development of its content and themes, is foundational to our personal identity, our sense of continuity over time, and our coherence in a multifaceted and often confusing world. A narrative life saver, it helps us keep our heads above the water as we paddle in the changing currents of circumstance, feeling, and maturity.

While the blank pages in my journals gave me space to develop my uneven and sometimes inchoate self-understanding, my social world was its most fertile ground, as it is for us all. In our animated, whispered conversations, my friends and I were not just describing ourselves to each other but also co-constructing our identities, trying to get comfortable in our skins while positioning ourselves in relation to each other, besotted with the drama of being teen-agers in what, we were coming to realize, was a very large world. We are all of us, of course, narrative selves, our memories and identity inextricable from the stories that help us to make sense of who we have been and who we are becoming.

Memories and the stories we create with them never stand still, even when written down or recorded, because they meet both speaker and listener in the complexity of each person's history and hopes, her hurts and hauntings. The meaning of a memory can change over time, of course, harmonizing with the present situation and goals of the person remembering it, or tuning itself to others' persuasive interpretations. Changes in details or focus are natural, if not inevitable, and some of them signal healthy growth. Discrediting those interpretive shifts, or reifying a single grand narrative across time, is not so much a clinging to truth as it is a kind of narrative fundamentalism.

The personal memories and stories I first wrote down in elementary school, followed by the longer ones in high school and beyond, culminating in this book, are both as true as I can render them and inevitably reconstructed. My sisters and brothers, my cousins and friends, surely have different stories to tell, even about the same events. And that's normal. It's what we make of the experiences we foreground, and the ways we interpret them, that track the truths of our lives, every day. We yearn to remember well, and we thrive, in part, by also choosing well.

In my cousins' backyard tree, the summer I moved my bedroom to the cellar. South Wellfleet, MA, 1970. Photo by George H. Power, courtesy of Leslie H. Power.

# 7

# Wellfleetian, Old
# and New

~

As I was scribbling away at the pine desk in my cellar bedroom, I couldn't help but be responsive to, or react against, the other voices chiming in. While DNA writes code that influences who we become, it is not the only author of our identity, functioning instead in a complicated call-and-response with our environment, choices, accidents, and—most especially—interactions with others. As social creatures, our sense of self exists in a dialectical relationship with the stories that we tell about ourselves and the stories that are told about us, by those around us and by our culture. This is especially true when we are young, but it doesn't end there.

During my teenage years, when, without consciously understanding it I was taking my first serious crack at elaborating a narrative identity, I sometimes felt as if I had been handed a script with lines I did not want to follow. Once I left the familiar walls of Wellfleet Elementary School to trip down the halls of Nauset Regional Middle School, I felt newly labeled as a Wellfleetian, a lightweight, and—after my parents' divorce in ninth grade and my father's death nine months later—a castaway from a shipwrecked family. I picked at the edges of those labels, but peeling them off felt impossible.

Though high school would ultimately become a refuge, on the first day of sophomore year my math teacher put me in my place.

Like our middle school, Nauset High tracked students, and I had landed in the advanced geometry class. Following in my father's footsteps, I loved math and chose a seat as close to the front as possible, eager to dive in. As our teacher scanned the roster before roll call, he flicked his eyes in my direction and tapped a sharpened pencil on his clipboard. He was obviously contemplating a problem of some sort, considering the possible angles. With a slight shake of his head, a gesture of resolve, he took two long strides to my desk, grasped both sides with his hands, and leaned his face close to mine. His limp brown hair, a shade darker than his eyes, fell across an oily forehead just on the other side of adolescent acne. "You'll never pass this class," he hissed *sotto voce*, as if suggesting I should cut my losses and leave then and there. I looked down from his smirk to my notebook, empty but for the "Geometry I" proudly marching in block letters across the front cover. Was "stupid" stamped on my forehead? I wondered. Or "Blakeley"? Or "girl"? Or did they all mean the same thing when it came to math?

I flashed back to another first day, this one in eighth grade, when my homeroom teacher reached the B's and groaned aloud, "Oh no, *another* Blakeley." Was I never to escape? While I had cousins who would go to college, another would go to jail, and two of my siblings landed in the regional technical school, at that time the warehouse for problem students. Neither graduated. Plus, there were just *so many* Blakeleys (and siblings and cousins with other last names) sprouting from a tangle of marriages, divorces, and remarriages. Teachers thought themselves hilariously original when they joked, "I'll never figure your family out!" I could relate. Only in adulthood did I realize that two of my cousins, who lived in different houses, were half-sisters.

The pigeonholing, however, made me fight back, first with inappropriate behavior in middle school, then with studying in high school. Wanting to belong to some place other than home, to thwart the low expectations of me, I threw myself into books, sports, student government, and the drama club, becoming a regular on the late bus and having recurring nightmares I would miss it, knowing there was no one to pick me up if I did. I remembered the joys of elementary school, my young astonishment that Emily Dickinson had lived in Massachusetts but never seen the sea, or that a soggy ball of Wonder bread in the science room cupboard would produce spectacular mold. Though freshman year was full of missteps (such as taking my Spanish final stoned, and failing), those early joys ultimately found an echoing pleasure in my high school classes, heightened by a growing sense of agency, the realization that trying might actually bend the path that led to my future.

My first and best love was English. I learned that mindful punctuation lent order to my sentences, allowing them to flow without the stuttering effect of misplaced commas, while strong syntax made agreement among the parts possible, an elusive dynamic for anyone, but especially teenagers. New vocabulary mined from the dictionary I flipped through nearly every night did more than offer ways to describe my thoughts and feelings; it *created* meanings and content, beating back confusion with categories and insights. Words, I discovered, gave me boundaries and plot lines, and with those lines came awareness and focus.

Despite my geometry teacher's appraisal, math ran a close second. Few things were as satisfying as completing a proof or producing a page of calculations with the queenly $x = 4$ and kingly $y = 3$ enthroned at the bottom. I could use a few more right angles in my life, a few more elegantly simple solutions for convoluted problems. God knows I wasn't finding them on Lecount Hollow.

"Your mother looks like she's speeding her brains out twenty-four hours a day," a friend said after Dad died. During the hardest months, Mom used amphetamines to wake up in the morning and tranquilizers to fall asleep at night. Worst of all was seeing her in the middle of the day with a rye and soda in hand as she waited for Charles to pick her up after his ten-day fishing trips to Georges Bank on the one-hundred-ton *Rianda*. I knew there was slim chance of seeing Mom again until Charles returned to sea five days later, unless she stopped off to pick up her waitressing uniform for the Lighthouse or a different pair of shoes.

In tenth grade I mustered the courage to tell her I wished she'd sleep at home more. Mom sighed and said, "You have your whole life ahead of you. I'm close to fifty years old and have almost nothing." I understood she felt compelled to create some security in her life with Charles, quickly introduced to us as her partner after the divorce, and once again I saw her point, feeling as guilty for asking as I did abandoned by her choices.

My older sister Thelma had moved out as soon as she graduated from high school, my younger sister Beth was seldom around, and Dad was taking his eternal rest in the Blakeley plot in Pleasant Hill Cemetery. I felt uneasy being in the house alone, rummaging in the cabinets for cans of split pea soup for supper. Thank god I was on the free lunch program at school. I loved the array of selections in the lunch line and was furious at Beth for refusing to accept the assistance. She instead raided our meagre stash of coins in the Revere Sugar tin Mom had painted black and decoupaged with wood ducks and turtles. After Mom's shifts at the Lighthouse, where she often had to wait on Charlie Frazier—the lawyer who had skewered her in a courtroom—she would sit at the kitchen table and sort through her change, dropping enough into the can to cover our thirty-five-cent lunches.

Beth's mortification was foreign to me. It wasn't shame that I felt in the lunch line but fear: fear that the dimes and quarters would run out, that we would lose the house, that someone would break in while Mom was with Charles in Orleans and Beth was who-knows-where. *Should I leave the bathroom door open?* I wondered on solitary nights when washing up for bed. Not a good idea; someone might stab me in the back while I bent over the sink. But if I shut the door, an intruder could pounce on me as soon as I walked into the hall. On those nights I was alone in the house, few things caused me as much anxiety as taking a shower or washing my face.

"Mom is drunk again," I'd tell my journal. "I hate it! She makes me sick." These were new, awful feelings.

I had no idea that knocking my mother off her pedestal was a developmental milestone and that most of my friends were surely trashing parental altars as well, all of us wrangling to give independence a foothold. I imagine several of them kept journals like mine. The only thing that came more naturally to me than running and wrestling was writing, and I wrote and wrote and wrote, talking myself out of despair, telling myself I'd be okay, and comforting myself with inspirational prose, especially these lines from Samuel Ullman's "Youth":

*In the center of your heart . . . is a wireless station; so long as it receives messages of beauty, hope, cheer, courage and power from men and from the infinite, so long are you young.*

Like a determined Marconi hunched over his spark-gap transmitter to rescue a sinking ship, I radioed myself this and other such messages over and over again, even as I understood that truths ran in more than one direction. "Mom seems so bad," I wrote, "while my heart is screaming out—no! she is good . . . I can't face the reality of my mother being bad."

Mom knew she was reaching the end, and so did we. After she was fired from the Lighthouse for showing up to work slightly drunk (the only way she could get into the car), she told me, "I don't know how much longer I can go on." She woke up one morning at 5 a.m. gagging, sure she was having a heart attack. She shook my sister out of bed, who somehow had the presence of mind to avoid calling 911 and to feed Mom some tranquilizers.

"I would be so lost if Mom died," I wrote. "What would the family do? Where would we get money? How would we keep up the house? . . . I feel so sorry for her it makes me want to wither up and die to extinguish the sadness."

I don't know why I felt more sorry for than angry at Mom. I overidentified with her, yes, but I also dreaded her detaching herself from us, from me. I knew that Mom could disappear, and might even do so voluntarily. Had I been more confident of Mom's attachment to her life at home with us, I might have risked testing it with anger. But my grief over the difficulties of her life elbowed aside adolescent rage.

This grief, however, is only part of the story of those years. I loved my life in high school: my friends and teachers, track and gymnastic meets, drama rehearsals, basketball games, and student government meetings. Teenagers, we had a life. We were the athletes who strode onto buses and ferries and turboprop planes to play games in Harwich and Martha's Vineyard and Nantucket. The dancers tapping and twirling across the stage. The contestants in VFW speech contests. The adventurers willing to miss a class or two to debate existential truths at Nauset Light Beach, a short mile down the road from our algebra and chemistry and Latin classes, which pedaled different kinds of truths. At night, we knew to look for the number of police cars parked at the Eastham station—two, and we were golden. We could then race with impunity between the Wellfleet Drive-In and the Orleans rotary, young and fast and free. The Cape was ours, every glorious inch of it: the dunes where we drank, smoked joints, and made out; the bars in Provincetown where we danced; the ponds in Wellfleet where we skinny-dipped under velvet skies; the restaurants where we dined with our prom dates, their boutonnieres matching the color of our floor-length dresses, the height of sophistication.

*How awful it must be to be an adult on Cape Cod,* I used to think. *What in the world do they do?* But I knew what they did. They came home with sore feet from their waitressing shifts or long hours behind a counter. They fell asleep on the couch after dawn treks to the flats. They fixed engines and built houses and shaped clay. One or two reset broken bones or sold insurance. Many more stretched their summer earnings catering to tourists to last the winter. And during those long, icicled months they distracted themselves with television or night classes or a few too many cocktails. Or so it seemed to me, at seventeen.

One day walking to my European History class in Nauset's B Building, I passed a chronically depressed classmate and gave her a friendly wave. A smile flickered in response, the dullness lifting for a moment, and I was struck by the realization that though my home life was shit, I still felt happy much of the time. One of my English teachers that year, a British man from Cambridge with an aristocratically hyphenated last name, had called my writings "life-enhancing"—like the paintings, he said, that the art critic Bernard Berenson most admired. "Don't lose this quality," he said. Though only half understanding what my teacher was talking about, I did wonder how I stayed so positive. Part of that noisy happiness, I decided, must be the dumb luck of chemistry, and feeling lucky only added to my sense of well-being.

As did the promise of change. While unexpected expenses sent Mom spiraling ("Mooney Fuel and Grain owns me," she used to moan), one such flash point sparked a different sort of crisis. The summer after my sophomore year, our Hoover vacuum broke, and when the repairman made a house call, he and Mom dove into conversation. Mom loved men, and men loved Mom, even if just to talk. She tried to get him to have a glass of wine with her, then found an Alcoholics Anonymous pamphlet on top of the bookcase after he left.

When Dad had told Mom that she was drinking too much, she divorced him. This time she picked up the phone. "I'm going to die if I don't stop drinking," she told the answering service.

It was Fourth of July weekend. No one returned her Mayday call, no one swooped by to rescue her. Mom got drunk, swamped with self-pity because no one cared. Two days later, a woman knocked on the door and drove her to her first meeting, at the Eastham Methodist Church.

"I was so frightened I could hardly stand up," Mom remembers. "I cried during the entire meeting. I couldn't relate to any of the people there. They were really screwed up! But I wasn't going for the company—I went for survival."

Against the odds, Mom found her higher power and a load of new friends to ferry her to daily meetings. What she also found was a new script, a way of framing her story and her experiences that brought revival within reach, and I believe that this new script helped save her. Nana's disapproving voice still clanged in her head, but it now had competition. In AA, Mom found a vocabulary and a story-centered community that helped her name and change the path she was on. She had hit "rock bottom" and was climbing out. Instead of an embarrassing anomaly, her tale of personal wreckage was a variation of nearly every story she heard at her meetings, the one place she felt recognized.

As is typical for an American redemption narrative, Mom did not stay on the receiving end. Even during her hardest drinking days she had felt compelled to help others, especially the elderly and shut-ins. As soon as I received my learner's permit, she deputized me to drive her on many of these errands. My favorites were to the house of an ancient couple who kept a basket full of *Life* magazines next to their moldering couch, where I'd lean against a snaggled, hand-crocheted afghan and pore over "The Year in Pictures" while Mom put the casserole she had made in the fridge and chatted away.

Mom was, of course, partially meeting her own needs by tending those of others. This was most obvious in her decision to start taking in boarders while I was in high school. Driven mostly by the never-ending scramble to make ends meet, but also by the shards of herself she saw in others, Mom began renting out any spare bedroom in the house, as well as the unheated summerhouse and top garage, into which she tossed a bed and chest of drawers. She liked not only the income but also the company, so much so she kept it up for the next forty years. Some renters stayed for just a few months, others for decades. Once I left for college, I braced myself for an eclectic assortment of housemates on every visit home.

The first boarder, a new waitress at Mom's job, showed up the summer after Dad died and Mom was largely AWOL, living parttime with Charles in Orleans. Thelma and I decided that Stacey must have recently left a cult, because she seemed to come from nowhere, smoked pot like Mom drank, and didn't believe in possessions. With her long sandy hair and sylphlike form, she had the beauty of a target and the evasiveness of an escape artist. Beth, thirteen and cratered by the divorce and Dad's passing, had fled to Paine's Campground to live with one of the owner's daughters, so Mom offered her room to Stacey.

As might be expected, Mom and Beth's relationship never really recovered. It's one thing to want the freedom to escape home and another to have your mother choose a rent check over you. But Mom was, after all, Henrietta's great-granddaughter, and just as she had said about her own mother's choice to take in seventeen foster children, Mom was "earning a buck the best way she knew how." Beth, however, got her room back when she returned home just before Labor Day to start eighth grade, and Stacey moved out to the one-room summerhouse in the backyard. Sometime that winter she heard the call and left as suddenly as she had arrived, carrying nearly nothing. Thelma and I sorted through the things she left behind, including a leather belt with a silver buckle I snagged for my closet, perfect for an aspiring hippy.

Impecunious relatives moved in and out over the next couple of years, and then spring of my senior year I came home late one night from a party and found a strikingly handsome twenty-year-old in my cellar bed. "Oh hi," he said, long lashes fluttering over cornflower eyes. "Your Mom said I could sleep here tonight." He was a summer server at Chillingsworth, the haute cuisine French restaurant in Brewster where Mom waitressed on week-ends during the tourist and shoulder seasons. Dressed as a Marie Antoinette milkmaid—with a yellow-and-white striped dress held aloft by crinoline, a sheer organdy fichu encircling her shoulders, and a wreath of silk cabbage roses bobby-pinned to her hair—she earned more in two nights than in a month of morning shifts at the Lighthouse. Even then, we still lived well below the poverty line for all my years of high school.

The waiter in my bed, divested of his black knickers, white hosiery, and *citron* waistcoat (because why say "yellow" when a French word will do?), looked like a Hummel doll come to life in my pink flowered sheets. I couldn't believe my mother. But if I were to complain, she'd guilt-trip me into kindness, so I climbed upstairs and slept on the couch. The next day Lovely Hummel moved into the summerhouse out back until Labor Day and the cold hit.

After I graduated from high school, the onslaught began. Our house became what one friend dubbed "The Blakeley Hilton," home to a string of the temporarily dispossessed. They slept in the pine room upstairs, my cellar room, the rough studio in the top garage, and the summerhouse, which my brother and various renters expanded and winterized. Mom's only rules were no selling drugs out of the house and no drunkenness.

John moved out to the summerhouse sometime after the waiter, with his ruffled shirts and white stockings, left. From a distinguished Melrose family—John's mother was the first woman to serve in the Massachusetts House of Representatives—he was well educated and enjoyed just enough trust fund slush to make working a choice. I learned about "tough love" from Mom's dealings with John, who often slipped off the wagon and was in and out of detox (and it felt, our house) a dozen or more times. He was an irresistibly sweet and funny person, with white, fly-away hair and thick Mr. Magoo glasses that he often misplaced or stepped on, unable to see them. "Oh shit," he would mildly lisp, "I have lost another pair." On visits home, I loved to listen to John's stories over a cup of coffee or a bowl of his chilled avocado soup. In his sixties, he was often smitten by younger bad boys, some of whom led him into snags with the law.

One such misadventure involved a friend who had lost his license (to drunk driving, what else?). John gave Nicky a ride to the Cape Cod Five Cents Savings Bank in the center of town one afternoon and waited behind the wheel of his convertible while Nicky took care of business. But instead of making a legitimate withdrawal, Nicky told the teller he had a gun and ordered her to hand over all the money in her drawer. Catching a whiff of Nicky's breath as she stuffed a sack, the quick-thinking teller asked, "But wouldn't you like to deposit this in your account?"

Nicky thought for a moment. "I don't have an account here anymore."

"Surely someone in your family does?" the teller asked.

"Yeah, my daughter does," said Nicky, swaying slightly. "Put it in her account."

Hours later, the Wellfleet police released John, who breathlessly told Mom, "I had no idea I was driving the get-away car!"

Bob, a plumber wanting easy access to Provincetown, exchanged rent for remodeling jobs Mom couldn't afford. Like other boarders, he often ate supper with Mom, sighing, "Ambrosia, pure ambrosia" over her Swedish meatballs or boeuf bourguignon. Charles made it his nickname. Mom and Ambrosia parted ways a year or two later, after she realized he had plumbed the summerhouse sink to drain into the marsh out back. He moved to Provincetown and then Boston, where Mom called him every evening as AIDS ravaged and then claimed his young, handsome frame.

She also took in artists, recovering addicts, diehard surfers, and runaway teenagers. Two of my cousins lived with us at various times, as did a friend of my sister Beth. One day Mom asked the friend to be sure to stay upstairs while she met with a sewing client, a closeted cross-dresser who sought absolute privacy for his fitting of women's attire. Hearing the crunch of gravel as Mom's client pulled into the driveway, Beth's friend couldn't resist peeking out the upstairs window. "Oh my god!" she later told me in good-natured disbelief. "It was my boyfriend's father!"

One young woman, a beautiful, doe-eyed blonde trying to outrun heroin, asked Mom to co-sign a loan so she could consolidate her debts and straighten out her life. Perhaps she sensed Mom's soft spot for young women in trouble. A year later all of Mom's bank accounts, including the one Uncle Clyde had added her name to, were sucked dry when the loan defaulted. The girl was long gone, and her wealthy, flamboyant father refused to help. "I've bailed out my daughter often enough," he sighed. We were devastated. It was the winter I was living at home between graduate programs, when I had no waitressing work and hadn't yet started the law firm job. I had less than $300 in the bank.

Thelma was sewing in a leather factory up-Cape and had a little more, and she offered all of it to Mom, who now had nothing.

Truth be told, Mom's house felt more like a halfway house than a home, and I was sometimes weirded out by the disfigurements and delusions Mom lived with so easily. A former nurse turned waitress coughed incessantly, gutturally, as she scurried between my old room in the cellar and the bathroom, her skin preternaturally orange from a year-round QT tan. But she was kind and practical and, as Mom pointed out, "didn't have mental problems" like another one of her tenants that year. One man was so obese he broke the upstairs toilet when he sat on it. Another, a gaunt chain-smoker who subsisted on coffee and donuts and stayed for over seven years, arrived in Wellfleet from parts unknown. Thelma and I decided he must have been in the military or prison, because he folded his blankets every morning and placed them neatly at the foot of his bed.

Though hardly older than I, this boarder had pure white gums. When I finally dared to ask about it, he said he had dentures. "I used bleach to whiten the teeth, and then the gums turned white, too," he explained, then added, "but I didn't think it was noticeable."

He couldn't afford to replace the dentures, so his gums looked like paste for as long as I knew him. Though he survived on odd jobs at gas stations and restaurants, he'd tilt back his head and say, "I keep bankers' hours, Cynthia, bankers' hours," then flash me a snowy smile. Like most year-rounders on the Cape, he had plenty of hours to spare in the winter, when he'd stretch out in the living room, light up, and watch television into the wee hours, transfixed for the hundredth time by the starship *Enterprise*'s intergalactic battles or Tom Cruise's twirls though the sky in *Top Gun*, the throttling and gunfire shooting spikes into my brain while I hid in my room, jimmied a window for fresh air, and tried to read.

None of this bothered Mom. Reaching into her bulging sack of AA mottos, she'd sigh, "Live and let live, Cynthia." Wise counsel, but it also meant living in a fog of cigarette smoke, scrubbing

nicotine stains off the walls of the upstairs bathroom I unluck-
ily shared with Mr. Banker, and seldom knowing which bed I'd
sleep in on later visits home. I was out of place, and most everyone knew it. Like a hapless Marilyn Munster, I both belonged
and didn't belong, an oddball in this alternate universe. My relatively well-organized life—my vitamins, my dental floss, my Estée
Lauder skin products, my balanced checkbook—made me an
exotic bird, an interloper, as if our house were not my native
place. "I'm actually kind of normal!" I wanted to shout at the
everchanging cast of quirky housemates. But they wouldn't have
known what I was talking about. As far as they were concerned,
my standards were impossible, my needs frivolous, my love of
school seriously strange. On summer breaks from college I pinged
between resentment that home served as other people's way station, self-chastisement over my annoyance, and amusement over
the wackiness of it all. Plus, I genuinely liked several of Mom's
tenants and dated one of them. In the end, who was I to begrudge
a mother's openheartedness toward others? So I tolerated the
inconveniences, not to mention the headshaking, the jokes, and
even the occasional caution when renters crossed paths with me
in the kitchen, as if Mom's typically genial herd were not quite
sure what I might say or do or expect next.

Mom instinctively sided with the marginalized, those in
need, but she also kept a calendar on the wall with a meticulous
record of who paid rent on what day. When I was home from
school and working, my name appeared in Friday's box. We all
had to contribute. Though the money was critical in keeping
Mom afloat, it was evident even then that her attachment to
her boarders went deeper than this. She watched movies with
them, fed them, fixed their clothing. Exchanged long letters after
they moved away. Only once did she evict a lodger, a teenage
boy who was selling drugs out of my old bedroom in the cellar, the bulwark door to the backyard too great a temptation.
Mom had few hard lines, but pedaling dope on her property
was one of them.

One of the most significant advantages she found in renting out rooms, especially to fellow recovering alcoholics, must have been hearing the uncensored stories of others, be it at AA meetings or the kitchen table. These stories, I believe, helped her to recast her own, allowing her to reassemble her fractured past in ways that brought her meaning and coherence and hope. Growing up in the house on Rogers Street, Mom had been hounded into a conformity that only made her more rebellious, then ashamed of her rebellion. How was she to gain perspective or to understand her own experiences? How was she to free herself from conventional narratives that had framed her as a headstrong teenager, a sexual renegade, a middle-age drunk?

This was before Oprah, before the Internet, before reality television, before the surge of confessional memoirs. The only shrinks we knew were the high-maintenance psychoanalysts substituting spinach for rice at the Oyster House on busy August nights, when the sous-chef was as likely as not to stab a butcher knife into the cutting board if I asked where that order of steamed mussels was. Mom looked to Katherine Chancellor in *The Young and the Restless*, which she watched religiously, and D.H. Lawrence's *Lady Chatterley's Lover*, parked on her bedside table for years, as guides for sorting through thoughts as jumbled as her embroidery threads. Once Mom opened her house to boarders and joined AA, she heard countless other stories smeared with impulsive decisions, bad luck, and destabilizing losses. These dramas contextualized her own and provided the kind of perspective another drink or another man never could.

The friends Mom made at meetings, but most especially the renters she took in, also made her a pivotal player in others' stories, where her kindness and tolerance helped make their survival, and sometimes even healing, possible. She had boarders who had been homeless, who had escaped an abusive parent, who had lost marriages and careers and possibly minds.

Some, of course, simply needed a bed and pillow given the Cape's chronic housing shortage for workers. No matter the reason, she accepted nearly everyone who walked through her door, even if they had to sleep in the sewing room. For several, that alone was enough to fix her in the tale of their recovery.

I imagine that knowing she was part of her boarders' stories gave Mom narrative substance, anchoring her in a far more affirming script than the ones she'd been handed by her mother, by Ben Harrow, and by the courts. We all need a story in which we matter. And for her friends in AA and her dozens of boarders over the decades, Mom mattered.

I now see that both Nana and Mom, in their own ways, filled their homes with living refractions of their earlier selves and treated those household members in the ways they wished they themselves had been treated. Nana cared for her seventeen foster girls with scrupulous efficiency and discipline, while Mom's open-door, anything-goes policy and sloppy housekeeping accommodated her boarders' foibles and their struggles to get by as best as they could.

I wonder if this is another version of the save-yourself mode of parenting. In treating our children in the ways we wish we had been cared for in our earliest years, we find portals into the impossible: another crack at childhood, even if at one remove, the nearest we'll ever come to healing ourselves through loving a creature whose cells were fearfully and wonderfully cast by our own.

Of course, some parents descend in a different direction, projecting their disappointments and unhealed wounds onto their children, sculpting a new generation along the lines of their old pains, holding fast not to love but to resentment of another person's easier start.

Though Mom found a supportive community in her boarders and AA pals, her inner alcoholic still held court. During those first years of sobriety, her panic attacks were worse than ever. A house repair was a crisis, grocery shopping a terror. Pushing herself out the door and nearly always relying on someone else to drive, Mom waitressed, made house calls to measure for drapes and upholstery, attended AA meetings, and visited elderly shut-ins. Between fishing trips, Charles drove her to and from his house in Orleans, a stretch of road he could navigate in his sleep.

Before the vacuum repairman's house call, before the AA meetings, I knew better than to hope Mom would come to my basketball games or track meets. My friend Diane's parents were the ones who cheered me and snapped the photos. Mom floated outside the frame, her agoraphobia and anxiety making every car ride a white-knuckled accomplishment. I can only wonder what it must have cost her, newly sober, to sit in a darkened theater my senior year to watch me chase a worthless Nathan Detroit as Adelaide in *Guys and Dolls*.

When I made the leap to think beyond the bridge and apply to college, however, Mom had little encouragement to offer. I pleaded with her to complete the financial aid forms, left them in strategic places, then finally ambushed her in the living room with the papers in hand. I had filled in every blank I could but still needed the numbers. I knew they couldn't amount to much.

Mom glanced at the sheets as if they were another unpayable bill, another stone I was asking her to carry. She hesitated a moment, then shook her head and said, "You'll never go to college."

It was a gut punch. I searched Mom's face, hoping she'd think twice, take it back, but she couldn't meet my eye. I had no rebuttal. I desperately needed Mom to step up, but my persistence and naïve teenage optimism seemed to exhaust her, only adding to the burden of what it took her to get through the day.

Over the next week I was sick with worry I'd miss the mailing deadline. Though I felt guilty for bothering Mom, an equally familiar self-preservation kicked in, questions prowling like hungry cats in my head. How hard could I push without cracking her? Did she have tax returns stashed away somewhere? Should I go through her dresser drawers? But even if I found the returns, would they tell me what she owed on the house and had in the bank? Could I submit partial information? I had no answers.

On the last day the aid application could be postmarked, Mom emerged from her bedroom, still in her floor-length nightgown, and handed over the completed forms. Relief flooded me. Then I saw the numbers on the page. I'm not sure what I was expecting, but Mom's declared income for the previous year barely topped $2,000. I knew we were poor, but I hadn't realized we were *that* poor. Maybe she wasn't counting the cash she earned in summer tips or through sewing. Maybe this was why people left garbage bags filled with clothes on our doorstep.

I only now realize how demoralizing Mom must have found that application. On good days she could throw a supper party with scallops fresh off Charles's boat, or slip into a dress she had expertly tailored and spritz herself with French perfume before one of their dates. But behind and between the lines on that official form, she was a divorced seamstress and seasonal waitress with seven kids, two of whom dropped out of high school. Neither she nor my father had ever attended college. Charles, who left school at fifteen to earn his keep in a shipyard, put food on our table.

Then Mom shot me a look and said, "I'm proud of you."

Mom's phobia cure began the morning a friend waited in a doctor's office and idly picked up a copy of *Psychology Today*. Flipping the pages, she came across an article on panic disorders. Thinking of Mom, she ripped out the article and stashed it in her purse.

Mom raced through the accompanying anxiety quiz, her perfect score an epiphany. On those torn pages she found the words for what was wrong with her and learned that other people had similar debilitating fears. She was not alone, she had a disease, and that disease had a name. Although she couldn't imagine how she'd afford treatment, that diagnosis offered a sliver of hope. The article featured Dr. David Sheehan, a Harvard-trained psychiatrist at Massachusetts General Hospital who was organizing a blind study of pharmaceutical and behavioral treatments for severe anxiety. He was looking for participants. But Boston was a hundred miles away. Mom couldn't drive to the end of the street.

Her AA network rallied. A fellow member introduced her to a gay gardener twenty-three years her junior who also had agoraphobia. Dick could drive but was terrified of entering restaurants or stores. Mom panicked in the driver's seat, but as a waitress and hostess, she'd made restaurants her stage set. They decided to team up and apply to Dr. Sheehan's study—an impossibility for either of them alone.

Mom was still hesitant, though. "I wish I had a good family doctor," she wrote me the evening after her initial three-hour evaluation and acceptance into the study. She had been without health insurance for years, and primary care physicians on the Outer Cape were nearly as scarce then as they are now. "What do you think about all this?" she asked. "I have a month to decide. It would be so wonderful to be normal."

I didn't know what to think. I had recently graduated from college and was teaching in Bordeaux, but I remembered what prescription drugs had done to Mom when I was in high school. Would these drugs be different? Would she be treated like a guinea pig? Could she handle the stress of traveling to Boston? I waffled, afraid that Mom might mess up her life even more, so I simply said, "It's hard to know."

Six weeks later, Mom and Dick drove to Boston to officially enroll in Dr. Sheehan's study. Mom wrote me a detailed letter in the car, distracting herself. "I expect to have a good trip, as I have spent a long time preparing myself spiritually." She felt as if she were embarking on a life-changing journey, and truth be told, she was. When she and Dick arrived at Mass General, however, she nearly backtracked out the door after catching sight of the reporters and cameramen packing the lobby. "Who could find phobia patients this interesting?" she asked Dick, panic spiking. Someone then told her they were awaiting not the arrival of anxiety-crippled test subjects but news of Henry Kissinger's bypass surgery that day.

Too spooked to enter an elevator, Mom and Dick slipped by the photographers and climbed the stairs to Dr. Sheehan's office on the fifth floor. Dr. Sheehan had selected approximately one-hundred patients and divided them into four groups. Three of the groups would take different medications, the fourth a placebo. Over the next ten weeks, then during a year of follow-up appointments, Mom and Dick would have myriad physicals and vials of blood drawn, as well as reams of paperwork to fill out. Smaller behavior therapy groups offered emotional support in which participants shared the results of their "homework assignments," attempts to deflate phobias by facing them repeatedly in real-life situations. One of her first—designed by Dick—was crossing a pedestrian bridge over a highway near the hospital.

"I won't be able to breathe!" Mom cried when he pointed to the bridge he had chosen for her to cross. "There's only a tiny rail to hang onto. I'll die on that walk!"

Dick insisted she try and reminded her this was part of the process of getting well.

Mom's legs had turned leaden, as in a nightmare when you can't run. Straining, she lifted her right foot onto the first step. She began hyperventilating, her heart pounding. "I'm going to pass out," she croaked.

Dick assured her he was right behind her, she was safe.

Mom made it to the top of the steps, clinging to the rail as other pedestrians strolled by. Too frightened to cry, she forced herself to take baby steps toward the middle of the bridge. Cars and trucks streamed beneath, horns tooting and brakes squealing. She wished she could jump into the traffic and be done with it.

Losing heart, she turned to hold onto Dick, but he hadn't moved from the top of the steps. *I'll never forgive him!* she thought. She told herself she would have *never* tricked him into entering a restaurant; how could he abandon her on a bridge?

As Mom later put it, a lifetime passed in that crossing. She made it to the opposite end and sat on a large rock in a patch of grass, where Dick, trotting confidently across the bridge, joined her. She was too upset to speak. They waited for a long while, Mom catching her breath and trying to calm herself.

"Please find us a cab to get us back to the parking lot," she panted.

"You're going back the way you came," Dick said.

"Never," Mom replied. "I will never walk across that bridge again."

Dick coaxed and encouraged, held her arm and guided her as they retraced her steps. Back in the parking lot, she sank into the car, depleted.

Years later, Mom recalled that crossing in her journal. "It was the beginning of a long fight for freedom," she wrote, "and the biggest risk I've ever taken."

Mom was lucky and responded well to the tricyclic drug that her trial group was assigned. "The medicine makes me awfully drowsy," she admitted in a postcard, "but I'm also working in my sewing shop during the day and at the Oyster House six nights a week." She began to practice driving short distances, and while Dick still sat behind the wheel on their weekly trips to Boston, the journey grew easier. Dick, who had lived in Boston, shared his favorite places with Mom: Copley Square, Trinity Church, the Public Library, Faneuil Hall, Newberry Street, the fabric district. They adored each other and began vacationing together, driving to Maine in the summer and Florida in the winter, where they heard the occasional tut-tut as Dick, handsome and young, with his tiny Dachshund tucked into a shoulder bag, escorted my scandalously older mother in and out of hotel rooms and restaurants. For one vacation, Dick arranged for the two of them to fly on a puddle jumper to Nantucket; Mom hadn't boarded a plane since her escape from Germany twenty-five years earlier. As she rumbled above the calm inland sea of Nantucket Sound and spotted Great Point Lighthouse on the northernmost sliver of the island, she felt as if she were conquering the world.

Though Mom's horizons were expanding by the week, it would be months before she could ride in an elevator. After yet another long hike up the stairwell at Mass General, she blurted to Dr. Sheehan, whom she worshipped, "I can't believe a psychiatrist specializing in phobias would put his clinic on the fifth floor!"

"Anyone who wants to get better," he replied, "will climb those five flights of stairs."

While my mother was feeling her way into a changed story, a new kind of script utterly seduced me. My junior year of high school, a year-long substitute Algebra II teacher filled in for a teacher on maternity leave. I liked Mr. Caldwell, who was patient, and I liked algebra even more. One day a couple of months into the school year, Mr. Caldwell stood in front of a chalkboard wiped clean of equations. He had an important question for us:

"Who do you think Jesus was?"

I looked down at my homework, dumbstruck. I'd solved for $x$ and $y$ the afternoon before in the school library. Why couldn't we stick to math? I would have slid under my desk to die before starting a conversation about Jesus with a room full of eleventh graders and fifty minutes before the next bell.

"So, who *do* you think Jesus was?" he repeated.

Mr. Caldwell's light brown hair grazed his collar, and his hazel eyes studied us through nearly rimless glasses. He had the build of a fastball pitcher and had been at Nauset High long enough for us to know he could outwait us.

A brave soul two rows over said, "A religious guy, a good man."

"I have no argument with that," replied Mr. Caldwell. "He was a perfect man."

A jock I had made out with over the weekend scoffed, "Perfect? No one's perfect."

*Especially you*, I thought, pissed that he hadn't talked to me since the party.

"Jesus was." Our teacher's voice rode a comforting wave between certainty and gentleness.

"But Jesus was a man," said the jock, familiar with masculine failings.

"A man *and* God," Mr. Caldwell corrected. "He told people he was the way, the truth, and the life."

I thought Jesus sounded stuck up.

"That's why he called himself the Son of God."

"Aren't we all children of God?" asked a girl I sometimes partied with.

"Yeah, but back then it meant something different," said Mr. Caldwell. "It was enough to get you nailed on a cross."

I grew up attending Wellfleet's First Congregational Church, a Greek Revival building on a hill in the center of town, with a steeple clock that keeps ship's time—from one to eight bells every half hour, in keeping with port and starboard watches. The very British Reverend Leonard Heap and his wife Lucy arrived from South Africa to lead our church when I was a toddler. Reverend Heap's sermons, delivered in a rich, baritone voice, were liberal and erudite, a comfort to himself, if not to his listeners. My mother cleaned the sanctuary on Saturdays when I was in elementary school, and she and Reverend Heap sometimes fell into conversation between the empty pews while I straddled the large iron heating grate in the red carpet, my skirt billowing into a parachute, the warmth soothing my thighs. "We can do things we don't mean to," he'd tell her, catching the scent of her hangover, perhaps hearing stories. "God is very forgiving."

Lucy Heap, a thin, graying woman who smelled of mutton and smoked like a fiend, led the Junior Choir. Thelma and I, along with our girl cousins and friends, walked after school from Wellfleet Elementary to the church, which we all called "the Congo," every week for practice, and we punished the minister's wife for this. We tied our shoelaces together on the way so we'd be late and stuck our forbidden chewing gum on the church columns and piano keys. Aiming spitballs at Mrs. Heap's tweedy back while we all climbed Jacob's Ladder, we calculated how many shots it would take before she spun around and cracked.

We probably sent our Sunday School teacher home with headaches, too, but unlike the minister's wife, Mrs. Villeray loved teaching children. Our talks became more contentious, however, as we reached middle school and *Jesus Christ Superstar* started spinning on turntables. "See, Jesus didn't really want to die!" my cousin Holly announced one Sunday morning. She believed, as did I, that song lyrics were at least as reliable as Scripture, and indisputably more compelling. "And he and Mary Magdalene were in love," I added.

Mrs. Villeray looked apoplectic, but rock theology won out. When I was twelve, Mom told me I could choose whether to attend church, so I happily pushed my Sunday dresses to the shadowy end of the clothes rack. A few months later, I climbed into the closet with a flashlight and huddled under a wool blanket to tickle my legs with Mom's electric razor. Time to move on to bigger things.

Soon after Mr. Caldwell's Jesus bomb in Algebra, the principal called him into his office. A surfer in the back of the room had complained.

"Listen, Fred," began the principal, reddening. Mr. Caldwell, who later described the meeting to me, gazed steadily back at him. "We hired you to teach algebra, not to talk about Jesus Christ."

The next day before the end of class, Mr. Caldwell asked, "Have you thought any more about who Jesus Christ is?

Silence.

"Why should we believe he was God rather than deluded or dishonest?" I asked.

"Because he rose from the dead."

"Could be a myth."

"Except there were eyewitnesses. The first were women, which broke all sorts of cultural barriers, since their testimony was worth about as much as a pig in those days. And a whole bunch of men believed them. The resurrection is so important because otherwise we'd all be dead in our sins, with no hope of salvation."

"I live a decent life," said a kid from Orleans, shifting uneasily in his seat.

"Decent isn't good enough for God," said Mr. Caldwell.

Saved by the bell, we scrambled to our feet and rushed out the door like minnows streaming through a crevice to escape a striper. But a few brave souls stopped at Mr. Caldwell's desk—the daughter of a Baptist preacher, a guy we had all pegged as a narc, and a prim blonde who wore blouses buttoned to the top (*what century is she from?* I used to wonder as I adjusted my cropped halter top). Within a couple of weeks, a small Bible study had begun. There were no more religious discussions during math class—the department chair had hauled Mr. Caldwell into his office after the second round of God talk—but if we had a question, we knew where to go. Mr. Caldwell's desk was Bible Central, and he always had time.

I had thought about the divine off and on during my apprenticeship in adolescent mischief, but even at thirteen I knew my relationship to God was self-serving. I sucked up and walked a straight line when eager for a favor, only to return to business-as-usual as soon as the emergency passed. As Orleans cops chased a gang of us running in all directions one Halloween night, I hid behind a bush and promised God I'd never throw another egg or toss another roll of toilet paper into trees, if only he'd keep me from getting arrested. God, unlike me, kept his end of the bargain.

Although my friends and I often took God's existence for granted, as I got older faith turned elusive. "Why are we here?" I wrote in my journal. "Where did we come from?" Those questions felt unanswerable.

"Why do *you* believe in God?" I asked a friend dabbling in hard narcotics.

"How could anything but God create a sunset?" she asked dreamily. I think she was stoned. "Evolution couldn't possibly create something that beautiful."

Proof enough for her, but I needed more.

When I walked into my first Bible study at Mr. Caldwell's winter rental in Chatham, I said, "Listen, Mr. Caldwell, I'm not really interested in religion or the Bible; I'm just here to take a look."

"That's fine," he replied. "Glad you're here."

In the center of the sparsely furnished living room sat a cardboard box. Mr. Caldwell pulled out fresh copies of a paperback called *Good News for Modern Man*, handing each of us one as we plopped down on the second-hand furniture and the blue and green braided rug. No one I knew dealt out books like playing cards.

I cracked the gray spine to stick figures preaching, healing, and raising the dead. The New Testament made easy. Scanning a few lines, I was startled by the language. Where were the "thou's," the "saith's," the "virgins"?

My math teacher folded himself onto a stool and said, "Let's start with a short prayer." I closed my eyes, embarrassed to be in such a compromising position. "Lord," began Mr. Caldwell, "thank you for the kids coming tonight. I just ask that you open their hearts and minds to you and what's true. In Jesus' name, Amen."

Short and sweet.

"Let's open our Bibles to the Gospel of John."

Bette, a beautiful, brown-eyed Baptist, helped me find my place.

Mr. Caldwell's voice, disarmingly earnest and certain, led us through the Gospel. Over the weeks that followed, he offered his own story as Exhibit A.

"People come to Christ for all kinds of different reasons. I did because I was screwed up and knew that life made no sense."

Did life make sense? I didn't know where we came from, but life didn't feel meaningless. Shitty sometimes, fun other times, beautiful, cruel, complicated. A surfeit of meaning I tried to decipher through poetry and history. Was there a God at the center? The question nagged me.

"Have any of you heard Peggy Lee's song 'Is That All There Is?'" asked Mr. Caldwell. "It's about the pointlessness of life, and how we might as well just booze it up and party all night. That song haunted me, because it said exactly what I was thinking. My parents pummeled me into being a perfect boy. I won all sorts of awards and went off to Dartmouth, but still I was lost. No one had an answer. I didn't know anything about evangelicals. I thought they all wore Hawaiian shirts with striped ties and coke bottle glasses. You know, screwballs and whackos."

Yup.

"I drank like a fish, but that didn't help. I played minor league baseball, but that wasn't the answer. Sex felt good for a while, but the relationship part was horrible. I had that love bucket with a hole in it."

My math teacher, at thirty-three, didn't seem to notice the difference in our ages. I'd never met anyone like him.

"By the time I met my second wife, I was a mess. But she was a Christian, and on our first date she introduced me to Jesus Christ."

I glanced over at Mrs. Caldwell, rocking in a chair, hands resting lightly on a swollen belly. How had Mr. Caldwell liked having another man elbow in on his first date?

"She and I stayed up half the night talking. She had the answers I'd been looking for. I couldn't eat, I couldn't work, I couldn't sleep. For nearly a week I fought off God. When I finally got down on my knees, the reality of Jesus swept over me and I just sobbed like a child."

By New Year's, Mr. Caldwell's Bible study group was meeting regularly. Less than half a dozen attended, and Mr. Caldwell sometimes drove the length of the Lower Cape to ferry us to and from his ranch house. His devotion baffled and moved me. I didn't know what to do with his stories, with his kindness, with the verses we studied or his assertion that no decision was a decision. And both alternatives depressed me. I could turn my back on God, or I could become a weirdo, born-again Christian.

One late January evening we discussed the third chapter of John's Gospel, in which Jesus tells Nicodemus that he must be born again to enter heaven, and my ambivalence stretched to a breaking point. As the meeting broke up, I nibbled chocolate chip cookies and silently fenced with God. The others stood around bantering, apparently unaware that eternity was on the line. Mr. Caldwell picked up his keys, and three of us climbed into his Volkswagen squareback for the forty-minute drive to Eastham and Wellfleet. Route 6 was desolate, cottage colonies and motels closed for the winter, the Wellfleet Drive-In a ghostly set piece. I was the last to be dropped off. After the girl before my stop climbed out, I fell silent. The concern emanating from Mr. Caldwell blanketed me with a confused immobility.

"You're really on the fence, aren't you?" he finally asked.

"Yeah, I am." I remembered an illustration I had seen in Sunday school, Jesus knocking on a closed door, a plaintive look in his eyes. What the hell was I going to do?

Soft rock spilled out of the radio, tuned to WQRC. Mr. Caldwell kept his eyes on the road, his mouth uncharacteristically shut.

"Please let me off at the Black Duck," I said. I needed time to clear my head before going home.

"Cindy, it's nearly ten. I'd rather not drop you there."

"I'll be fine, Mr. Caldwell. Really."

We pulled into the long hollow, and Mr. Caldwell parked in front of the bait shop.

"God bless you," he said as I opened the door.

Mr. Caldwell's white car faded up the hill and past the brown, ice-tinged grass of Blackfish Creek as I walked between the bait shop and phone booth toward a stand of locust and scrub pine. Kicking grainy chunks of snow, I huddled on a felled tree trunk in the middle of the frozen back lot. Looking up, I scanned a night sky pinned with constellations I could not name.

"Okay, God," I said. "You win. I believe in you."

Then I burst into tears.

My stomach was killing me.

When I walked in the kitchen door, Mom and Charles were sitting at the table, an ashtray spilling cigarette butts between them. Mom had been to two AA meetings that week, after a drunk so bad I had cried my heart out on the phone to Diane. I mumbled a hello. Charles, registering the strain and emotion streaking my face, said, "Allo, Miss Santia," unable to pronounce the "th" in my name, too polite to ask more. Mom was oblivious. I retreated to

my room in the cellar and climbed into bed, feeling slightly confused, irritated even. The boundaries of my world had shifted, and
I wasn't sure where they lay.

I didn't write about that night in my journal. I wrote instead
about boys and school and how depressed I felt. It was as if I had
moved into a new house and was struggling to feel at home. I
wasn't even sure of the address.

Looking back, I can see that as a meaning-driven teenager
with a disorienting homelife, what I needed was a therapist, or a
philosophy primer, or young adult novels with heroines I could
relate to and admire. But none of these were at hand, so religion
stepped in, as it so often does for those with modest means and
a spinning compass.

I didn't say anything to Mr. Caldwell after math class, but at
the next Bible study he looked up in surprise when I talked about
a verse as if I understood it.

"Cindy, did something happen last week?" he asked.

"Yeah," I said, reddening. "I told God I believe in him."

Two girls shrieked, Mr. Caldwell hugged me, the others circled
'round.

I was in.

It took me a while to figure out what had happened on that log
behind the Black Duck. I was frustrated that our Bible studies
focused so much on Jesus, who seemed like an unhinged narcis-
sist. I was looking for God, for a way of believing that love, not
exploitation and indifference, lay at the heart of the universe. It
was only as I watched Mr. Caldwell reel in other teenagers that it
dawned on me: God was a package deal.

After some hesitation, I began to tell friends about my new
faith. On a sleepover at Diane's, I told her something big had happened. Could she guess? She narrowed it down to the letters
O-G-D. "A dog, you got a new dog?" she asked excitedly.

My heartthrob from elementary school, Paul Holbrook, miraculously started talking with me again, and we launched into debates

on the existence of God during late-night back rubs. He began attending Mr. Caldwell's meetings and became a Christian a few months after I did. He dragged in two or three of our Wellfleetian friends, guys we used to get high with. They became Jesus freaks, too. By April, there were twenty or thirty kids at some meetings. Many were simply curious, while others, a dozen or so, accepted Christ. After Bible studies, several of us would pile into Paul's rusting 1963 Ford Fairlane for the ride back to Wellfleet, harmonizing evangelical ditties like "Seek Ye First," "One in the Spirit," or "I Shall Be Released." Another kind of high.

My journal entries began to change a few months after my conversion, but it would take me many years to understand that I had not adopted a faith so much as a new script. I was learning a foreign language and it showed. Curlicues of praise punctuated heartfelt prayers sporting words like "conviction," "backsliding," and "spirit-filled."

"I am so glad I've changed," I wrote. "Ever since accepting Christ, I have so much more love for others. People are bossy and angry at drama practices, and I see a reflection of my old self in them. But life has become something I can actually grasp and cope with."

Mrs. Emerson, our drama teacher, didn't have much patience with the crop of new Christians sprouting in Algebra II, especially when we took up do-gooding. When I told her I might have to miss a dress rehearsal to raise money in a charity bike ride, she scowled, "You're *not* riding. You'll get TB or flunk out or both if you do!"

Although the language in my journals turns more euphoric in the months after I became a Christian, it's as hard a read today as my angrier or more despondent writings from earlier years. Raw honesty is gone. Dishonesty did not take its place, but something more subtle: a structuring of feeling to reflect what I believed, rather than an outpouring of uncensored emotion. I used Bible-babble to rearrange and rename experience, funneling it through phrases and code words any evangelical could have penned. It was as if most entries were Holy-Ghostwritten, an admixture of my own feelings and those I thought I should feel.

God's love for me meant every trial I faced was for the best. One spring afternoon, I rode Beth's ten-speed to the beach. While I was talking with some guy, the bike was stolen. "Thank God (I mean it)!" I chirped in my journal, inwardly chanting the mantra that "all things work together for good to those who love God."

My sister didn't see it that way; the bike had been one of her last gifts from Dad, and we couldn't afford to replace it.

My twisting of experience to align it with belief would one day prove too contortionist, but in high school, evangelicalism's comprehensive script lent coherence to what felt like competing and uncertain identities. Was I a nerd, a jock, a hopeless case? Evangelicalism gave me an identity that could gather and organize all these other ways of being, because I was first and foremost a Christian. Operating on an existential and eternal plane, the defining power of religion pasted over all the other labels I had chosen and had been chosen for me.

Religion is not so much the opiate of the masses (though it's that, for sure) as it is the story of the people. That story is not only about the world, allowing us to make sense of it, but also about ourselves, allowing us to make sense of our lives. What God had to say about me—that I was loved despite my failings, that I was his vessel for goodness—felt more significant and more true than any worldly versions, which were by nature changeable and transient and full of misinterpretations.

"The very hairs on your head are all numbered," writes the Apostle Luke. I might not have counted for much at home, but God had "knit me together in my mother's womb" and called me his own. This was as close as I had ever come in my short life to the curative power of unconditional love.

Years later, I would discover in the writings of cognitive psychologists and neurophysiologists the notion that actions help shape emotions. In other words, smile and something like happiness will begin to creep in. When I was a sixteen-year-old

Christian, I didn't consciously rearrange my face or "decide" to parrot cheerful, evangelical certitudes, but in smiling and believing, I began to change. I tried not to lie or gossip, stopped stealing, quit smoking pot, drank less, hoped more. And I had a passel of new friends who were loving and openly generous, allowing me to risk an unfashionable, vulnerable goodness.

The hardest place to be a Christian is at home. Although I was bold enough to join hands with friends and risk social ridicule by praying in a circle on the grass in front of Nauset High's E-Building, I didn't know how to communicate my newfound faith to my family. Perhaps they'd roll their eyes or tell me I'd gone bonkers. Or more likely, my behavior at home was still too reactive to convince anyone I had changed. I tried to be kinder, especially to my younger sister Beth, whose recklessness—she nearly ruined our temperamental Buick by driving it up a sand dune—enraged me, because it threatened to snap the fragile string of our family's survival. I made little progress.

Over time, my Christian faith became less a new way of relating to my family and more a wall I used to protect and distance myself from a whorl of family problems, a way of escaping the house without actually leaving it. Like my cellar hideaway, my new faith, shared by a circle of trustworthy friends, offered a space apart for growing up, a well-ordered refuge when events upstairs ricocheted off the walls, each unpredictable trajectory the strand of a web that might snare and bind me.

It didn't help that there were now seven of us crammed into the main house. My older half-brother Ted, a bartender at the Oyster House, had fallen in love with one of the summer dishwashers, a beautiful redhead from Mississippi, and she and her two children by previous boyfriends had moved in for lack of an affordable rental. Everyone shared a bedroom, except for me. Cellar-living had its advantages.

Ted and Jeanne married in our yard the summer after I became a Christian, just before my senior year of high school. The bride, twenty-seven, carried a bouquet of daisies. In between waitressing shifts, Mom made the wedding dress, the flower girl's dress, the mother-of-the-bride's dress, her own dress. She was exhausted. I read a rhapsodic, spiritual poem I'd written. Jeanne's children, eight and six, called Ted "Dad" with shy pleasure, and her strawberry-blond daughter crayoned notes of love to me after our coloring sessions and spelling games.

As winter fell, so did moods. Mom tumbled off the wagon and got drunk one night after an argument with Jeanne, throwing up all over the living room couch. It would be the last time she took a drink, although none of us knew that then. Jeanne was home-sick for the South and sank into silence as she fried chicken and applied lipstick to her flawless, doll-like face. "The atmosphere in your house is so depressing," said a friend spending the night. I had lived in the fog for so long, I no longer registered it.

One cold January afternoon, a year to the day after I yielded to God behind the bait shop, Jeanne's children and I came home from school to an empty house. There was no sign of my sister-in-law, who I figured must be out. Mom walked in from bringing food to an elderly couple and asked, "Where's Jeanne?"

"Don't know," I said. "Haven't seen her since I got home."

"But her car is here."

Jeanne's daughter looked from Mom's face to mine, searching for reassurance, unable to speak.

We called upstairs to Jeanne and Ted's small bedroom, across the landing from the pine room. No answer. Mom and I climbed the stairs and knocked on the door. Locked. I didn't know that door could lock. Not even our front door locked. Why in the world would that door be locked?

Mom and I looked at each other, and I felt her panic shoot through the roof. We turned and banged on the door, shouting my sister-in-law's name, ears pressed against tired wood. Silence.

My step-niece, eight, watched from the bottom of the stairs, terror seeping into her freckled face, her large, green eyes fixed on Mom and me. Her younger brother, a blond wisp of a boy, had run into the living room, where he sat inhaling television cartoons in willful oblivion.

Sick with foreboding, I told Mom to stand back and kicked the door, just below the cut glass handle. It didn't budge. A second desperate strike made a loud crack. I kicked harder and faster, until the door flew open and hit the night table.

Mom rushed past me as I held back, afraid to enter, afraid of what we might find. Peering cautiously into the room, my heart dragging to a thud as I crossed the threshold in slow motion, I saw an empty bed. *Thank God!* The locked door must have been a fluke, the old house playing tricks on us, the ghost having its fun. Then Mom screamed as she grabbed Jeanne's foot and started shaking it, trying to rouse the lifeless body splayed on the floor between the bed and the closet. I ran to Jeanne and saw that her eyes were nearly closed, her mouth slightly open. Slits of possibility.

Later she told me she had wanted to stab herself, but chickened out and swallowed every pill in the house instead.

Mom started moaning and pacing. I had just finished a CPR unit in a survival course at school, so I knelt next to Jeanne's body, swept my finger along the inside of her mouth, tilted her head back to establish an airway, and checked her pulse. It beat frantically against her thin, pale wrist, as if trilling for death's release. I felt unnaturally calm, as if the slightest panic on my part would be the end of us all.

Mom, watching over my shoulder, cried, "Call the rescue squad! Now!"

*God, what was the number?* I had no idea. I'd have to call the operator. I ran downstairs to our rotary phone, passing Jeanne's daughter, still frozen at the bottom of the stairs, tears streaming down her cheeks. Picking up the heavy receiver, I spun the dial, the slow, clicking turn from zero to help an eternity. The operator connected me to the fire department, another delay, a new mental image to haunt me. For years I dreamed of misdialing numbers, misreading telephone books, or slurring urgent, unintelligible pleas into a receiver that might be dead.

Back upstairs, Mom was pacing and wailing. I sat her on a chair and told her to stay put while I rushed the children to neighbors. It would be too awful for them to see their mother carried out on a stretcher.

Once the kids were safely out of the house, I held Jeanne's limp hand until the rescue squad and its entourage ducked inside. Their bodies were too big for our small rooms, their uniforms and equipment foreign, official, humiliating. After the men maneuvered the stretcher out the low kitchen door and the ambulance pulled away, I ran to the pay phone near the Black Duck to call Diane. Only in the shelter of the telephone booth, away from the craziness at home, could I begin to unclench, to cry, to give in. Even with God on my side, escape felt impossible. For Jeanne, for my family, for me. We were all of us caught in misfortune's crosshairs.

Ted, who had arrived home by this time, rode in the ambulance with his wife to Cape Cod Hospital, forty-five minutes away. Mom hightailed it to an AA meeting and wouldn't return for hours. My two sisters drove to Hyannis with clothes for Ted. The house fell silent. Alone with Jeanne's two children, I sang to them over the clatter of dishes and the snarl of the vacuum, making a stab at the only kind of order I was capable of.

Sometime after nine I curled up with the children under Mom's blankets and read Bible passages aloud. My step-niece, still sniffling, nestled under my arm, we three children adrift on the unmoored raft of my mother's bed. But as sleep slowly enveloped the other two, something else, something unexpected, came for me.

Earlier that week, sitting at the kitchen table as he meditated his way through a pack of Marlboro Lights, Ted had told me about a series of reported UFO sightings, subtly unnerving me with his inclination to believe them. As the kids drifted off and I laid my copy of *Good News for Modern Man* on Mom's bedside table, my conversation with Ted flared back to life, torching any comfort I might have found in verse or prayer. *Could UFOs and God co-exist?* I wondered. Then I panicked. *It can't be true. Impossible.*

I pulled the top blanket closer to my chin. *Oh god, was it sacrilegious to even ask this question?* This was bad. *Sorry, God!! But if they did co-exist*—I couldn't help myself—*was one of them more real? More powerful?*

For a brief, disorienting interval, there seemed no way to know, and a haunting doubt seeped through the crevices of that leaky house, swirling otherworldly molecules in the air of Mom's low-ceilinged room. Trapped in her bed, not wanting to leave the children alone, I lay vigilant during the warped hours of that night, under the floor where Jeanne had tried to die, awash in fear that at any minute aliens were going to land in our backyard. I imagined them docking by the locust tree outside the bedroom window, a blinking, silent disc skimming the mid-winter snow. Hideous nonhumans, gray, dispassionate, invincible, would march out and spirit me and the children away.

It was the logic of displaced chaos, which would make me laugh if I could forget the dread.

I sleepwalked through school the following day, unsure whether Jeanne survived the night, wanting to blurt to teachers, *My sister-in-law tried to kill herself last night!* just to relieve the awful pretense of normalcy. Jeanne pulled through but made a second attempt just a week later in the same upstairs room. While Ted was scrambling to ready his wife for another trip to the Hyannis hospital—the cost of a second ambulance ride would be ruinous—our white miniature poodle, Pierre, backed himself into a kitchen corner and howled with eerie, instinctual unease. No treat, no threat, no pleading would shut him up. He was channeling the voice of our dumbstruck family in that moment, the disordered energy of self-destruction slinking down the stairs, and he couldn't rest until something in the air changed.

It did. Ted, desperate to relieve his wife's sadness, packed up their belongings after Jeanne's release from the psychiatric hospital in Taunton and moved with his new family to her hometown in rural Mississippi, a universe away from the Outer Cape.

After their departure, I threw myself with even more energy into my own world. Our born-again contingent at Nauset started Bible studies and prayer groups and potlucks followed by songs, prayers, and freewheeling communion. Several of us created a singing group and performed at weddings, in Sunday services, and on boats during Provincetown's Blessing of the Fleet. Reverend Heap sent me a note after our visit to the Congregational Church:

"Dear Cindy," it read. "I am more delighted than I can say that you have arrived at a point of decision and dedication. Stick to it and you will never regret it. There will be ups and downs to encounter, but there will be true joy, and a sense of adventure to sustain you. May I make one small suggestion? When you sing, determine to be God-conscious rather than audience-conscious. You will find it a great help. Thank you for last Sunday. Sincerely, Leonard Heap."

The summer after Jeanne's suicide attempts, friends and I attended a Christian camp in Saranac, New York, immersing ourselves in a week-long Jesus-fest. Brightness and light. Hot chocolate and hugs. A faith that, whether I understood it or not, could and would explain everything. I talked and read and listened, eager to learn everything I could about my faith and God, the only convincing security I knew.

I also began a long, neuroticizing process of trying to fit every detail of life into God's plan for me. It led to ridiculous prayers, which I wrote in my journal because my mind hopped around so much. In the space of a paragraph, I could travel from the sublime to the trivial: "Lord, I give my life to you. . . . Wilt Thou heal the wart on my knee?"

God's will led to the tyranny of The Right Choice, made anxious by my frequent inability to divine The Right Choice. Should I go out dancing with friends at the Back Room, a gay bar in Provincetown—in the world, but not of it—or stay home in pious isolation? (I danced.) Fast every week? (Hardly.) Audit sociology, or take it for credit? (Audits were for slackers.) Paul Holbrook adopted a useful strategy: when he wanted to kiss a girl, he'd flip a coin to see if it was God's will. If the toss went against him, he'd give God two-out-of-three.

In September of my senior year, nine months after my conversion, Mr. Caldwell met several of us at the South Wellfleet General Store and drove with us the short mile to the beach at the end of Lecount Hollow. Our feet sank in sand as we descended the dunes and walked across the nearly deserted shore. A friend pulled out her guitar while our Bible study band formed a half-circle. As choruses of "Pass It On" floated on the breeze, a pair of morning beachcombers stopped several feet away, mystified.

Mr. Caldwell turned to me, his gaze steady, his soft, manly voice the tone of all I found most reassuring in the world. "Are you ready?" he asked.

I nodded, and together we waded waist-deep into the chill waters of the Atlantic. Mr. Caldwell put his right hand behind my shoulders and his left on the crown of my head. A breeze slapped the collar of his light-blue dress shirt. He looked me in the eyes and said, "Cindy, I baptize you in the name of the Father, the Son, and the Holy Spirit." My toes curled in rocky sand, my hair spread like seaweed tendrils, my breath stilled. Three seconds of gliding between water and air. Lifted with a wave into skylight, I opened my eyes and shivered with joy.

# 8

# The Opposite
# of Memory

~

While moments like my ocean baptism still thrill me—despite my later loss of faith—going back is not for the faint of heart. There are reasons we forget, many of them good ones. Sometimes I find myself *believing* rather than *feeling* that the more we mine our pasts and those of our family members, the stronger our sense of self becomes.

Many of my stories have indeed anchored me: the visitation of ghosts that I took for guardian angels; Nana's resilience despite eight years in charity institutions, then her fostering seventeen abandoned girls; Mom's decision to join AA and to chart a healthier path for herself; my unlikely climb into college and graduate school. While such stories are points on my compass, they are not the landscape itself, which quietly thrums with less momentous happenings: playing jacks and pick-up-sticks with my sisters and cousins, swatting mosquitos while watching movies at the Drive-In, digging for clams, hitting golf balls at the Eastham driving range with Dad, making Swedish meatballs with Mom, listening for the call of the whip-poor-will and bobwhite, circling fantasy items in the Sears catalog for Christmas, checking my bed for Geoff's frogs, and cutting up paper bags at the kitchen table to make covers for my school books, searching for the rare markers that hadn't yet dried up.

These memories offer color and flow, filling in my mental images of the past. Unremarkable as they may be, they allow me to feel I have existed, that I have historical dimensionality. The more singular memories, however, some of which are negative—splitting apart on Willy's lap, watching my scary cousin roast a songbird he shot over an outdoor fire, discovering a revolver in the rag pile under our bathroom sink—blot that portrait of the past like spilled ink, drawing my eye away from what is more lovingly sketched. I have sometimes chastised myself for too often seeing these blots, though we are all susceptible to that diversion of the eye.

I could attempt to paint over the negative scenes, of course, but this would also come at a cost. We carry difficult stories with us one way or another: through a conscious remembering and telling, or through choices and actions that tell the story for us, be it on Halloween or at the wedding altar.

Social scientists have long touted the mental and physical health benefits of personal writing, especially when trying to process and integrate painful experiences. While the effect of such writing tends to produce short-term emotional distress and physical symptoms, long-term reverberations often result in a greater sense of well-being.

I do believe that keeping a journal throughout high school helped me to understand my life and my desires better. In college and later, when friends asked how I managed to leave my family situation to travel and study, I would tell them that I wrote my way out. Most of my siblings were at least as smart as I was, and my brother Geoff far smarter; why didn't they go to college? Lots of reasons, of course, but I knew in my gut that putting words to paper had allowed the chaos and fear and hopes and enthusiasms in my head to sort themselves out, my sentences plotting the lines of a chart I could then navigate. Without those words, that sequentially unfolding map, it would have been hard to find my way or to persuade others that I had a future worth investing in.

I would love, however, to see expressive writing studies conducted on memoirists. My guess is the findings would not replicate those for short-term journaling. As Mary Karr puts it, memoir writing is like "knocking yourself out with your own fist, if it's done right," and I have felt pummeled by the writing of this book. Emotional distress? Yes. Physical ailments? Too many. Hard words from family members? Wrenching. I can't honestly say if these days, months, and years of research and writing have been worth the disruptions, those of the heart and those of the body. I only know what I have felt compelled to do. And in recalling and fleshing out the past, I have gained a new and abiding appreciation for forgetting.

It's nearly impossible to write about what I have forgotten and have no record of, but like most people I can write easily, and passionately, about what others have forgotten and I have not.

About ten years ago an unexpected message popped up in my Facebook Messenger app, a hand shooting through the grass from its shallow resting place. "Hi Cynthia," it read. "I don't know if you remember me. . . ."

*Remember you?* I thought, a riptide of panic and curiosity lashing my ankles and tipping me into a current I knew instantly I would have to ride out. It's not as if I hadn't wanted this; I had searched online for Samantha Smith over the years, had asked others about her, but I invariably hit dead ends. Sam had vanished when her family moved off-Cape after eighth grade. Forgetting her, however, had never been an option.

Sam's family lived "on base" at the Cape Cod National Seashore Headquarters, near the old Marconi wireless station in South Wellfleet. We could hike between each other's houses on the trail through the White Cedar Swamp, an ambitious ramble but nothing an unsupervised kid couldn't pull off on a boring summer day. Sam's father was an earnest park ranger, a straight arrow who loved the outdoors. Her mother, not long for the marriage or Cape Cod, was a beautiful, dark-eyed songbird desperate for, and deserving of, some other stage than the Congregational choir stalls.

Sam was one of my closest friends, but I grew apprehensive when she began harassing a new girl, Nancy North, who joined our class at Wellfleet Elementary in third grade. Nancy's father, an Air Force colonel, had gone missing just before the start of school, after the Viet Cong shot his single-seat F-105 fighter-bomber out of the sky on his thirty-fourth mission. For three years our new schoolmate and her family would not know if he had survived. In sixth grade we—his family, the town of Wellfleet, the nation—learned he was still alive. He was caged in the infamous "Hanoi Hilton," enduring unerasable tortures.

But during Nancy's first few years at Wellfleet Elementary, all anyone knew was that her dad was MIA. And that she was struggling. Sam made that fragile transition harder, lobbying well-aimed verbal darts and isolating her. I want to say I was kind to Nancy, who later became a good friend, but when I picture those months, I see myself skirting trouble from the sidelines, no better than a collaborator.

Early in fourth grade my number came up. While I can't recall the exact timing of my visit to the barbershop, I believe it was the summer between third and fourth grades, in part because it would have created in me the kind of vulnerability that makes for an easy target. Why else would Sam's arrow shift to me? She must have sensed my new brokenness, the pain that had seeped into my bones. I don't know. I only know that Sam made fourth grade miserable for me, bullying and isolating me as she had our classmate.

One mid-quarter morning in fourth grade, another new girl joined our class, and I looked hopefully at her as she stood in front of the class with her bob haircut and plaid skirt, a large gold pin lying neatly along the pleat, her matching shirt and shoes a fashion marvel. I told myself she wouldn't know the schoolroom's hierarchy or that I was an outcast. And we shared the same first name! *Maybe, just maybe*, I thought, *she'll play with me at recess.* Mrs. Snow even directed this new Cindy to a desk near mine, sending a slight, anxious thrill through me. But Sam, alas, sat closer to the front than I did. As Cindy passed her desk, Sam leaned over, pointed at me, and warned, "See that girl? Don't like her."

Paul Holbrook sat behind me, straight blond hair falling across beautiful, stubborn brown eyes. I had loved Paul in kindergarten, when we sat together in the dunce's corner, and I loved him in sixth grade, when our math teacher announced we were destined to marry. Charmed by how much we liked each other, he arranged a wedding ceremony during class, positioning the desks like church pews with a central aisle for me to walk down. As Jono Brock, the gender-bending "mother of the bride," theatrically wept, Paul slipped a ring he had stolen from his sister's jewelry box onto my finger, and our towhead minister, the class nerd, proclaimed us husband and wife, eliciting cheers from the pint-sized congregation. In fourth grade, Paul was the only one in the class, or so it felt, to ignore Samantha Smith's orders.

One wintry evening that year, I stood on the toilet seat after a bath while my mother buffed me dry with a scratchy green towel. "You never have any friends over to play," she said, a question in her voice.

Her comment startled and embarrassed me. My mother seldom seemed aware of what was going on in my life. What had she noticed? Had she heard anything? Had my teacher spoken with her? Unlikely. Mrs. Snow was the ice queen of Wellfleet Elementary, maintaining military-like discipline. After recess or gym class, she lined us at the bubbler and commandeered the handle, allotting us each, no matter how sweaty or hot, a split-second of water, just enough to wet our mouth while minimizing visits to the restroom. Few moments were as alarming as Mrs. Snow's pause while sitting at her large desk after lunch and reapplying red lipstick in the reflection of a silver spoon, inquisitorial glances shooting over her glasses.

The first day of school that year, Mrs. Snow had given me notice and exiled me to the hall for accidently elbowing a ruler off my desk as I bent over my worksheet, eager to fill in the blanks as perfectly as possible. As she barked "Out!" and snapped her arm toward the classroom door, perhaps she was remembering the day ten years earlier when my older brother Geoff came early to school with a friend to rub all the desktops in her classroom with raw onions, or the time he loosened the bolts on her desk chair during recess so it would collapse when she next sat on it. Alone in the hall, not sure of where to go or what to do with myself, I fumed over the unjust punishment but also understood it for what it was: both a warning that branded me and a badge of honor I would crow about as soon as I walked into the kitchen after school. I didn't know *anyone* who had been thrown out of class on the very first day. This was even more impressive than my first day of kindergarten, when on a dare I shimmied like a salamander under the seats of the school bus from the back to the front, smearing dirt and grease down the front of the new dress Mom had sewn for me and popping up with a smile for the aggravated bus driver.

So I stayed silent about Sam, Mrs. Snow, and my loneliness as Mom finished drying me off and pulled a flannel nightgown over my head. But she added a special treat and fetched her favorite powder puff, the one she kept high on the top shelf, to dust my exposed chest. Plumes of Chanel N°5 wafted toward my chin, a silent kindness. I understood Mom was not going to press me for more, and I loved her for it.

A month or two later, I stood behind Sam at the bubbler after another humiliating gym class. Though an equal in sports, I was no match for Sam's barbed wit, and she had been vicious during our game of dodgeball. As she lowered her mouth into the brief, arcing stream of water, our PE teacher leaned down and whispered in her ear, "You are a cruel little girl, Samantha Smith."

Sam's dark brown eyes—lashes bewitchingly long—shot sideways as the water tumbled over her pursed lips. She let go of her hair, shielding her cheek with a cascade of straight brown strands I had fruitlessly tried to copy by singeing my curls on the ironing board. I stood silent next to the bubbler, stunned a teacher would say such a thing. Had I dared, I would have hugged her. I hoped the girls in line behind me had heard the teacher, or at least understood that the queen bee had been stung.

Too bad she took it out on me. One day soon after, I met Sam by accident near our lockers in the empty hall outside our classroom. Once again she taunted me, and for the first time I turned and fought back, flailing my skinny arms and trying to trip her onto the floor. Confusion, not anger, drove me, every scratch of my nails or yank of Sam's perfect hair a strangled *Why? Why? Why?*

I don't remember how the catfight ended, but I do know that, unlike the first day of school, I wasn't punished for it. This, too, felt like a mercy, a silent recognition by adults who couldn't, or wouldn't, intervene.

The summer after fourth grade, I sat entranced in front of our RCA television in the living room as I watched eight-year-old Rhoda Penmark, her dresses and curtseys impeccable, calmly murder her classmate to steal his penmanship award in *The Bad Seed*.

"That's Samantha Smith," I realized, horrified—but most of all grateful—to find a way to explain what I had been up against all year. Sam was, I decided, "a bad seed." I had no idea why she had chosen me, or the new girl whose father had vanished from the sky, but part of me, even then, realized that just like Rhoda Penmark, she couldn't stop herself.

In the way of young children, with their absorption in the present, Sam and I became fast friends again by sixth grade. We had sleepovers and squirt-gun fights, climbed trees and hiked through the cedar swamp, celebrated birthdays and traded secrets. We also hunched for hours over a Ouija board in the upstairs pine room to answer questions impossible to ask our parents, our longing all the more tender after floating on the sounds of Sweet Baby James and Cat Stevens. But I never understood what had happened two and three years earlier, what had driven her to hurt others and me.

Tracked in middle school, Sam and I saw less of each other, and then she moved off-Cape before high school, when I might have dared talk with her about fourth grade. With Sam's move, my chance at a reckoning, at an explanation, evaporated.

Four decades later, her note landed in my Messenger inbox.

My childhood friend was thrilled to have found me, and our story suddenly found its depth. We wrote long messages about our paths since elementary school, our memories of each other's families, our years together on the playground, in the cedar swamp, on the beach. But throughout the exchange of those first expansive missives, I kept wondering, "Doesn't she remember? Why is she saying nothing?

While I waited for the right moment to ask, Sam described how cold and unforgiving her homelife had been and how alienated from her mother she had felt, so much so that she kept to her vow never to have children. "I really believed that if I had a child, I would treat them the same way I was treated, and I never wanted that to happen to any child," she wrote. One morning, Sam said, her mother had pummeled her after catching her secretly switching out her school shoes for sneakers on her way to the bus stop. "Do you think I enjoy doing this?" her mother had cried afterward, holding out her swollen hands as if pleading for pity from the child she has just beaten.

As an adult Samantha could see that her mother was taking out her rage and powerlessness on her, but as a young girl all she understood was that her home was one of punishments for small infractions, of emotional rigidity and rules. "I will never forget how open and freewheeling your house was compared to mine," she wrote. Given my fear of my father, comments like this by Sam and other school friends have often surprised me, but when Dad was at work or golfing or asleep, we kids had the run of the place, as long as we didn't wake him up. Sam and I waged epic pillow fights in the cellar, raided the fridge for forbidden foods, and stayed up as late as we wanted. But most of all, she loved my mother, for her kindness and her ready affection. "I envied that," she wrote.

It was a possible answer.

But I still wanted to know: had Sam forgotten this thing that blighted my otherwise wonderful experiences at Wellfleet Elementary, this sliver forever under my skin? I finally floated a tentative question. "What do you remember about fourth grade?" I asked. "You and I had a painful breach in our friendship, and I don't think I ever understood what caused that. Do you remember it in the same way?"

"I guess we did diverge in our friendship, didn't we?" she replied, casting about for a way to agree with me. But she seemed to have no idea what I was talking about.

I typed up a draft letter that meandered through other aspects of our early years in Wellfleet—candy runs to the General Store, the dusty thrill of county fairs, missiles twinkling in the night sky as Navy pilots bombed the target ship anchored in the bay—before circling back to fourth grade. I decided to detail my memories of that year and then let the message sit overnight. The next morning I'd edit it into a more measured account before sending.

"I don't know how else to put it—I don't want to be unkind," I initially wrote, "but do you not remember organizing a year-long hate campaign against me? I didn't have a single girl friend the entire year." I reminded her of our cat fight in the hall and told her I had heard what the PE teacher said to her at the bubbler, the shocking charge of cruelty.

Even in this unedited version I was not seeking a "*j'accuse*" moment, but I couldn't continue corresponding without some acknowledgment of the way Sam had cratered my social life and, more enduringly, my self-esteem, in the middle of elementary school. I ended with, "Everything you've written to me so far tells me you're no longer that little girl. . . . So my telling you this story is not in any way a blaming. But not telling it would be dishonest."

I had said it. All that remained was to tone down the message in the morning and draft a few conciliatory, closing sentences. We had moved from Messenger to email, and as I guided my cursor to the "Save" button on AOL, a rogue imp magicked my screen into our old Ouija board and bumped the mouse to "Send" instead of the "Save" right next to it. I watched, horrified, as an email I had neither reread nor signed shot out of my past and into Sam's present.

Sam couldn't finish reading it. "Why a 9-yr old would inflict that kind of cruelty on others is mortifying," she wrote, "and it must have come from such complete lack of self-worth." She in no way disputed the details. "I am so ashamed," she confessed, "and the horrifying thing to me is that I don't remember it."

*She doesn't remember it.* I was dumbfounded. Yet to Sam's credit, she didn't express any doubt it had happened. Most people who have bullied others deny their behavior or challenge the other person's memories. Sam could have suggested I misinterpreted her actions, was misremembering, but instead she wrote, "I'm so very sorry, Cindy, that I hurt you and others. . . . There is something deeply messed up for a young girl to treat her friends that way."

Sam's graciousness and open apology moved me. Yet I was still stupefied that a long-lasting campaign to ostracize me could have been forgotten by the commander who waged it. How could something so consequential for my self-esteem and social relations evaporate from the memory networks of the very person responsible?

Emotion, once again, was likely pivotal. Especially when negative, emotion supercharges memory, and fourth grade was a year of sadness and loneliness and loss for me. Sam had been one of my best friends, and I didn't understand her behavior. I imagine she did not, either. My guess is she was caught more in the dramas of her home life than in those she was orchestrating at Wellfleet Elementary. I now believe that as an adult, Samantha recalled not the pain she had inflicted, but the pain she had endured. Those emotions must have obscured any memory of her strategic—or unthinking?—cruelties at school. I was simply a casualty of the pitched battles she was fighting on the home front, a way for her to exercise control when her parents granted her so little.

The past shifts and can even change as we grow and reinterpret the events of our lives, and learning of Sam's pain helped me reframe the story of that wounding year. The pain she caused was not erased, of course, but it became more complicated, more comprehensible. As with my father, my tight narrative of Samantha

Smith began to split at the seams, teaching me once more that we need to hold our stories of others lightly, that no one version tells it all.

This includes the versions we tell ourselves about ourselves. Perhaps Sam forgot about having bullied others in elementary school because remembering would have cost her more than forgetting did. In a normal eagerness to enhance our self-image, we have little incentive to summon our crueler moments, which typically shame us more than they teach us. In a kind of mnemonic mercy, the memories we neglect tend to fade, their neural networks weakening like beacons in the fog. Permanent memories make high storage demands on our brains; this is one of the reasons we have so few of them compared to the myriad things we could have remembered but don't.

We all differentiate, to varying degrees, between our past and present selves, and perhaps Sam's inability to recall her bullying maneuvers in elementary school arose not only from how much easier it is to recall being hurt than hurting others, but also from a disavowal of that earlier incarnation of self. Forgetting may have well allowed Sam to imagine, and become, a better version of herself. I have wondered if this is why she now uses "Samantha" instead of "Sam" in social media, just as I had claimed my full first name, "Cynthia," instead of the more girlish "Cindy" when I was halfway through college. It wasn't that I wanted to be a different person, but I did want to emphasize or develop a different aspect of myself: one more mature, one less easily diminished by a sweet nickname.

Narrative is as much an act of imagination as it is a factual recounting of what has happened, because the stories we tell create meaning as they interpret and fill in the gaps. In that imaginative space, tuned to our surroundings and hopes, we can reposition the props of our lives—experiences and relationships, behavior and clothing, even the languages we speak—to extract other meanings, to play with other ways of being, just as I began to embody a more substantial Cynthia at Trinity, much to my family's initial amusement, even derision. (In working-class families, sometimes

no one is more ridiculous than the person attending college.)
But my loyal band of college friends instantly dropped Cindy for
Cynthia, helping the narrative to shift ever so subtly as I moved
into the future, and I loved them for it.

Like many, I hoped to change in positive ways while growing
up, and I did so through turnings of every sort: religious conversion, education, a different social group, psychotherapy, a more
adult version of my name. But forgetting, I've come to learn, is
also a kind of turning. While we tend to lament that our memories
are not as robust as we'd like, forgetting can allow for personal
growth by muffling self-chastisement and, like negative space in
art, or silence in music, foreground something else—perhaps even
the belief that healthy changes in behavior are cumulative and
misdeeds don't necessarily shackle us forever. The self evolves in a
co-dependent way not only with the stories we tell but also with
those we forget, sometimes to good effect. In the words of the
psychologist Jacqueline Burkell, "A strong sense of self requires
that one remember what matters, and forget what does not."

The neurologist Scott Small concurs: he underscores the importance of normal (as opposed to pathological) forgetting not only
for our emotional well-being but also for our creative abilities.
Forgetting, he assures us, is a "cognitive gift."

Writing, I have discovered, is a way of both remembering and
forgetting. I write, in part, from a drive to give my personal history substance. I don't want to float shallowly on the present, like
a plastic fishing bob tossed by every whitecap. I find it anchoring
to keep a written calendar, filled with appointment dates, dream
fragments, lecture notes, ticket stubs, fabrics from sewing projects,
wine labels, and reading notes, a collage of my daily life. My stack
of bulging datebooks is evidence of past incarnations of myself,
all adding to the present version of who I am, which itself is in
subtle flux, as it is for us all.

But this ability to change over time does depend in part on the
undervalued mercy of forgetting, and writing, oddly enough, can
help us in that endeavor. Every writer chooses some experiences

and thoughts over others, allowing the latter to slip away. Yet the relationship between writing and forgetting goes deeper than this.

When I write about an event that has distressed me, or about a friendship that perplexes me, I am both processing my thoughts and weakening their hold on my attention. In other words, writing gives forgetting a foothold in events we want to acknowledge but not necessarily mentally rehash. By writing down a story, an event, or a dream, I am better able to let it go. Knowing the record exists means I don't have to mull over the details in my head, anxious to keep the story straight, because I can always return to it if I wish. But the benefits go beyond this. Without mental rehearsals, memories slacken. A journal can paradoxically loosen the hold of an episodic memory, just like the whiskey nip stashed in the glove compartment quelled Mom's panic after she became sober. Picturing the mini bottle nestled there and knowing she could drink it if necessary freed her from having to do so.

Writing may be a weight, but whether it sinks us or balances us depends on our relationship to the writing, not the writing itself.

So perhaps the idea is not so much that writing is a way of remembering, but that writing allows us to both remember and forget. Personal writing achieves some of the best effects of auto-biographical memory: a sense of continuity over time, a defined sense of self, evidence of existing. But it also allows us to leave the past behind. Unless, of course, you decide to write a memoir.

I am grateful for the thousands of pages of letters, dreams, and journal entries I have written over the past fifty years, but the effects of rereading them have varied wildly, contingent on who I am in the moment of my return. The same passages can make me cringe or laugh, depending not only on my temporal distance from an event but also on my emotional one. That said, time has a way of collapsing, and emotions are much more cyclical than they are linear.

When I reread my journals from elementary school and high school, I have much more compassion now for that earnest little girl and at times anguished adolescent. I appreciate the tenacity with which she clung to evidence of good in the world, even when her sphere tilted with vertiginous ills: alcoholism, drug addiction, suicide attempts, murder, abandonment. I used to hate sinking into my high school journals, letting years lapse between the readings. But I now see more clearly the differences between who that girl was then and who I am now, all the while marveling at her confused resilience and dogged optimism. The words have not changed. The person reading them has.

Just as Sam, the recipient of my unabridged account of her childhood cruelties, has changed. I held a mirror up to her and she found it excruciating. But she didn't look away. My better self hopes I haven't in turn wounded her. But I needed her to know what she had done. Our Messenger and email exchanges accomplished that, but I perhaps took it one step too far.

Our Nauset graduating class of around 160 students held reunions every five years until Covid hit. Our last one took place a year or two after Samantha and I started corresponding. The temptation was too great. Although Sam had left Cape Cod after eighth grade, most of the students who graduated with my class had been in the local school system since early childhood. Those of us from Wellfleet had Sam as a classmate for several years, while those from Eastham, Orleans, and Brewster crossed paths with her in middle school, two of the longest years in any kid's life. I knew one girl from Orleans who had suffered Sam's lash, and I guessed there might be others. "Where'd you get that shirt?" she'd taunt my friend. "The discount store?" On the mark.

I encouraged Sam to attend the reunion and said, with complete but not entirely transparent honesty, that many people in our class would remember her. I told her I'd love to see her in person—which was also true. What I didn't say: *part of me is still that little girl at the bubbler. Part of me hopes you discover I am not the only one.*

Sam bought tickets for herself and her husband. "For some reason, I'm kind of nervous about the reunion and not sure why," she wrote.

"It's natural to be nervous," I wrote back, skirting what to me seemed obvious. "But my guess is once you are on the Cape you will be struck by the deep familiarity of it all, how the place is in your bones."

It was a safe thing to say, because the Cape is often a place of profound nostalgia for those who have left or who spent childhood summers here. With over sixty percent of Wellfleet belonging to the National Seashore, much of the landscape of our earliest years is relatively unchanged, offering the exquisite pleasure of recognition. Place, memory, and emotion are inextricably entwined in our brains, and for many summer visitors, the Outer Cape is the one setting where childhood went spectacularly right.

As the reunion weekend unfolded, I caught snippets of conversations between Sam and others. At one party, I reintroduced Sam to one of the friendliest guys I knew in middle school, a redheaded athlete from Orleans who as an adult has tiled half the baths and kitchens on the Lower Cape. I wasn't sure he'd know who Sam was, as they would have crossed paths only briefly before her family moved off-Cape. Meeting her again, though, he gave a small start and blurted, first thing, "You made fun of me in seventh grade."

*Boys?* I silently marveled. *She even taunted boys?*

He later told me he'd had a crush on her.

"She hurt so many people," a fellow fourth-grade target told me over lobster and scallop rolls at PJs. I had never spoken with Lisa about Sam and, absorbed in my own experience, did not even remember that she had been mocked as well. "Sam was cruel to me," Lisa said, "but she was absolutely merciless toward you, making fun of your tiny size, your clothes, your hair, everything." Once again I felt that old amazement, even gratitude, that someone, anyone, had noticed.

After the reunion, Samantha told me it had been a moving and positive homecoming, full of reconnections. She had visited touchstones of her childhood: her family's former home on the National Seashore base; my cousin Richard, who had been her brother's best friend; and the cedar swamp where we once caught tadpoles among the graceful, lilting trees. Six years would pass, however, before Samantha wrote me again.

I've wondered if this was because she understood without articulating it that I had wanted her to learn the scope of the pain she had caused others, or if the return to the Cape was harder than she had admitted. But now her mother had died, and my childhood friend reached out to me. I had known Mrs. Smith when she was young and wore hip-hugging jeans, when her gorgeous black hair fell nearly to her waist, when she turned heads not only at church but on the stage as Anna in a local production of *The King and I*. Sam relished my memories, just as I had her remembrances of my mother. Like most children, we wanted more than anything to love our parents. It's why we eulogize the dead, of course. In their imperfection they may have hurt us, but stories, especially kind ones, can splint our brokenness.

Mary Karr calls the human ego "a stealthy, low-crawling bastard," adding that "for pretty much everybody, getting used to who you are is a lifelong spiritual struggle." Samantha and I made this both harder and easier for each other through our entwined forgetting and remembering. While Sam had effaced what I found indelible about fourth grade, her forgetting and my remembering are now colored by what we both have learned.

Some of the memories I shared about fourth grade wounded my friend, though that was not my intention. But I wonder: did they also help her to better understand her childhood self, to name an uneasiness that dogged her or to spot patterns she has broken? Such change is the work of a lifetime for many of us. The integrity, honesty, and remorse with which Samantha listened to my memories, and those of others, taught me, though, that I had been wrong about one thing. She was not a bad seed. She was just another bruised one striving to grow well.

Because of our unexpected and candid reconnection, new images from Samantha's early past have become part of the filmstrip that loads when I recall that hard year. I picture not only our cat-fight in the school hallway but her mother's battering hands. Not just the taunts in gym class but the sneakers hidden behind a bush. Not just my mother's concern that I had no friends but the fears that kept Samantha from having any children. While I can't erase my memories of being bullied, bringing Samantha's stories to bear on mine has cast a gentler, more emotionally forgetful light on the flickering scenes and backdrop of our interlaced childhoods.

# 9

# Memory and Forgiveness

~

*You would have to feel with me, else you would*
*never know.*
                                        —*George Eliot*


When I want to return in my mind to a happy, even ecstatic, memory, I sometimes conjure a midnight hour on a summer night in Wellfleet when I was twenty-seven. It was the year before I moved to Atlanta and the first time in a decade I had lived at home during the winter months. I waitressed at the Oyster House during the two summers bookending that year, as well as on weekends during the shoulder season. My mother, the restaurant's hostess, packed her crew with an assortment of relatives, from Thelma and me on waitstaff to my brother Ted filling in as needed behind the bar. Nana, eighty-four and determined to work, manned the dessert station.

The servers and busboys usually hung around the bar after closing, knocking back sweet concoctions while catching up on gossip or assessing that night's tippers. (Other servers were the most generous, psychoanalysts the least—but we had our theories why.) I tasted my first White Russian at the Oyster House bar, as well as its chocolaty, Irish-cream cousin, the mudslide. After one sugar high too many I switched to Cape Codders, the zing of cranberry and vodka on my tongue a welcome wash after an evening of reciting my way through oysters Rockefeller, paella, and prime rib.

One sweaty August night, instead of late-night drinking I turned my dinged but trusty Honda Civic, a gift from Mom's friend Milton, toward the beach at the end of our street. The Big Dipper and the Little Dipper, with its North Star asterisk, twinkled in the sky, reminding me, as they always did, of my father, who taught me how to spot them. I had packed my bathing suit in one of Mom's home-made beach bags and, peeling off my waitressing outfit, slipped it on.

Most people have a favorite side of the beach, ritually descending the steep dune to the left or the right, but there was only one path for me that night, and it led straight to a ribbon of light cast by the full moon on a risen tide. My feet sunk into still-warm sand as I skirted small piles of seaweed tossed with driftwood and razor clam shells, the sand turning cooler and firmer near the water. Hesitating briefly, I dove in where the luminous sea met the diamond-flecked sand, the water's silent, silky lift of my hair a caress. I kept my aim straight toward the horizon, my body immersed in liquid light, my nostrils tingling with salt, the spaces between my toes scoured and washed clean.

Memories like this one transport me into grateful wonder for life. As a child, my favorite time of day was dusk, when I would lie on the grass in the yard and stare into the dimming sky, its green molecules a mystery, the in-between world my cradle. I adored windy days, when I could set my mother's scarves free, tossing them into the air and watching jeweled colors pirouette on the impish breeze. Even the high winds of hurricane season thrilled me. When the lights flickered, Mom and Dad would set us to work filling the bathtub and lighting candles fixed to upturned jar lids with melted wax. Tucking myself under the covers in my twin bed upstairs, I'd listen to locust branches scratch the windows with the promise of a changed landscape come morning.

Memories, of course, cut in every direction. These are among my happiest. Others, however, have bullied me into self-reproach, into a shame I have found hard to outrun.

Over fifty years later, I am still working on forgiving myself for one aspect of what I remembered that night in Berkeley when caught in a tsunami of barbershop images. It's a detail I wrote down in my journal, communicated to others, and then, over the years, apparently let go because it did not seem particularly relevant. I am now astonished at how oblivious I was of its import, of its connection to the self-recrimination that has dogged me since childhood, the voice in my head that has pronounced my missteps—whether forgetting to use a coupon at the grocery store or pulling into traffic too quickly and causing an accident—as moral failings or proof of idiocy.

This Trojan detail is connected to the nature of memory, in that our recall of similar events—Thanksgiving meals, visits to grandparents—tends to merge repeated instances into one, creating a script for those occurrences out of common elements. But this is more true of routine happenings than for unusual ones, whose distinctiveness often makes them more memorable.

When I rose from my prayer in Berkeley with the memory reel still flapping, I knew I had found myself alone with Willy more than once. "Two or three times" is how I remembered it. What that meant to me at the time was that Willy had molested me more than once, even though I couldn't reliably differentiate between the visits.

What I never asked myself was *why*. Not why I was molested, or why I couldn't easily distinguish between these visits, but this: why had I returned? Willy had no physical control over my movements outside his shop, no way to command me. No parent or adult was telling me to run down to the barbershop on an errand. No cousin dared me to go there. Yet when he whistled for me, I parked my bike against the clapboard and walked inside.

When I recall sitting at our supper table that summer after sixth grade and hearing about Willy's death, the feeling infusing the scene is more than anxiety at the mention of his name, more than relief at his passing: it's also fury at his betrayal. But why betrayal? The only way I can make sense of that feeling is to assume that my first two visits to the barbershop were not traumatizing, did not involve a ripping physical pain but a jolly man tickling me briefly over my clothes, testing my response, dropping candy or coins into my hands. Perhaps I was even growing fond of Willy. He was so unlike other adults; he never treated children as nuisances.

Staring at my plate of summer vegetables as my parents spoke of the barber's death, I knew, with the hard bitterness of a scrappy child, that this old man, someone who had once treated me kindly, had not only injured me, but had also tricked me. And like any child who has been cruelly tricked, I seethed—at Willy for tearing my insides and for robbing me, as I believed, of ever having a child, and at myself, I only now realize, for letting him do so.

Revisiting those early feelings, the adult in me asks how the trick was managed, and the answer pops out of the proverbial hat, the way some truths do the instance they're given the chance. We had so little money in our lives. I scrabbled for the spare dime and guiltily stole coins from my mother's purse to plant near the summer house. I'd drag Holly to the spot, telling her we were going to dig for treasure, the two of us cheering as we caught the flash of silver in sand and ran to the General Store.

Far more devastating for my self-image and relationships, I had not only been tricked, but I had *become* a trick. I had been fooled into allowing my body to become part of a bargain, the field of an old man's desire, my tender flesh ploughed with bribes. While the candy and five-dollar bill disappeared, while the physical pain subsided and I stopped thinking about what had happened, crippling beliefs detached themselves from the version of myself I had left behind in that hard plastic chair, drifting into the future to haunt me: My insides were messed up. I might have to turn to a life on the streets. I was, at heart, a prostitute. And it was all my fault.

When I was seventeen, I had my first complete physical, a requirement for the year-long, foreign exchange scholarship to Finland I had received. A young doctor had set up a practice in an old house on Briar Lane, and I chose him over the A.I.M. Medical Center on Route 6, where I had received my sporadic medical care, because he didn't know me. The exam table was set up in what must have once been a living room, and I eyed it uneasily as the doctor told me to undress.

"All I need is this sheet filled out," I said. "I don't really need an examination."

He wasn't buying it.

Ten minutes later, the cold metal of the speculum split muscles stiff with anxiety, my thoughts popping like a cap gun off the white sheet obscuring the doctor's head. After the exam, as he stood checking a list of boxes certifying my good health, I spit out something long on my mind. "Excuse me?"

His eyes flickered as he continued scanning the list.

"I'd like to get sterilized."

Two beats passed before the doctor looked up from his clipboard. "What?" he asked, disbelieving.

"I'm sure I don't want to have any children, and I would like to take care of it now. Could you sterilize me?"

What I didn't say was I was afraid of getting raped, of not having a choice. What I didn't understand was that this conscious fear was the blind side of a suppressed one.

"There isn't a doctor in America who will sterilize a seventeen-year-old girl," he said, "so forget about it."

A few years later in France, I tried a second time to have my tubes tied—I think this was after I heard that crazy-making whistle on Cours Victor Hugo—but again met with dead ends. I did not remember, could not articulate, the dread that Willy had mauled my womb beyond repair, but I believe it fueled these unconscious attempts to make the choice my own. Control, at the price of becoming an unwitting accomplice.

This overdue questioning of the unquestioned—why did I return?—and the answers that leapt forward have helped me, finally, to make sense of the mental anguish that has drilled weak spots in a life otherwise filled with strokes of luck, generosity from others, the recompense of hard work, and the healing brought on by marriage to a goodhearted man and the ability to love our daughter in the ways I wished I had been loved. I would like to be able to say I have forgiven myself, but the habit of self-chastisement runs deep, softened only slightly by logic and compassion. Though I *feel* as if I deserve the blame, I *know* that Willy does. That knowledge will have to do.

I first started therapy in Berkeley after these childhood memories returned, and while becoming more conscious of how I felt and why could not inoculate me from painful emotions, it did open the door to other kinds of choices, better ones.

My mother was horrified that at twenty-five, I was still technically a virgin. "You'll never understand life," she warned me on the phone, "until you start having sex." I doubt she realized all the inventive ways evangelicals indulge in sexual pleasure outside of intercourse, and that I couldn't help but pursue nearly all of them with partners less plagued than I by guilt. Men, mostly, but also an irresistible Chicana I worked with at the Blood Bank ("No woman is straight around me," she'd joke, her pink lip gloss glistening in a sea of black curls. And she was right). But I also wonder if Mom framed my relative self-discipline as an implicit criticism of her extravagant attachment to men and her reliance on them for both good times and survival. I wanted anything but that for myself. But could I fault her? Though attractive and smart and creative, my mother could not survive on her waitressing tips and the hemming of pants for $3.00 a pair. A woman with no more than a high school diploma in hand, she balanced precariously on the lowest rungs of a very short ladder, especially in the Cape's seasonal economy.

I simply could not talk with my mother about sex, and I certainly wasn't about to confide in her once I crossed the line several months later. I wouldn't have been able to bear her welcome-to-the-club tone, her satisfaction. But most of all, I would not have been able to communicate the meaning of my encounter. Like many women, I never expected to lose my virginity in the moment or way that I did, and despite Mom's history, she would not have understood my experience—or worse, she would have cheapened it in the hearing, because we would have been speaking two different languages, and her translation would have made me cringe.

At the end of my block on Dwight Way in Berkeley stood Newman Hall, a Paulist center where five funny, spiritual, progressive priests celebrated the liturgy in a sanctuary of textured concrete, glass, and candlelight. The fired-clay altar, which looked like primitive stone, rose from the floor as if erupting from the soil itself, while the four soaring, freestanding walls overlapped with apertures of glass that seemed to whisper: *look beyond us.*

Although some evangelicals had warned me after I became born-again that the pope was the anti-Christ, I began attending services regularly at Newman Hall. The poetry of the liturgy, ancient and new, offered mystery instead of pre-packaged answers. I loved walking past scrappy parishioners having a quick smoke before mass as I entered the church's huge red doors, knowing I'd never see such a sight at First Presbyterian. Though a non-Catholic, I was never asked to explain myself, never felt defined in the ways I had defined so many others. Evangelical certitudes I had listened to and spewed for years were evaporating, and while this felt unsettling, it was the most honest response I could muster to what I was studying and experiencing in Berkeley.

Searching for a quiet space in my overbooked schedule, I signed up for a weekend retreat at a Trappist monastery in northern California. Four Newman parishioners and I drove north until we found ourselves on a gravelly country road leading to the monastery gates. Glancing to my left, I saw hundreds of acres planted in plum and walnut orchards against a backdrop of mountains tinged with falling light. To my right stretched fields that would one day become a vineyard.

We rang the bell at the gate and drove inside, parking next to a small, modern building of cement and glass. The guestmaster, a young, closely shaven, dark-haired monk in black and white robes, welcomed us. We unloaded our bags and entered the simply adorned foyer. While the four others stood silently in line to register in the guest book, I took a few steps away and gazed through a tall, narrow window into a circular pond, the water nearly impenetrable in dusk's ambiguous light. Clusters of green dotted the pond's glassy reflections, hints of orange and white flitting below the surface.

I heard a polite cough and turned to find the foyer empty, except for the guestmaster, Brother Sebastian. He smiled shyly, his right hand stretched toward the open guest book. His large, brown eyes shone with embarrassed happiness, betraying an unexpected, intimate openness. As I bent over the book and signed my name, unmistakable currents streaked through me.

In my single guest room, I flung myself on the narrow bed and prayed. I had come to the monastery for solitude and contemplation, not ridiculous distractions! Attracted to a monk? At first sight? *Get a grip, Cynthia.* Yet the connection electrified me, my fantasies skipping across the impossibilities between Brother Sebastian and me.

I rose at 3:00 a.m., in time for Vigils. In dim, candlelit space, I joined the monks and my fellow retreatants to chant the first office of the day. "Be watchful!" We sat by a side entrance to the right of the altar. Two dozen brothers arrived by a separate entrance and chanted in pews around the corner, mostly out of sight. Slim chance of glimpsing the handsome guestmaster. Quelling the nausea that hits when I get too little sleep, I flipped through a baffling array of chant books, gave up, and listened to manly voices echoing in antiphonal song.

Night prayers over, my fellow retreatants straggled back to the guest rooms to snooze until Lauds, at 6:00 a.m. I stayed in the church and bowed my head as white robes rustled out an unseen door. I wanted to mull over the dream I had had during my short stretch of sleep. I decided to use a Gestalt interpretive technique I had recently read about: viewing each character in the dream as an aspect of myself. I had dreamt that I needed intestinal surgery and had to choose between two surgeons: a black woman and a white man. I chose the woman, telling her I trusted her.

Jung would have had a field day with the dream, which took many turns and ended with me prepping myself for surgery. The dream's imagery seemed to suggest I was trusting an unconventional part of myself and had agency in my own healing. Sitting alone in the dim, marginal pews, I felt reassured, even emboldened.

The clatter of silver startled me. I looked up to see two elderly monks emerging from a door on the other side of the altar, cordoned off by a red rope. They, too, had stayed behind. Carrying a chalice and the host, they prepared communion at the altar. To my astonishment, one of them unlatched the protective cord and beckoned me.

*I'm not a Catholic!* I thought. But I rose to join the brothers in the altar's intimate circle, hoping God would not object. The three of us celebrated the Eucharist before dawn. Euphoria and gratefulness streamed through me.

During the rest of the day, I chanted the remaining Divine Offices, wandered in the orchards, and spoke with two or three monks as they went about their work. When I sat next to a small chapel to read, a middle-aged monk showed up with tools in hand to repair one side of the building. I helped him in his work, and we began to talk.

"I joined the order when I was eighteen," he said. "And now I'm fifty-five. When I first came to the monastery, I was walking on clouds. But I discovered some of those clouds had holes in them!"

I laughed. He asked me how my weekend was going.

"It's beautiful here," I said, "but I'm surprised at all the noise—tractors, carts, radiators, even planes flying overhead."

He paused, looking intently at me. "Most people can't stand being away from a radio or the television. You must be a true seeker."

"My love is books," I said. "If I could marry one, I'd be all set. Like Henri Nouwen's *Reaching Out*. There's a book I'd like to wed!"

The monk nodded, chuckling.

I gazed into this man's honest face and realized he was the age of my father when he died. Tears stung me. I felt as if this monk,

for a brief moment, incarnated another kind of father, offering a
new way of imagining a relationship cut short before I'd had time
to grow up.

The guestmaster and I crossed paths a few times during the
day and fell into long, open conversations. He had been in the
monastery for ten years, since his early twenties. He talked about
the confusion and unhappiness that had driven him to a cloistered
life, his fractured family, the acceptance he had found among the
brothers, the startling range of personalities and habits of those
bound together by monastic vows.

Later, warmed by the late afternoon sun, I wandered alone into
the orchards and sat under a plum tree. I wrote a long letter to a
college friend who had abandoned her Christian faith but not our
friendship. I described the monastery, the grounds, the profound
and unexpected pull I felt toward Brother Sebastian. "Does he
feel the same depth of connection?" I wrote. No matter, I added;
there was little chance of intimacy. The monks slept in a gated
enclosure, where no outsider was allowed.

At the supper table after Vespers, one of the male retreatants
asked petulantly, "Where has the guestmaster been all day? I was
hoping to talk with him."

I dipped my head and slid my fork under a fragrant mouthful of
vegetarian stew, silently musing, *I don't think the guestmaster's gay.*

Brother Sebastian and I spoke again before Compline, the last
prayer of the day. "Can I come to your office and continue our
conversation after chanting?" I asked.

He blushed, eyes widening, "Would you *like* to?"

After Compline, we sat on a couch in a sitting room off the
foyer where I had registered the evening before. The blinds were
lowered, the light dim. Sebastian did not turn on the lamp. We
talked, then fell into intimate silence. The evening turned to star-
lit night.

After an immeasurable interlude—was it twenty minutes,
sixty?—Sebastian offered an open hand, smiling radiantly, the
slight rise in his eyebrows a question, a curve of hopefulness. Dizzy

with astonishment and desire, I put my hand in his and asked, "Are you sure you want to break your vow?"

He drew me to him and kissed me with an engulfing passion. What a full, sensual mouth! So rich and present. Later, I would dream of his mouth, its sweetness like a nearly overripe fruit. His tongue slid from my lips to my legs, flesh pulsing with pleasure. "Beautiful," he whispered. Sensations nearly too intense to bear rippled across me.

The monk took my hand and led me through his office to a cell where he slept, apart from his brothers in the enclosure. So it *was* logistically possible. Stepping around his desk chair, I said, "You know, I've never done this before."

He paused, disbelieving. "You're a virgin?"

I nodded.

A sudden understanding swept across Sebastian's face, as if realizing this moment was more than the end of his ten years of celibacy.

In his small, Spartan room, my clothes fell to the ground. Brother Sebastian hung his white robe, black scapular, and wide leather belt on a peg next to denim work clothes, his only garments. A single mattress lay on the floor. We slid onto the sheets.

"Don't be afraid," he said, as he found his way inside me.

I gave myself over to pain and pleasure. When he came, a prayer burst from his lips: "Sweet, holy Jesus!" The sacrament of sex.

We lay in his bed and talked until near three in the morning, when we rose and walked to my room. The air was silent, but for the song of a night bird and the swish of Brother Sebastian's habit. As we passed the circular pond I had contemplated just after our arrival, he offered me his arm.

"Isn't it risky?" I asked.

"If anyone sees me even walking with you at this time of night, I'm in trouble," he said. "So, please, take my arm." He was utterly at peace.

I slept through the morning offices and hurriedly packed for the return trip to Berkeley. Popping open my contact case,

I discovered one of my lenses missing. I had taken them out in the ambiguous light of the sitting room, and it must be somewhere on the floor. Returning to the welcome center, I met Sebastian walking out of his office. We knelt to find my lens, shoulders brushing. Desire flashed. We slipped into his cell, once again naked, vulnerable, willing.

He asked me to stay longer, saying, "You could take a bus back to Berkeley."

But the weekend was over. I had crossed a threshold. Making love with Brother Sebastian had allowed deep-running currents of sex and spirituality—so long at odds—to flow in one stream. It was also the most healing, radical response I could make to Willy and his violations. Intercourse with a holy man transformed the space the barber had defaced, consecrated what had been desecrated by a prostituting old man. In the arms of a monk, I had crossed into terra incognita and found myself at home.

I hugged Sebastian goodbye and climbed into the car for the ride home. As we drove through the monastery gates, I looked out the back window. Brother Sebastian stood motionless, smiling, in the center of the road. Our eyes cradled each other in rising dust. The man sitting next to me turned, eyebrows raised. Unable to answer his questioning gaze, I lay my head against the seat and closed my eyes, wandering back through the unstained night as the car sped home.

Brother Sebastian and I corresponded for months. He wrote long, frequent letters; sent me gifts of pottery, mix-tapes, books, and art; asked me to return. I poured myself out to him. Over time, though, I grew uneasy as his questions became pointedly inquisitive, as if hammering out a theory of sexuality with me as his outside, human informant. Sebastian's other sources—Dr. Ruth and *Playboy*—turned me off. I sought to be present to sex, to its infusion with spirituality, while Sebastian seemed to want a catch-up course in male-female relations.

"I am a person, not an experiment," I wrote in a moment of irritation. "I don't want to be your sounding board for theories developed in that lonely, static distance between a radio and a monk's cell."

To be honest, I was disappointed I had not found a Thomas Merton, but a poor speller with detached, psychoanalytic approaches to sexuality and a fascination with *The Godfather*, which he'd read seven times. *The Godfather?* I asked myself. *Who is this person?*

Too many of Sebastian's letters hinted at a bitter, intellectualized skepticism over romantic relationships, rooted in his disappointments before the monastery. Yet other letters helped interpret dreams, spoke about life in the monastery, asked questions about my family, friends, and past. The monk, symbol of holiness, was as flawed as the rest of us.

During our correspondence I had a long dream of searching for Sebastian in a gilded, mountain monastery. Climbing over rocky paths, wandering through chapels and orchards, meeting others along the way, I failed to find him. In waking life, I was perhaps on an impossible search for a holy man and healer who would not make uncomfortable demands. Although I brought my first, brand-new diaphragm the next time I visited Sebastian in the monastery—we hardly got out of bed—what I prized most was his symbolic power as a priestly lover in response to a profane pedophile.

Our letters and phone calls eventually revealed how incompatible Sebastian and I were, how our relationship within monastery walls—so powerful—would not survive outside them. By the time Sebastian accepted that he was no longer a monk and left the order a year or so later, our correspondence was sporadic, measured, unpredictable in its affection. Yet the miracle endured: though we broke the rules of our faith, though we stumbled under the weight of our differences, for a brief, transformative season Sebastian and I had unexpectedly found each other—and ourselves—in a healing, sacred exchange.

"Life is definitely too short," Mom wrote me during this time, "especially if you don't grow up until your forties!" She was on her own journey. Now in her mid-fifties—sober, successfully treated for her agoraphobia and panic attacks, even driving again—Mom enrolled for the first time in college courses. She signed up for General Psychology at Cape Cod Community College in Barnstable, fifty minutes from Wellfleet. Thelma picked another course on the same evening to spare her the stress of driving at night. Mom proved as eager a student any professor could hope for.

She took one or two night courses each semester, studying communications, psychology, anthropology, world religions, and gerontology. "I just adore school!" she wrote me. She worked days in her sewing shop and hostessed at the Oyster House part-time during the off-season, what I now called the academic year. She missed one final exam in May because the restaurant had a stack of reservations but not enough waitstaff, a recurring shoulder-season dilemma. Her anthropology professor, a retired British professor from Oxford University, let Mom take the exam in her elegant Hyannisport home. In this marvelous new story she found herself in, Mom was there to measure not drapes but what she had learned from lectures and books.

Claiming a corner of our kitchen den as her study area, Mom dragged my scuffed pine desk up from the cellar and wedged it between the bookcase and the kitchen table. Her friend Dick gave her a gooseneck wall-lamp that she hung on the wallpapered Sheetrock. Mom filled the drawers with notebooks and pens, much as I had fifteen years earlier, and made a comfortable seat pillow for the hard pine desk chair. For one or two hours a day, in-between sewing jobs and weekend hostessing, she watched birds out the window and composed papers on my old manual typewriter.

"There is all kinds of wonderful hope for me in the future," she wrote me. "I am so-o-o-o-o excited, I have to calm myself down. It's wonderful to feel like there is some kind of plan and organization in my life."

After two years of part-time study, Mom waited for an hour in line to speak with a harried education counselor about pursuing a degree. He cut to the point. "You're in your fifties, but you're not too old," he told her. "Women will be working into their seventies by the time you graduate. You could have a twenty-year career."

"I'll cross that bridge (the Sagamore? Ha!) when I get to it," Mom wrote as she tried to plot her study plan. "Maybe it's crazy, but I have a goal."

She knew she wanted to work in social services. She had been volunteering at the Cape Cod Council on Alcoholism's hotline for years and began looking for a paid position so she could give up year-round sewing. In 1987, the year Uncle Clyde moved into our house for his final months, Mom started working for Elder Services, coordinating the Meals on Wheels program at the Wellfleet Senior Center. She was now sixty years old and for the first time in her life had a job with sick leave, vacation time, and retirement benefits. Salary was low, but self-esteem was shooting high.

Mom began taking on new positions within Elder Services, and a year or two later she spotted an internal office posting for a full-time geriatric case manager. The job listing specified "a bachelor's degree or equivalent" among the qualifications. "I went up to the main office in Dennis," Mom says. "I didn't have a bachelor's degree, but I made damn sure they knew I was equivalent. They gave me the job!"

With it came a computer, office space, and colleagues Mom grew to love. Over the next fifteen years she tended to the Lower and Outer Cape's needy elderly, driving herself to house visits. When she left in the morning for work, she carried a new briefcase filled with intake forms, information sheets, and a calculator, at long last transformed from a case to a case worker.

The work was fascinating and demanding, with Mom often juggling more than seventy clients. Some were destitute, others were hoarders, several were flashers, and an unexpected number had been successful—the "other" Cape Codders—before their savings had run out or been passed on: well-known writers, artists, and business owners. A few were retired fishermen with scant Social Security, though more often it was the widows of fishermen lost at sea or in hardscrabble living who needed assistance.

Most of Mom's new clients were strangers, but once in a while a familiar name would rattle her voicemail. One day it was the former owner of the Lighthouse Restaurant, the woman who had fired Mom from her waitressing job over twenty years earlier.

"She was hard as nails," remembers Mom, "and living mainly off Social Security because her husband George, who was dead, had loved to play the races."

"We never talked about the Lighthouse," she adds. "I was determined to be gracious and professional. And I was glad she could see I had made something of myself—certainly a hell of a lot better than a hungover coffee maker!"

Mom tried to retire in her mid-seventies, but her supervisor talked her out of it. Finding a social worker able to cover the Outer Cape is still no easy task. When you're not a tourist, driving to Provincetown is a haul and finding parking spaces a nightmare. Elder Services set up an office phone line in Mom's sewing room and installed the necessary computer software so she could semi-retire by working part-time from the house. She drove to the main office in Dennis once a week, visited clients from Eastham to Provincetown, and took care of paperwork—often in her nightgown—at her sewing room desk, with mounds of fabric piled high next to her and the ironing board petrified in place by the front window. Just a few feet away on a shelf sat a roll of her blue and gold tailoring labels, "Shirley Original," and a stack of leftover Wellfleet police badges, emblazoned with six red bolts of electricity zigzagging from a Marconi radio tower and "1763," the date of Wellfleet's incorporation. Years earlier she had been hired to sew the badges onto uniform sleeves by the department that had once arrested her.

Even at part-time, however, keeping up with client visits was challenging. Although Mom hadn't picked up a cigarette in years, decades of smoking had left unerasable marks, and asthma settled in. Blasts of winter cold knocked the breath out of her as she walked to her car; the heat of summer pressed hard as she sat in crowded, unairconditioned living rooms. Finally, at seventy-eight, she declared, "I don't want to be the oldest social worker in America!" and fully retired. Her colleagues threw a huge party at work, showering her with cards and a gold and silver bracelet. That night a friend hosted a buffet dinner party for fifty, with Mom as guest of honor.

"Don't worry," she said, as the jokes flew. "I'm not going to sit around and mold. I plan on seeing the world!"

And she did. On a friend's dare a few years earlier, she had set up a profile on a dating site. She was still with Charles, but theirs was a relationship of habit. And he hated to travel, insecure about his broken English and attached to his little skiff anchored at Orleans Town Cove. Just around sunrise he'd don one of the many black wool berets he ordered from France and harvest his allotment of clams for the day, selling most while keeping some for himself and us. He and Mom had a regular schedule of dinner out on Wednesday nights and Chinese takeout on the weekend, with other dinners and family celebrations mixed in.

Their routine—like the fishing news—bored Mom. Though she was chronically short of breath and sometimes needed supplemental oxygen, the air she craved most was male appreciation. "When I turn ninety, I want to have a drink and sex!" she announced to the Congregational minister's wife as they chatted at our kitchen table and I stood nearby washing up the dishes. The minister's wife laughed, knowing that Mom had a slight crush on her much younger husband. *It's not over til it's over*, I thought as I rinsed Mom's mismatched mugs.

I don't know how my mother described herself on the dating site, but instead of a photo of herself she uploaded a shot of my gorgeous, twenty-year-old niece, her flaxen hair and sapphire eyes swamping Mom's in-box with so many messages Thelma had to shut down the account and help her create a new one. But in the end Mom met someone her own age, a Christian, Republican, exotic-animal rancher from Texas. And despite their astonishing differences, they fell in love. For six years, until Mom was in her early eighties, they visited each other and traveled by plane, car, and cruise ship to far-flung spots in the US and abroad.

Charles simply waited it out. He might have been able to give up Mom, but he couldn't give up our family, his family. And most especially he could not give up Thelma, who would care for him for the rest of his life. A few days before he died at eighty in the Orleans nursing home that his carpenter brother had helped build decades earlier, a chaplain kindly asked Charles if he had any questions about death or the afterlife. Charles raised his sea-blue eyes to the priest's and asked, "Can Thelma come, too?"

I don't know how Uncle Clyde felt about his encounter with the ghost in Mom's house, but I do know he spent his last days and hours retracing the spirit he cared most about: Aunt Persis. "You know what love is?" he asked me, lifting his trembling, gray head off his pillow. "It's an itch on your heart you can never reach."

I couldn't scratch that itch, so I said, "Roll over, Unk, and let me rub your back." I reached for a gadget he'd ordered through the mail, an electric, handheld heat massager I could slide over his dry, emaciated shoulders. Murmurs of relief and comfort seeped into his pillow. After a few minutes he turned toward me and asked, his voice hoarse, "You know what I'd really like?"

"What Unk?"

"Pork chops."

I laughed and a few days later picked up a couple of center-cut chops after my day job in Orleans, where I worked as a legal secretary. I cooked them up that night, but Clyde's shriveled stomach had the last word, and he pushed his plate away.

On evenings I wasn't waitressing that year, I'd curl up on Uncle Clyde's bed and tell him about the lawyers I worked with and the clients I met. Though he and they lived worlds apart, any detail could spin him into well-worn memories. Clyde had a circuit of stories he rode, revisiting past wrongs as if they were watering holes. He hated lawyers, but he especially enjoyed abusing doctors. One afternoon he wagged an arthritic finger toward Mom's painted green dresser and told me to fish out a packet from the top drawer. Flipping through folded bits of paper held together by a cracked rubber band, he pulled out a copy of a letter he had sent six months earlier to a specialist who, Clyde believed, had overcharged him.

"You think that you have hit a pot of gold, the prices you charge Medicare," he wrote. "I have been to Dr. Peabody quite a few times and never charged more than $35., if you think that you are a better doctor than him you better never go to buy a hat, because you will never find one to fit that big head of yours."

Clyde's doctor on the Cape—one of the "good" ones—had warned us that lung cancer would render his last moments ugly. "Clyde will essentially drown," the doctor said. But it was life my great-uncle railed against, not death. "Goddamn it, if I had a gun, I'd kill myself now," he'd mutter. And he would have.

Though later than he had hoped, Clyde passed sooner than any of us expected. Six of us happened to be at home on that July day: my mother, yet to leave for her new job with Elder Services; my sister Thelma, normally at an industrial sewing machine in a leather factory; Nana, who had spryly hopped off a puddle jumper in Provincetown two months earlier to help nurse her brother; Clyde's hospice worker; my sister-in-law; and myself. I'd called in sick to the law firm when I heard Clyde's guttural, gasping breaths, knowing the end was upon us.

We fastened an oxygen mask over Clyde's mountainous nose and thin, cracked lips, streaked with white. We propped his sunken, translucent body onto pillows piled high. Clyde began to breathe more calmly, as if pacing his inhalations by an inner clock near the end of a long crank. We six women circled his bed, touching his wasted shoulders, holding his rough hands, massaging his bony feet. In urgent, tender tones, one of us said, "It's all right to let go, Clyde."

Another, "You can quit fighting." A third, "We love you, we're all here, you can go."

My sister-in-law, undaunted by Clyde's atheism, said loudly and clearly, "Move toward the light, Clyde. Persis is there."

Clyde nodded, hearing us but unable to speak. We held on, suspended with him during the long, still pauses between each exhalation. In his last minute, my uncle's pale blue eyes brightened and focused on a spot through and beyond us. We caught the shift in an instant, recognized his foot at the threshold, the anticipation coursing his wrecked frame. Bitterness evaporated. Clyde's connections shifted, as if we were falling away and something else streaming in. Were his unwavering eyes on the form of the woman he loved? Clyde lifted his head slightly, almost smiling, and stopped.

How is it death can feel like a birthing? None of us had expected the passing of our cantankerous uncle to unfold in such a sacred manner. We looked down at his motionless form in wonder.

Needing time alone, I hopped on my bike and pedaled to the beach, tingling with life. I settled into a hollow on the dune, wept, and looked out over the water. Clyde's spirit met me on the crest, then expanded to fill the sky from the horizon to endless blue. For half an hour it filled me, then whooshed in a last goodbye toward and beyond bursts of clean cloud.

Nana lived for another dozen years after her brother's passing. At ninety-three she rolled onto a plane in Florida and flew to Atlanta to attend my PhD graduation. We were four generations together: Nana, Mom, myself, and my young daughter, Hannah Rose. Despite the stresses of the past, the cords binding us felt strong and reaffirming.

During the visit, Nana, slowing down but still lively, sat on our brown leather living room couch and gave me the most meaningful gift I'd ever received from her. Though she had but an eighth-grade education, she read every page of my dissertation on twentieth-century dream theories, from Freud and Jung to present-day cognitive psychologists, philosophers, and sleep researchers. This is the most lasting, most moving, image I have of my grandmother: her silent and rare approval, even appreciation, as she tilted her head under the wall lamp and labored through the words it took me years to write.

Not long after, Nana was devastated when my aunt could no longer care for her and moved her, with Mom's help, into a nursing home. Nana, I imagine, felt abandoned all over again, once again the small girl whose mother had left her, unwanted and consigned to an institution. She remembered her brother Clyde's death in Mom's home, envied it, but it was one inheritance she couldn't force.

Mom flew south two or three more times to visit her mother in the Florida nursing facility. "I wish God would take me," Nana cried as Mom held her hand. Nana, who had biked and swum through her eighties, was now a broken-winged bird trapped in a wheelchair.

"You're going to have to wait until he's ready for you," Mom said.

"We'll see about that," Nana snapped.

Curved like a waning moon with osteoporosis, Nana stopped eating and did, indeed, die on her own terms. On my mother's last visit, Nana turned toward the daughter who could never please her and said, "You know, Shirls, you are the kindest of my three children."

*It's a little late for that*, thought Mom. Stanching a surge of resentment, she saw before her a frail, vulnerable creature whose earliest years had been blighted by miserliness and hard-fisted care.

"Thank you, Mom," she said, and bent to kiss the old woman goodbye.

When I was in tenth grade, my mother gave me one of my favorite Christmas presents: my own set of sheets, blue flowers on a white background, for my twin bed in the cellar. No more scratchy or mismatched linens for me. I carried that set to college and even to graduate school, relishing the cool, smooth percale finish. Forty years later, my twin beds long gone but reluctant to throw away the sheets, I cut them into strips to tie heirloom tomato vines to green metal stakes in our southern garden. Sitting on our back porch, I'd watch the blue and white strips flutter in the breeze, whitecaps of another sort, and think about the teachers and events and lucky breaks that led me from that bed in the cellar to college, to Europe, to graduate school, and finally to a home of my own, one mercifully free of ghosts.

In the intervening decades, I've come to understand that our family's past, or even our own, is never handed to us, whole and intact, on a platter. It takes work to sketch the scenes that inspire or justify or redefine the lives we are leading. Historians talk about the "usable past," one that offers generative connections to the present and hopes for a better future. Even here, though, effort and choice are involved. Which stories? Which events? Which ancestors? Raymond Williams writes that we create our cultural traditions by continually selecting and reselecting our ancestors, and in the writing of this book, I have made my choices.

I have also sought to better understand my life through exploring the intersections of science and memory. It is still my best hope. This is not so very different, however, from my drive as a teenager to find answers in religion, groping toward belief in a divinely organized universe like a blindfolded girl touching faces, windows, and doorknobs to gain her bearings. Later, in my twenties and thirties, psychotherapy became a powerful explanatory force, filling me with wonder as I overlay my current mental state on my childhood experiences to trace a map of trajectories, of cause and effect. Along the way I dove into nineteenth-century literature, thronging with fictional characters whose personalities, insights, and foibles threaded themselves into my inner dialogue and imaginings.

Science, religion, psychotherapy, literature—each tantalizes with the promise of a portal to understanding. But like Eliot's keen, blinkered Mr. Casaubon and his contrived "key to all mythologies," I have not, of course, been able to rely on any one source for a comprehensive answer to the existential questions that dog us: Who am I? What is my purpose? And how did I arrive, for good or for ill, where I have?

The answers, like our stories, lie behind doors of many shapes and sizes, much as we might wish to wield a single key. With my yearning for a clear-eyed sense of self and faithful boundaries, that multiplicity can feel unsettling. Integration, I have come to accept, is a lifelong task. My stories are both a map of my being and an ever-shifting point of intersection, my inner sense of sameness and continuity inextricable from the questioning, choices, reinterpretations, and unexpected experiences that effect subtle, or not so subtle, changes.

While stories, both our own and those of others, connect our past, present, and future, they can also change the past and present and future through the work of asking and remembering, researching and writing, even forgetting. In writing this memoir I have come to appreciate the power of multiple voices in telling the tale not only of a place, but also of a family and my co-remembered life. When we seek out stories with curiosity and compassion, they have the power to knit us together as individuals and families, as communities and as sentient beings in relation to nature. Some of these stories might also divide us, of course, as anyone writing a memoir would admit. But each of us memorializes—or forgets—in our own way. Each of us loves—or stumbles toward love—in our own way. This is mine.

# CAPE COD REGIONS AND THE OUTER CAPE

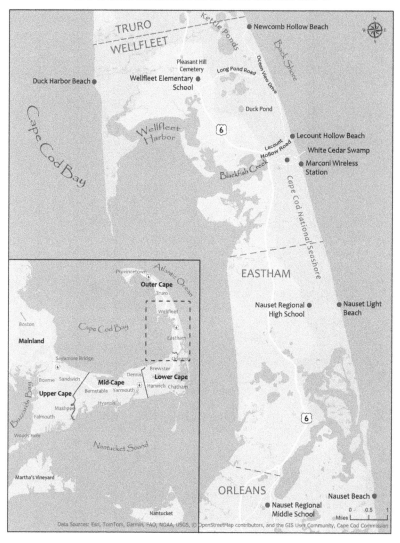

Map created by Megan Slemons, Emory Center for Digital Scholarship.

# Notes

## Preface

xiii **The Outer Cape.** Though the geographical designation of the Outer Cape has varied over time, the most common now comprises the towns of Eastham, Wellfleet, Truro, and Provincetown, which contain 40 miles of undeveloped ocean coastline belonging to the Cape Cod National Seashore.

xiv **"These sands might be the end or the beginning of a world."** Henry Beston, *The Outermost House: A Year of Life on the Great Beach of Cape Cod* (New York: Viking Press, 1928), 2.

## 1
## Impossible Memories

4 **Hundreds of synapses a second.** Or approximately 40,000 synapses per minute. See Vivette Glover, Kieran O'Donnell, Thomas O'Connor, and Jane Fisher, "Prenatal Maternal Stress, Fetal Programming, and Mechanisms Underlying Later Psychopathology—A Global Perspective," *Development and Psychopathology* 30, no. 3 (August 2018): 843.

**As Mom's cortisol levels spiked, were mine shooting high?** In all probability, yes. "Maternal cortisol crosses the placenta and maternal and fetal cortisol levels are strongly correlated." Elysia Poggi Davis, Kevin Head, Claudia Buss, and Curt A. Sandman, "Prenatal Maternal Cortisol Concentrations Predict Neurodevelopment in Middle Childhood," *Psychoneuroendocrinology* 75 (2017): 61. Interestingly, in low-risk and "normative" pregnancies, higher (but still within a normal range) levels of cortisol late in gestation have beneficial effects on brain development and cognitive functioning, but exposures to more extreme levels "may induce neurotoxicity with detrimental long-term consequences" (ibid., 60). Thus the timing (early or late gestation) and levels (beneficially high or toxically high) of cortisol exposure influence the positive or negative consequences for the developing fetal brain.

4    **Carving enduring pathways in my gray matter.** The brain of a fetus is under construction, and thus particularly plastic, throughout a woman's pregnancy, and its development—even its structure—can be affected by the biological signals it receives from the mother. As Alexandra Lautarescu et al. write, "In vivo brain imaging research reports that maternal stress is associated with changes in limbic and frontotemporal networks, and the functional and microstructural connections linking them. The structural changes include cortical thinning and an enlarged amygdala. . . . The amygdala is a brain structure involved in emotional regulation, and larger amygdala volumes are associated with behavioral disorders." Alexandra Lautarescu, Michael C. Craig, and Vivette Glover, "Prenatal Stress: Effects on Fetal and Child Brain Development," *International Review of Neurobiology* 150 (2020): 17–18. That said, "changes in the womb do not mean that they cannot be altered again later. For example, some of the neurodevelopmental effects of prenatal life event stress or raised in utero cortisol can be buffered by sensitive attachment between the mother and the child postnatally" (ibid., 19). See also Scott A. Small's excellent discussion of the effects of fear on the amygdala, which renders it more hypersensitive to danger. Small, "Fearless Minds," in *Forgetting: The Benefits of Not Remembering*, 84–105 (New York: Crown, 2021).

**Impossible memory.** For a discussion of the phenomenological qualities of "memories" of things that could not have happened, see Mary Ann Foley, "Setting the Record Straight: Impossible Memories and the Persistence of Their Phenomenological Qualities," *Review of General Psychology* 19, no. 3 (2015): 230–48.

5    **Most events in a person's history can be framed in varying ways.** This framing is in part related to personality, in part to choice, and it has an accretive effect on our mental health. "The way we narrate our experiences is related to well-being. Also our stories do not just reflect the raw data of experience: The meaning in life stories is continually constructed by emphasizing some parts of autobiographical memory (while ignoring others) and by selectively interpreting the causes and consequences of events." Dorthe Kirkegaard Thomsen, Martin Hammershøj Olesen, Anette Schnieber, and Jan Tønnesvang, "The Emotional Content of Life Stories: Positivity Bias and Relation to Personality," *Cognition & Emotion* 28, no. 2 (2014): 260–61.

**Our private stream of self-talk.** In reference to this inner voice and the conversations most of us hold with ourselves, the psychologist and neuroscientist Ethan Kross writes, "Our verbal stream plays an indispensable role in the creation of our selves." Kross, *Chatter: The Voice in Our Head, Why It Matters, and How to Harness It* (New York: Crown, 2022), 15. Kross's research underscores how destructive negative internal "chatter" can be, and his book offers effective strategies for changing patterns of self-talk in ways that lead to better mental and physical health.

7 **From letters and diaries to travel logs and court records.** An avid journal keeper, I also kept copies of the hundreds of letters I wrote and received from the time I graduated from high school on. I also found Ancestry.com an invaluable aid in my research. Through Ancestry's library edition, I was able to determine travel dates (from flight manifests), jobs held by ancestors, where they lived and when, and marriage records, among other valuable information.

**We collaborate . . . on our autobiographical stories.** See, for example, Charles Ferneyhough's discussion of the collaborative nature of memory in *Pieces of Light: How the New Science of Memory Illuminates the Stories We Tell About Our Pasts* (London: Profile Books, 2012), especially his chapter "Negotiating the Past."

**Recall is a collaboration of different parts of the brain.** As the researcher Jiawei Zhang and others point out, memory is a coordinated, brain-wide process: "Memory is, at its simplest, a set of encoded neural connections in the brain. It is the re-creation or reconstruction of past experiences by the synchronous firing of neurons that were involved in the original experience. . . . Because of the way in which memory is encoded, it is perhaps better thought of as a kind of collage or jigsaw puzzle, rather than in the traditional manner as a collection of recordings or pictures or video clips, stored as discrete wholes. Our memories are not stored in our brains like books on library shelves, but are actually on-the-fly reconstructions from elements scattered throughout various areas of our brains." Jiawei Zhang, "Cognitive Functions of the Brain: Perception, Attention and Memory," *IFM Lab Tutorial Series #6*, Copyright ©IFM Lab (2019): 15. See also Signy Sheldon, Can Fenerci, and Lauri Gurguryan, "A Neurocognitive Perspective on the Forms and Functions of Autobiographical Memory Retrieval," *Frontiers in Systems Neuroscience* 13 (29 January 2019).

20 **Children whose mothers were depressed or abused while pregnant.** See Glover et al., "Prenatal Maternal Stress," 846. See also Anqi Qiu et al., "Effects of Antenatal Maternal Depressive Symptoms and Socio-Economic Status on Neonatal Brain Development Are Modulated by Genetic Risk," *Cerebral Cortex* 27, no. 5 (May 1, 2017): 3080–92.

**The cognitive and emotional lines of our lives.** This is referred to as "gene-environment interdependence" in the literature.

**Photographs or corroborating witnesses.** Photographs and witnesses can also be untrustworthy, however. See Annette Kuhn's essay on the complicated and ambiguous relationship between photographs and memories in "She'll Always Be Your Little Girl . . ." in *Family Secrets: Acts of Memory and Imagination* (London: Verso, 1995): 11–20. Social psychologists have demonstrated that eyewitness testimony is often rife with mistakes and mis-identifications, a result of the variable and subjective nature of human perception and memory, our susceptibility to suggestion, and changes wrought by the passage of time, among other factors. See, for example, Jed Rakoff and Elizabeth Loftus, "The Intractability of Inaccurate Eyewitness Identification," *Daedalus* 147, no. 4 (Fall 2018): 90–98.

20 **Imagined memories that feel real . . . can affect our psyches and behavior.** See, for example, a discussion of Freud's changed perspective on the aetiology of hysterical symptoms (actual early childhood sexual assaults and/ or fantasized ones) in Joel Kupfersmid, "Freud's Rationale for Abandoning the Seduction Theory," *Psychoanalytic Psychology* 10, no. 2 (1993): 283.

**Not everyone visualizes to the same degree.** The first person to describe and quantify "the great variety of natural powers of visual representation," or what scientists now call aphantasia and hyperphantasia, was Sir Francis Galton in "Statistics of Mental Imagery," *Mind* 5, no. 19 (July 1880): 301–18. The term "aphantasia" was coined over 120 years later, in the early 2000s, by Adam Zeman, Michaela Dewar, and Sergio Della Sala. See their "Lives without Imagery—Congenital Aphantasia," *Cortex* 73 (2015): 378–80. For a popular account, see Anna Clemens, "When the Mind's Eye Is Blind," *Scientific American*, August 1, 2018. Approximately three percent of the population has aphantasia, or "blind imagination." Brains, however, have multiple ways—including conceptual and linguistic—to imagine, and many demonstrably creative people, such as artists and animators, are aphantasic.

**Severely deficient autobiographical memory.** Daniela J. Palombo, Signy Sheldon, and Brian Levine, "Individual Differences in Memory," *Trends in Cognitive Science* 22, no. 7 (July 2018): 583–97.

21 **Hyperphantasia.** Carl Zimmer, "Many People Have a Vivid 'Mind's Eye,' While Others Have None at All," *New York Times*, June 8, 2021.

**Correspondence to actual events.** See Martin A. Conway and Jefferson A. Singer, "The Self and Autobiographical Memory: Correspondence and Coherence," *Social Cognition* 22, no. 5 (October 2004): 491–529.

22 **One of several possible true versions.** See Lad Tobin's essay "The Permission Slip," *The Sun* (November 2015): 27.

# 2
## Proof of Other Worlds

24 **The glue that holds families together.** Sharing family stories also strengthens children's sense of self and resiliency. Studies show that children who know pivotal details of their parents' and grandparents' pasts, such as how their parents met, where their grandparents grew up, and how older family

members navigated difficult times, have demonstrably higher self-esteem and a greater sense of control over their lives. Robyn Fivush, Marshall Duke, and Jennifer Bohanek, "'Do You Know?' The Power of Family History in Adolescent Identity and Well-Being," *Journal of Family Life* (2010) and Robyn Fivush, Jennifer Bohanek, and Widaad Zaman, "Personal and Intergenerational Narratives in Relation to Adolescents' Well-Being," *New Directions for Child and Adolescent Development* 131 (Spring 2011): 45–57.

27    **The naked slate of a newborn child.** See Kuhn, *Family Secrets*, especially chapter four, "A Credit to Her Mother": "The baby's body is quite literally a blank canvas, screen of the mother's desire—desire to make good the insufficiencies of her own childhood, desire to transcend these lacks by caring for her deprived self through a love for her baby that takes very particular cultural forms" (45).

33    **Mr. Ayer's death from insanity in 1878.** Two years before his death in 1878, Dr. Ayer, who had unsuccessfully run for Congress in 1874, became uncontrollably violent and was committed to a private insane asylum in New Jersey for several months. He then moved to and died at "a family home for the treatment of mental and nervous diseases" in Winchendon, MA, run by Ira Russell, MD, a Union Army surgeon and the author of *The Borderland of Insanity* (1884). As Ayer's obituary in the *New York Times* adds, "it was clear that the mind, once so active and vigorous that it seemed as if no obstacle could conquer it, the indomitable will that could brook no opposition, and the splendid business talent that could organize and manage stupendous business transactions for so many years, had all been wrecked by disease; the strong, clear-headed man had again become a child." "Dr. James C. Ayer," *New York Times*, July 4, 1878. He left his wife, Josephine Mellin Southwick Ayer, $15,000,000. "Mrs. Ayer Was Famous," *Chicago Daily Tribune*, January 6, 1898.

**Mrs. Ayer's lavish spending, brilliant jewels, and magnificent parties.** See "The Richest Children in the World Today," *Birmingham Age Herald*, February 6, 1898.

**Mrs. Ayer . . . transferred Stone House to a struggling local orphanage.** "The 'Home for Young Women and Children' first occupied a house on John Street until October, 1892, when it moved to the beautiful Ayer Home on Pawtucket Street, the generous donation of Mrs. Josephine Ayer, of Paris, and her son, Mr. F. F. Ayer, of New York. . . . The purpose of this excellent institution is to provide a temporary home for young women and children at a moderate expense; or, according to circumstances, 'to help others to help themselves.' This has been its motto. It also assists in obtaining employment and in giving advice in time of need. It is likewise a temporary home for unfortunate and destitute children, who, on account of the loss of both parents or one, are left helpless and uncared for." Courier-Citizen Company, *Illustrated History of Lowell and Vicinity, Massachusetts* (Lowell, MA: 1897), 852.

33    **On her death in 1898, Mrs. Ayer . . . bequeathed $100,000 to Lowell's Ayer Home.** "Mrs. Ayer's Bequests to Charity," *New-York Tribune*, February 4, 1898.

      **Richest children in the world.** "The Richest Children in the World Today," *Birmingham Age Herald*, February 6, 1898.

34–35    **"Paid for by wealthy people in Boston."** The Ingleside School for Girls was founded in 1895 by Georgie McClure Lee, the daughter of Colonel George McClure, one of the founders of Tiffany & Co. "Mrs. James Stearns Lee: Boston Philanthropist, Daughter of a Tiffany Co. Founder," *New York Times*, June 7, 1938. The school was run by the Ingleside Corporation in Boston, which raised most of the funds for its maintenance.

35    **"Young, neglected girls . . . in danger of falling into evil ways."** "Home Free of Debt: Aim of Ingleside, in Revere, Wholly Preventative," *Boston Daily Globe*, January 21, 1910.

      **"Threatened by the undertow of life . . . a power for good in the world."** *Record of Christian Work* 27, no. 5 (May 1908): 310.

      **Mission of preventing marginalized girls from turning to such work.** My grandmother entered the Ingleside Home for Girls at the height of the American Progressive Era (1900–1918), ignited in large part by the late-nineteenth-century social purity movement. The historian Ruth Rosen notes that the first two decades of the twentieth century entertained "one of Western society's most zealous and best-recorded campaigns against prostitution," considered not only a moral problem but "a national menace," which resulted in "a deluge of committee reports, surveys, studies, and official public records"—including those on the need for schools like Ingleside. Rosen, *The Lost Sisterhood: Prostitution in American, 1900–1918* (Baltimore: The Johns Hopkins University Press, 1982), xi. A 1902 article in the *Boston Daily Globe* documents the Ingleside Home's turn from the rescue of "fallen women" to a wholly preventative mission, "with the hope of saving them to themselves." The article explicitly notes "the practical and patriotic motives" of such work. "Helps Young Girls," *Boston Daily Globe*, January 30, 1902.

      **Ingleside believed that showing love and kindness to children was as important as their practical care.** As the *Congregationalist and Christian World* reported in 1902, Ingleside "is a home where the girls are loved as well as cared for. This is important, as some are mere children." *Congregationalist and Christian World* 87, no. 7 (February 15, 1902): 251.

38    **Family storytelling over the supper table.** See Merrill and Fivush on the importance of intergenerational narratives for both the older family members telling the stories and the younger ones hearing them: Natalie Merrill and Robyn Fivush, "Intergenerational Narratives and Identity across Development," *Developmental Review* 40 (2016): 72–92.

38    **"Narrative ecology."** "In the simplest terms," writes Kate McLean, "the narrative ecology comprises the stories that are available to a person as he or she develops, the stories that form each person's particular narrative landscape." Our narrative ecology interconnects stories of our personal experiences; stories of the people in our life; cultural stories; and family stories, about both ourselves and other family members. McLean, *The Co-Authored Self* (Oxford: Oxford University Press, 2016), 5.

      **While perhaps vicarious.** See Pillemer et al.'s fascinating discussion of vicarious memories, which they argue "share basic phenomenological and functional properties of memories of events experienced firsthand." The authors accordingly find "current models of episodic memory, which include only past events that happened directly to the self" as "too restrictive." David B. Pillemer, Kristina L. Steiner, Kie J. Kuwabara, Dorthe Kirkegaard Thomsen, and Connie Svob, "Vicarious Memories," *Consciousness and Cognition* 36 (2015): 243.

      **The "warmth and intimacy" of episodic recall.** William James, *The Principles of Psychology*, Vol. 1 (New York: Dover Press, 1950/1890), 650.

      **As if what is most hidden were most true.** See Michel Foucault's discussion of Catholic confession and the construction of truth in *The History of Sexuality*, Vol. 1: *An Introduction*, trans. Robert Hurley (New York: Random House, 1978), especially pages 58–63.

# 3
## The Memory Keep

49    **The nation's capital, then swarming with young women supporting the war effort.** For an engaging description of the American women flooding Washington, DC, during the war, see Liza Mundy's *Code Girls: The Untold Story of the American Women Code Breakers of World War II* (New York: Hachette Books, 2016).

55    **The most buried family secrets.** See Ashley Barnwell, "Family Secrets and the Slow Violence of Social Stigma," *Sociology* 53, no. 6 (2019): 1111–26.

56    **Many family secrets are badly kept.** See Carol Smart, "Families, Secrets, and Memories," *Sociology* 45, no. 4 (2011): 539–53. Smart argues that while some kinds of family secrets, especially those concerning sexuality and reproduction, can restructure all the relationships in a family or rewrite the family story, some family secrets may also be "a way of sustaining kinship relationships" (540, 550). Fivush et al. identify "three major ways in which families express secrets across the generations—through collusion, through confusion, and through whole-family secrets." They note that "the stories that families tell are as much about who we want to be as who we are; family stories embrace how families imagine themselves." Robyn Fivush, Helena

McAnally, and Elaine Reese, "Family Stories and Family Secrets," *Journal of New Zealand Studies* NS29 (2019): 21–23.

61  **Known as the "Boss," Charlie [Frazier].** The writer, editor, and lawyer Ike Williams, long a part-time resident of Wellfleet, describes Frazier as the town's "legendary all-powerful town counsel," who was "universally feared for his skill as a lawyer and his powerful political influence." John Taylor Williams, *The Shores of Bohemia: A Cape Cod Story, 1910–1960* (New York: Farrar, Straus and Giroux: 2022), 294.

**The year I was born, Charlie was waging a vitriolic battle against the proposed Cape Cod National Seashore.** The journalist Seth Rolbein writes that "[Charlie Frazier's] influence within Wellfleet was so strong and he was able to stir up such staunch and loud local opposition that when President John F. Kennedy signed the Cape Cod National Seashore into law in 1961, he is reported to have said, 'We got the Seashore in spite of Charlie Frazier.' Years later, Charlie would say, 'To me, that was a compliment.'" Rolbein, "The Two Charlies of Wellfleet," *Boston Magazine*, July 1986, 222.

73  **No one needs to justify a convention that society tells us to expect.** See Robyn Fivush, "Speaking Silence: The Social Construction of Silence in Autobiographical and Cultural Narratives, *Memory* 18, no. 2 (2010): 88–98.

**My grandparents' . . . fiftieth wedding anniversary.** "Tewksbury Golden Jubilarians Presented Trip to Hawaii," *The Sun*, Lowell, MA, October 20, 1975.

# 4
# Memory's Angles

86  **The recovered memory / false memory debates.** Steven M. Smith and David H. Gleaves, "Recovered Memories," in *The Handbook of Eyewitness Psychology*, Vol. 1, edited by Rod Lindsay, David Ross, J. Don Read, and Michael Toglia (New York: Routledge, 2007).

89  **Like much recovered memory, mine had the qualities of a flashback.** See Robyn Fivush and Valerie J. Edwards, "Remembering and Forgetting Childhood Sexual Abuse," *Journal of Child Sexual Abuse* 13, no. 2 (2004): 3.

90  **Like many adults who recover genuine memories of early sexual abuse, I soon realized I had never completely forgotten it.** In their study of twelve middle-class women who had suffered severe sexual abuse as children by a family member, Fivush and Edwards found that half of the women underwent long periods during which they did not recall the abuse. The researchers note "the difficulty describing a very real subjective memory phenomenon, that of both remembering and not remembering simultaneously." Fivush and Edwards, "Remembering and Forgetting," 9–10.

92   **The rancor of the controversies . . . over the possibility of accurately recalling long-forgotten instances of childhood sexual abuse.** Writing in 2019, Otgaar et al. argue that "the debate concerning repressed memories is by no means dead" and that the term "dissociative amnesia" has largely replaced the more controversial "repressed memory," though they share many characteristics: the inability to recall traumatic autobiographical information during a period of time, despite this information having been "successfully stored" in the brain and remaining potentially recoverable in intact form, often as a result of retrieval cues. Henry Otgaar, Mark L. Howe, Lawrence Patihis, Harald Merckelbach, Steven Jay Lynn, Scott O. Lilienfeld, and Elizabeth F. Loftus, "The Return of the Repressed: The Persistent and Problematic Claims of Long-Forgotten Trauma," *Perspectives on Psychological Science* 14, no. 6 (2019): 1079.

# 5
# Dreams of Memory

107   **The powerful link between emotion and memory.** While this link tends to privilege negative emotional events, research shows that it doesn't always. Compared with neutral events, emotional events are typically recalled with more perceptual detail. The clarity of negative and positive emotional memories does not differ significantly, but some studies show that our memories of positive events include more sensory details, such as smells, sounds, touch, and taste. See Victoria Wardell, Christopher R. Madan, Taylyn J. Jameson, Chantelle Cocquyt, Katherine Checknita, Hallie Liu, and Daniela J. Palombo, "How Emotion Influences the Details Recalled in Autobiographical Memory, *Applied Cognitive Psychology* 35 (2021): 1455. I wonder if this is because of the stress involved in negative events and the way the brain focuses (and screens out irrelevant details) in situations where fear is involved. As Daniel Reisberg writes, "Emotion typically improves memory for an event's gist, but undermines memory for more peripheral elements within the event." This is especially true in cases of trauma. Daniel Reisberg, "Memory for Emotional Episodes: The Strengths and Limits of Arousal-Based Accounts," in *Memory and Emotion: Interdisciplinary Perspectives*, edited by B. Uttl, N. Ohta, and A. L. Siegenthaler (Malden, MA: Blackwell Publishing, 2006), 15.

108   **We might forget what a person has done, but not how they made us feel.** This quote is often attributed to Maya Angelou, but it has been credited to others, as well, including Carl W. Buehner, a high official in the Mormon Church. See Richard L. Evans, *Richard Evans' Quote Book* (Salt Lake City: Publishers Press, 1971), 244.

111   **Sherry Turkle . . . an "evocative object."** Turkle, a social science and technology professor at MIT., writes about such objects "as companions to our emotional lives or as provocations to thought." She adds that "we think

with the objects we love; we love the objects we think with." She connects these evocative objects to Claude Lévi-Strauss's notion of bricolage, which she describes as "a way of combining and recombining a closed set of materials to come up with new ideas." Sherry Turkle, *Evocative Objects: Things We Think With* (Cambridge, MA: The MIT Press, 2011), 4–5. See also her fascinating memoir, *The Empathy Diaries* (New York: Penguin Books, 2021).

121 **How profoundly experiential dreams can be.** Though it is well established that some form of dreaming can take place during various stages of sleep, I am speaking here of typical REM dreams: ones that are vivid and follow a narrative, even if a bizarre one. Dreams vary in quality and length from realistic simulations of waking life to fragmentary images and repetitive thoughts. Lucid dreamers are aware they are dreaming and can typically change their dream experience, but I am not addressing lucid dreams here. For a discussion of the "real-world simulation" inherent to many dreams, see Jennifer M. Windt, "Dreaming: Beyond Imagination and Perception," in *The Cambridge Handbook of the Imagination*, edited by Anna Abraham (Cambridge: Cambridge University Press, 2020), 659–75. And, as Harry Hunt points out, "dreaming can operate both as mnemic imagery and as perception." *The Multiplicity of Dreams: Memory, Imagination, and Consciousness* (New Haven: Yale University Press, 1989), 41.

**Dreaming is its own world.** Or, as Foucault writes, dreaming is "a primary state of existence." He argues that a dream is not a way of experiencing another world but "a radical way of experiencing its own world." Michel Foucault, "Dream, Imagination, and Existence," trans. Forrest Williams, in *Dream and Existence: Michel Foucault and Ludwig Binswanger*, edited by Keith Hoeller, a special issue of the *Review of Existential Psychology and Psychiatry* 19, no. 1 (1986): 73, 59.

122 **Waking imagination can be characterized as a weak form of perception.** "Research supports the claim that visual mental imagery is a depictive internal representation that functions like a weak form of perception. Brain imaging work has demonstrated that neural representations of mental and perceptual images resemble one another. . . . Common sets of neural structures are employed during both events [i.e., mental images and externally triggered perceptual representations]." Joel Pearson, Thomas Naselaris, Emily A. Holmes, and Stephen M. Kosslyn, "Mental Imagery: Functional Mechanisms and Clinical Applications," *Trends in Cognitive Sciences* 19, no. 10 (October 2015): 590, 599.

Another group of researchers has attempted to show correlations between dreaming and waking neural activity using a different methodology, that is, applying transcranial direct current stimulation (tDCS) over targeted brain areas during sleep to influence certain types of dream content. Their findings support the notion that "the neural correlates of specific dream content match the neural correlates of corresponding cognitive and behavioural functions during wakefulness." Valdas Noreika,

Jennifer M. Windt, Markus Kern, Katja Valli, Tiina Salonen, Riitta Parkkola, Antti Revonsuo, Ahmed A. Karim, Tonio Ball, and Bigna Lenggenhager, "Modulating Dream Experience: Noninvasive Brain Stimulation over the Sensorimotor Cortex Reduces Dream Movement," *Science Reports* 10, 6735 (2020): 9.

These connections between imagination and perception have inspired therapeutic interventions using mental imagery to mitigate the effects of PTSD, depression, and anxiety disorders, especially in cases that involve upsetting imagery. Three of the most effective interventions are repeated "imaginal exposure" to lessen anxiety about feared things or contexts; "imagery rescripting" to heighten comfort or performance in future events; and "systematic desensitization" to deflate the negative emotional valence of a feared object or situation by pairing its image with a relaxation response. See Pearson et al., 598.

122 **Dreams, which are far more vivid and realistic than most waking imagery.** Except, of course, in hallucinatory states such as those produced by illness (e.g., schizophrenia) or drugs (e.g., psylocibin). Those with hyperphantasia (see Chapter 1) also come close to producing, while awake, the realistic mental imagery of dreaming.

**Stress often enhances memory, though it can also impair it.** For the positive effects of acute stress on memory, see Elizabeth V. Goldfarb, "Enhancing Memory with Stress: Progress, Challenges, and Opportunities," *Brain and Cognition* 133 (July 2019): 94–105. Yet chronic stress can lead to memory deficits, especially in depressed patients. See Daniel G. Dillon and Diego A. Pizzagalli, "Mechanisms of Memory Disruption in Depression," *Trends in Neurosciences* 41, no. 3 (2018): 137–49. As the Irish psychiatrist Veronica O'Keane succinctly puts it, "Memory, like many physiological systems, works best at moderate levels of arousal." She explains that too little or too much of the stress hormone cortisol impairs memory function. Neurologically speaking, "a minimum threshold of cortisol is necessary for memory formation," which O'Keane calls "good stress." But constantly high levels of cortisol, or over-arousal, mean that hippocampal neurons are "stuck in a hyper-fired state" and cannot absorb new memories. "We know intuitively that we cannot learn if we are not paying attention or, at the other extreme, if we are over aroused and anxious." Veronica O'Keane, *A Sense of Self: Memory, the Brain, and Who We Are* (New York: Norton, 2021), 120–23.

**Mental imagery and varying types and degrees of emotion have long been linked.** Simon E. Blackwell, "Emotional Mental Imagery," in *The Cambridge Handbook of the Imagination*, 241–57.

**Emotion is a cardinal characteristic of our most memorable dreams.** The psychiatrist and dream researcher J. Allan Hobson lists the five cardinal characteristics of dream mentation as: intensity of emotion; bizarre content and illogical organization; sensory impressions; uncritical acceptance (except, of course, during lucid dreaming); and difficulty of recall. See J. Allan Hobson, *The Dreaming Brain* (New York: Basic Books, 1988), 9.

123 **The point is not that dreams are inherently dramatic or pedestrian, comprehensible or bizarre.** Harry Hunt offers a sophisticated account of the varieties of dream experience: "There do seem to be relatively distinct types of dreaming, each with its own line of development. . . . There are relatively mundane dreams that seem to be based on mnemic consolidations and reorganizations; Freud-type relatively fantastic, pressure-discharge dreams, often based on complex rebuslike wordplay; dreams based on somatic states and illness; dreams based on aesthetically rich metaphor; dreams based on problem-solving and deep intuition (perhaps extrasensory?); lucid-control dreams; the varieties of nightmare; and a Jung-type archetypal-mythological form of dreaming. These forms potentially overlap, and all may have in common some background mnemic reorganization, but each also has its own prototypical exemplars. It may be because dreaming has no fixed function that it is open to so many different uses. Not only do these potentialities of the dream . . . argue against any one deep structure for dreaming, they are also fully consistent with the recent view . . . that there is no single deep structure for symbolic cognition generally. Rather we find multiple and potentially independent symbolic faculties—each developing a reflexive recombinatory capacity in its own fashion." Hunt, *The Multiplicity of Dreams*, 76.

**I may be remembering what I remembered.** Robyn Fivush argues that autobiographical memory, a cognitive achievement, is more complex and multifaceted than episodic memory alone, which helps us to understand the difference between knowing what happened and re-experiencing our past self within the context of a personal history. While I have a clear memory of the what, where, and when in this dream experience, I no longer have what is called autonoetic consciousness of it. Robyn Fivush, "The Development of Autobiographical Memory," *Annual Review of Psychology*, 62 (2011): 560.

124 **That counts for something, and that something feels very much like a memory.** But is this so very different from the way we imagine and construct those around us in waking life? As Will Storr writes, "The world we experience as 'out there' is actually a reconstruction of reality that is built inside our heads. It's an act of creation by the storytelling brain." Will Storr, *The Science of Storytelling* (New York: Abrams Press, 2020), 21.

126 **Freud's assertion that "the most trivial elements of a dream are indispensable to its interpretation."** Sigmund Freud, *The Interpretation of Dreams*, trans. James Strachey (New York: Avon Books, 1900/1965), 552.

**The ability to generalize from myriad details is necessary to engage flexibly with the world.** Forgetting, it turns out, plays an indispensable role in this process. The neurologist Scott Small explains that normal forgetting is critical for seeing patterns and for generalizing. Computer scientists, he writes, have shown that "the most effective way to artificially create human computational flexibility is to force the algorithm to have more forgetting." He adds that "the capacity for generalization that comes with cortical forgetting allows us to . . . arrange the clutter and squelch the clang of an external world sensed only as parts." Small, *Forgetting*, 58, 63. This is analogous, I would argue, to ignoring the distraction of extraneous dream details in order to better understand a dream's gist.

126  **The competing interpretations that most dreams can absorb.** Ken Frieden cites a story in the Mishnah in which a rabbi visits 24 different dream interpreters, presenting the same dream to each. The dream is interpreted in 24 different ways, and each interpretation comes true. While Frieden's argument is that "dream interpreters perform self-fulfilling prophecies," the underlying point is that the interpretation of a dream, as of many waking experiences, is convincingly pliable. Frieden, *Freud's Dream of Interpretation* (Albany: State University of New York Press, 1990), 79.

129  **How confounding, though, that taking control of one's life could well mean ending it.** In her brilliant memoir, the philosopher Susan J. Brison writes movingly of her survival of a rape and attempted murder, noting that the goal of a survivor is not, ultimately, to transcend trauma but to endure its aftermath. "This can be hard enough," she writes, "when the only way to regain control over one's life seems to be to end it." Brison, *Aftermath: Violence and the Remaking of the Self* (Princeton: Princeton University Press, 2002), 65.

130  **The immersive, perceptual experience of these dreams.** "This immersive here and now quality, as described in dream reports, is widely regarded as a defining characteristic of dreaming . . . ; with few exceptions, both the virtual world and the virtual self in dreams are experienced as real." Noreika et al., "Modulating Dream Experience," 2.

**Caused them to exert enduring effects on the present.** The Austrian psychiatrist Alfred Adler considered this one of the primary functions of dreams, that is, arousing feelings that effect changes in waking life—some of them adaptive, others delusional. Adler was fascinated by dreams but also suspicious of them. See Alfred Adler, *What Life Should Mean to You*, edited by Alan Porter (Boston: Little, Brown, and Co., 1931), 98, as well as Alfred Adler, "On the Interpretation of Dreams," *International Journal of Individual Psychology* 2, no. 1 (1936): 7–8.

131  **Recalling past experiences recruits the same network of brain regions as imagining future ones.** See, for example, Roger E. Beaty, Preston P. Thakrall, Kevin P. Madore, Mathias Benedek, and Daniel L. Schacter, "Core Network Contributions to Remembering the Past, Imagining the Future, and Thinking Creatively," *Journal of Cognitive Neuroscience* 30, no. 12 (2018): 1939–51. Or as Charles Ferneyhough eloquently puts it, "Memory is Janus-faced, looking both to the past and the future." Ferneyhough, *Pieces of Light*, 127.

131 **Dreams . . . insist . . . on our presence.** Presence is a key concept for memory. It is the feeling of being there, and it incorporates "first-person perspective, interactivity, emotion experience, and attentional engagement," which are cardinal aspects of most dreams. Dominique Makowski, Marco Sperduti, Serge Nicolas, and Pascale Piolino, "'Being There' and Remembering It: Presence Improves Memory Encoding," *Consciousness and Cognition* 53 (2017): 195.

# 6
# Found by Stories

135 **A marionette of veiled emotional memory.** O'Keane notes "our tendency to be guided unknowingly by emotional memory. Many of us, after all, do marry our 'fathers' or 'mothers.' It is memory that partly makes us the unknowing victims of our passions." O'Keane, *A Sense of Self*, 78.

140 **Mr. James's advocacy for a "more Indian America."** Among other papers, the *Cape Codder* and *Boston Globe* published Frank James's censored speech, in which he decries three centuries of "battles . . . atrocities . . . [and] broken promises." Though "our lands have fallen into the hands of the aggressor," he writes, "today we work toward a more humane America, a more Indian America." Instead of celebrating the 350th anniversary of the landing of the Pilgrims, Mr. James, also known as Wamsutta, proposes celebrating "a beginning of the American Indian, particularly the Wampanoag, to regain the position in this country that is rightfully ours." Frank James, "Our Beginnings: An Indian's View," *Boston Globe*, October 8, 1970. For twenty years following this speech, Mr. James served as the moderator of United American Indians of New England, the group that organized the now annual National Day of Mourning protests in Plymouth, MA. He remained a music teacher, then director of music, in our Nauset Regional school system until 1989. He died in 2001.

**A throng of national tribal members, led by a Sioux, buried Plymouth Rock.** For more details, see "Mourning Indians Dump Sand on Plymouth Rock," *New York Times*, November 27, 1970.

142 **The archive corrects and instructs, reveals and surprises.** Or as the historian Clifton Crais puts it in his elegant memoir, "the archive disciplines and provokes." Crais suffers from severe childhood amnesia, which he attributes to chronic childhood trauma, and his book narrates his attempts to reconstruct his personal history through interviews, letters, photographs, hospital reports, and visits to childhood places. Clifton Crais, *History Lessons: A Memoir of Madness, Memory, and the Human Brain* (New York: The Overlook Press, 2014), 141.

**The pages of my journals . . . tingling with an existential joy.** My friend Robyn Fivush, a social psychologist, has suggested that the journals from my preadolescent and teenage years show that I was intuitively engaging in positive psychology exercises, including finding gratitude and benefits. I think my natural extroversion and excitable nature played a role, as well.

147    **Changing physical scenes alters mental ones.** Or as James Somers writes, "passing through the doorway brings one mental scene to a close and opens another." Somers, "Head Space," *The New Yorker* (December 6, 2021), 33.

148    **Adolescence and . . . an internalized "narrative identity."** Dan McAdams has written extensively on narrative identity, a concept first developed in the 1980s. Narrative identities, McAdams writes, "reconstruct the autobiographical past and anticipate the imagined future to provide the self with temporal coherence and some semblance of psychosocial unity and purpose." McAdams, "'First We Invented Stories, Then They Changed Us': The Evolution of Narrative Identity," *Evolutionary Studies in Imaginative Culture* 3, no. 1 (December 1, 2019): 2. He argues that narrative identity first emerges during adolescence, and he points to work by Habermas and Bluck that suggests this is, in part, because of the cognitive challenge of producing autobiographical stories that exhibit both causal and thematic coherence, which are essential markers of narrative identity. Dan P. McAdams and Kate C. McLean, "Narrative Identity," *Current Directions in Psychological Science* 22, no. 3 (June 2013): 235. See also Tilmann Habermas and Susan Bluck, "Getting a Life: The Emergence of the Life Story in Adolescence," *Psychological Bulletin* 126, no. 5 (2000): 748–69.

**The fashioning of that life story . . . is foundational to our personal identity, our sense of continuity over time, and our coherence.** I have long appreciated the cultural anthropologist Katherine Ewing's insights on our sense of enduring boundedness and consistency, an affective state that ignores contradictions but is "an essential illusion for ongoing experience." She suggests that the self is constituted as a string of highly selective memories, and that each of us contains multiple "strings" or selves that, although perceived as timeless and continuous while experienced, shift rapidly and are context dependent. This perspective is not unlike Jung's notion of personae, although Jung reifies unity in his postulation of the Self, while poststructuralists deconstruct that unity as a Cartesian illusion. Ewing instead proposes a model of the self that "accounts for the important phenomenon of the experience of wholeness and self-continuity without falling into the error of reifying a unitary self." Katherine P. Ewing, "The Illusion of Wholeness: Culture, Self, and the Experience of Inconsistence," *Ethos: Journal of the Society for Psychological Anthropology* 18:3 (1990): 251, 263, 267–68.

**Memories and the stories we create with them never stand still.** Like Ewing, the philosopher Susan Brison does not believe in the self as "a single, unified, coherent entity." Brison, along with many others, argues that we are socially constructed, "in large part through our group-based narratives." The structure of the self, she writes, "has harmonious and contradictory aspects, like the particles of an atom, attracting and repelling each other, hanging together in a whirling, ever-changing dance that any attempt at observation—or narration—alters." Sounds a lot like being a teenager. Brison, *Aftermath*, 95.

149 **The personal memories and stories . . . are both as true as I can render them and inevitably reconstructed.** O'Keane writes that "we may intuit that our past drives the present, but the events of the present also change past memories. . . . Present experience and memory are in a never-ending dance of construction and reconstruction." She thus considers the phrase "true event memory" a contradiction in terms: "All biographical memory is false to some degree, because of the imperative of change, the changing networks caused by ongoing events and experience, and the human drive to self-narrativize." O'Keane, *A Sense of Self*, 205, 207–8.

# 7
# Wellfleetian, Old and New

150 **While DNA writes code that influences who we become, it is not the only author of our identity.** I am persuaded by the work of the behavior geneticist Kathryn Paige Harden, who argues that DNA matters for social, educational, health, and personality outcomes—though it works in tandem with and does not erase cultural and psychological effects. As a "hereditarian leftist" scientist committed to social justice, she writes that "insisting that DNA matters is scientifically accurate; insisting that it is the only thing that matters is scientifically outlandish." Quoted in Gideon Lewis-Kraus, "Can Progressives Be Convinced That Genetics Matters?" *The New Yorker* (September 6, 2021). See also her recent book, *The Genetic Lottery: Why DNA Matters for Social Equality* (Princeton: Princeton University Press, 2021).

The political scientists Rose McDermott and Peter Hatemi concur with Harden, writing that "no single genetic marker will regulate complex social or behavioral traits in a meaningful way. . . . Humans are not slaves to their environments or their genotypes; rather, behavior is shaped by both factors in circuitous and interactive ways." McDermott and Hatemi, "DNA Is Not Destiny," in *Oxford Handbook of Evolution, Biology, and Society*, edited by Rosemary L. Hopcroft, 241–63 (New York: Oxford University Press, 2018), 242.

**Stories that are told about us, by those around us and by our culture.** As McAdams writes, "The authorship of a life story is, in a deep sense, joint—shared by the narrator whose life it is and the social world within which the story is made and told. Put differently, life stories are 'psychosocial constructions.' As such, they reflect much more than the narrator's own efforts to make sense of his or her own life. They reflect social norms, gender stereotypes, historical events, cultural assumptions, and the many and conflicting narratives that people grow up with and continue to hear, experience, appropriate, and reject as they move through the life course;

and life stories continue to change as the narrator's social world changes and as new stories about how to live come to replace old ones." Dan McAdams, "The Redemptive Self: Generativity and the Stories Americans Live By," *Research in Human Development* 3, no. 2 & 3 (2006): 95.

152 **Words, I discovered, gave me boundaries and plot lines, and with those lines came awareness and focus.** As the philosopher Ludwig Wittgenstein writes, "Die Grenzen meiner Sprache bedeuten die Grenzen meiner Welt" *Tractatus Logico-Philosophicus* (New York: Harcourt, Brace & Co.: 1922), 5.6. Though often translated as "The limits of my language are the limits of my mind. All I know is what I have words for," I prefer a more succinct and literal translation: "The boundaries of my language comprise the boundaries of my world."

156 **The dumb luck of chemistry.** It turns out that human happiness is, indeed, strongly influenced by one's genetic make-up, though the significance of that predisposition is, like any complex trait, affected by one's environment. Studies on people of European ancestry, including identical twins raised apart, find that "approximately 40% of the differences in happiness are accounted for by genetic differences between people while the remaining variance is accounted for by environmental influences that are unique to an individual." There's no one "happiness gene," however; scientists believe thousands of genetic variants are involved. Meike Bartels, Ragnhild Bang Nes, Jessica M. Armitage, Margot P. van de Wijer, Lianne P. de Vries, and Claire Haworth, "Exploring the Biological Basis for Happiness," *World Happiness Report* (2022): 105–26. See also Jared K. Rothstein, "Pollyannas, Pessimists, and the Science of Happiness," *Journal of Mental Health and Social Behavior* 3, no. 2 (2021): 144.

157 **As is typical for an American redemption narrative, Mom did not stay on the receiving end.** Studies show that redemption narratives, "highly favored" in American society, are "strongly associated" with a generative concern for others' well-being. See McAdams, "'First We Invented Stories,'" 14.

179 **"All things work together for good to those who love God."** Romans 8:28.

**"The very hairs on your head are all numbered."** Luke 12:7.

**God had "knit me together in my mother's womb."** Psalm 139:13.

# 8
# The Opposite of Memory

188 **We are all susceptible to that diversion of the eye.** Social scientists have conducted myriad studies—and numerous debates—on positivity and negativity biases. It has been theorized that a negativity bias among adolescents might offer an evolutionary advantage, because "negative information has stronger effects on attention, perception, memory, physiology, affect, behavior,

motivation, and decision-making than does equally extreme and arousing positive information." Catherine Norris, "The Negativity Bias, Revisited," *Social Neuroscience* 16, no. 1 (2021): 68. That said, as we get older and focus more on the emotionally meaningful aspects of our present and past, a well-documented "positivity bias" sets in. See, for example, Susan Turk Charles, Mara Mather, and Laura L. Carstensen, "Aging and Emotional Memory: The Forgettable Nature of Negative Images for Older Adults," *Journal of Experimental Psychology: General* 132, no. 2 (2003): 310–24. See also Dorthe Berntsen, "Tunnel Memories for Autobiographical Events: Central Details Are Remembered More Frequently from Shocking Than from Happy Experiences," *Memory & Cognition* 30, no. 7 (2002): 1010–20.

188  **We carry difficult stories with us in one way or another.** In addition to influencing choices and behaviors that might not serve our best interest, repressed or intentionally forgotten negative memories can work on us physiologically: "A crucial finding is that repressors exhibit physiologically high levels of anxiety-related arousal despite their low self-reported anxiety. Thus . . . repressors have high levels of unacknowledged anxiety. Importantly, repressive coping style has been associated with deleterious effects on physical well-being, most consistently an increased risk for hypertension, cardiovascular diseases, and cancer." Lauren L. Alston, Carissa Kratchmer, Anna Jeznach, Nathan T. Bartlett, Patrick S. R. Davidson, and Esther Fujiwara, "Self-Serving Episodic Memory Biases: Findings in the Repressive Coping Style," *Frontiers in Behavioral Neuroscience* (September 3, 2013): 1.

**The mental and physical health benefits of personal writing.** Many of these studies compare writing about painful topics to writing about neutral ones, with the long-term effects more positive (and notable) for the former. See, for example, Karen A. Baikie and Kay Wilhelm, "Emotional and Physical Health Benefits of Expressive Writing," *Advances in Psychiatric Treatment* 11 (2005): 338–46. Some researchers suggest that writing in the third person may be more beneficial than writing in the first person. Patricia Fergusson proposes that writing in the third person "serves a psychological distancing function that permits individuals to reframe, 'work through,' and ultimately leave painful experiences behind them. . . . Third-person narratives may be effective, in part, because they enable individuals to view negative experiences as occurring to a different self." Anne E. Wilson and Michael Ross, "The Identity Function of Autobiographical Memory: Time Is on Our Side," *Memory* 11, no. 2 (2003): 144.

189  **As Mary Karr puts it, memoir writing is like "knocking yourself out with your own fist."** Mary Karr, *The Art of Memoir* (New York: HarperCollins, 2015), xx.

193  **In the way of young children, with their absorption in the present.** As O'Keane writes, "Time seems to stand still during childhood, in fact it doesn't exist experientially. The time is all 'present,' days seem endless and events just end and move onto the next one. Children are not so much

adaptable as partly amnesic." O'Keane, *A Sense of Self*, 112. The queer Belgian novelist Amélie Nothomb captures this phenomenon beautifully, and succinctly, in her autofictional *Loving Sabotage*: "To be children, that's to say, to be." Nothomb, *Loving Sabotage* (New York: New Directions, 2000), 83.

The ability to narrate personal stories that are linked across time and incorporated in one's self-identity is a cognitive achievement. Children do, of course, tell stories about their experiences, though they tend to be brief and elliptical, and "most findings suggest that prior to adolescence, there is no life story to develop." Monisha Pasupathis, Emma Mansour, and Jed R. Brubaker, "Developing a Life Story: Constructing Relations between Self and Experience in Autobiographical Narratives," *Human Development* 50, no. 2/3 (2007): 86. Fivush notes that "The ability to create an autobiography, a personal history of self that is continuous in time, with specific events experienced at particular points and linked both to each other and the present, is a complex human skill that relies on multiple component developmental skills. . . . Thus, the question is not when children 'achieve' autobiographical memory, but rather, how these sets of complex skills develop across age and become integrated into an emerging autobiographical memory system that continues to develop and evolve across the lifespan." Fivush, "The Development of Autobiographical Memory," 561.

196 **Most people who have bullied others deny their behavior.** In their analysis of 96 school-classes in Germany, the sociologists Travis Tatum and Thomas Grund write that "individuals in a dyad rarely agree on who bullies whom and who is bullied by whom." They find that only 26% of bullies identified by their victims admit to bullying behavior. Even more fascinating, only 18% of victims identified by their bullies recognize the bullying for what it is. Tatum and Grund, "Accusation and Confession Discrepancies in Bullying: Dual-Perspective Networks and Individual-Level Attributes," *Social Networks* 60 (2020): 66–68. In my case, it wasn't until I was middle-aged that I realized Samantha's behavior toward me bore all the hallmarks of bullying: harmful, aggressive behavior repeated over time, manifesting in physical acts (such as the fight in the hallway), verbal teasing (my size, clothes, and looks), and social exclusion (instructing classmates not to like me).

**Emotion, once again, was likely pivotal.** As the neuroscientist Lisa Genova, in her smart and accessible book on memory, explains, "Emotion and surprise activate your amygdala, which then sends a loud and clear message to your hippocampus: Hey! What is going on now is extremely important. Remember this! And so emotion and surprise strongly facilitate the consolidation of new memories." Genova, *Remember: The Science of Memory and the Art of Forgetting* (New York: Harmony Books, 2021), 239.

**The past shifts and can even change.** As the sociologist Peter Berger writes, "common sense is quite wrong in thinking that the past is fixed, immutable, invariable, as against the everchanging flux of the present. On the contrary, at least within our own consciousness, the past is malleable and flexible, constantly changing as our recollection reinterprets and re-explains what has happened." Peter L. Berger, *Invitation to Sociology: A Humanistic Perspective* (Harmondsworth, England: Penguin Books, 1963), 71.

197 **We have little incentive to summon our crueler moments, which typically shame us more than they teach us.** Or we never fully encode them in the first place. Genova notes that "we tend to limit the consolidation of negative information about ourselves, and so this information is never stored long term." She cites studies that show we are more inclined to "remember the good qualities about ourselves and actively exclude and therefore forget the bad." Genova, *Remember*, 159–60. The social scientists Jonathan Fawcett and Justin Hulbert write that one of the advantages of normal forgetting is that "it often guards us from our past and helps us to build a stable, positive representation of our present and future. . . . Our ability to forget when advantageous is a major determinant of mental health." Fawcett and Hulbert, "The Many Faces of Forgetting: Toward a Constructive View of Forgetting in Everyday Life," *Journal of Applied Research in Memory and Cognition* 9 (2020): 4–5. See also Yanchi Zhang, Zhe Pan, Kai Li, and Yongyu Guo, "Self-Serving Bias in Memories: Selectively Forgetting the Connection between Negative Information and the Self," *Experimental Psychology* 65 (2018): 236–44.

**We can reposition the props of our lives . . . to extract other meanings, to play with other ways of being.** The psychologist Ruthellen Josselson writes, "The self . . . might best be viewed as a kaleidoscope, with continuity in its elements but change in their arrangement and in the dominance (or inertness) of certain elements at different times. Identity is a lifelong process of rewriting the texts of one's experiences, assigning different roles to the various aspects of the self. . . . The meanings of the past are reshaped to hold aspects of a multivocal self that are either consistent with, foils for, or lost aspects of the contemporary self." Ruthellen Josselson, "The Present of the Past: Dialogues with Memory over Time," *Journal of Personality* 77, no. 3 (June 2009): 665.

198 **"A strong sense of self requires that one remember what matters, and forget what does not."** Jacquelyn Ann Burkell, "Remembering Me: Big Data, Individual Identity, and the Psychological Necessity of Forgetting," *Ethics and Information Technology* 18 (2016): 17.

**The neurologist Scott Small.** See Small's engaging and accessible book on the differences between normal and pathological forgetting, and the importance of emotional forgetting: Small, *Forgetting*, 5, 38.

200 **The words have not changed. The person reading them has.** Josselson has conducted a fascinating thirty-five-year study of a woman's evolving memory and reframing of a significant teenage romantic relationship, analyzing the woman's reconstructions in tandem with changes in her circumstances and self-understanding. In explaining how one might, over time, assign

markedly different meanings to the same event or relationship, Josselson writes, "Across the life span it is the meanings assigned to memory rather than the contents of the memory itself that are reworked in order to anchor, illuminate, counterpoint, disavow, or otherwise enter into dialogue with current self-experience." Josselson, "The Present of the Past," 664.

201 **Place, memory, and emotion are inextricably entwined in our brains.** In her chapter "A Sense of Place," O'Keane examines the dominant role of place, and its entanglement with emotion, in memory construction. The brain's place cells, which comprise "the unique identifier, or cell memory, of a specific external place," are primarily located in the hippocampus, where new memories are organized before their ultimate storage in the cortex. "Emotional memory," O'Keane writes, "is knitted into the neural connections between the hippocampus and the amygdala so that seeing that place will subsequently fire an emotion." This is why revisiting the physical landmarks of our past can be such a moving experience. "Places . . . are, experientially, the anchor for memory and feeling." O'Keane, *A Sense of Self*, 92, 97, 98.

202 **Mary Karr calls the human ego "a stealthy, low-crawling bastard."** Karr, *Art of Memoir*, 153.

# 9
# Memory and Forgiveness

225 **Historians talk about the "usable past."** Coined by the early-twentieth-century literary critic Van Wyck Brooks, a "usable past" provides historical antecedents and interpretations that often do not appear in dominant accounts but offer support for present endeavors and hope for a changed future. For example, Alexandria Griffin writes about the use of queer, vernacular Mormon histories to imagine and make possible a more inclusive future for LGBTQ+ Mormons. Griffin, "Queer Mormon Histories and the Politics of a Usable Past," *Dialogue: A Journal of Mormon Thought* 54, no. 1 (Spring 2021). The "usable past" is inevitably caught up in the politics of memory, charges of manipulation and selectivity (by both sanctioned histories and counter-histories), and debates over objectivist accounts of the past versus the inherent subjectivity of historical interpretation. See Casey Nelson Blake, "The Usable Past, the Comfortable Past, and the Civic Past: Memory in Contemporary America," *Cultural Anthropology* 14, no. 3 (1999).

**Raymond Williams writes that we create our cultural traditions by continually selecting and reselecting our ancestors.** "The cultural tradition can be seen as a continual selection and re-selection of ancestors. Particular lines will be drawn, often for as long as a century, and then suddenly with some new stage in growth this will be canceled or weakened, and new lines drawn." Raymond Williams, *The Long Revolution* (New York: Columbia University Press, 1961), 52–53.

**225 Science, religion, psychotherapy, literature—each tantalizes with the promise of a portal to understanding.** Peter Berger has described our "deep human need for order, purpose and intelligibility," noting that this need draws us to meaning systems that are "capable of ordering the scattered data of one's biography." He adds that none of these socially constructed meaning systems is final (though religion would like to present itself as so), suggesting a "vexing connexion between what we think and who we sup with." Berger, *Invitation to Sociology*, 77–79. We have no other way to exist, of course; as with memories and ancestors and friends, choice matters.

**Like Eliot's keen, blinkered Mr. Casaubon and his contrived "key to all mythologies."** George Eliot, *Middlemarch* (New York: Random House, 2000/1871–72), 58ff.

**226 My stories are both a map of my being and an ever-shifting point of intersection.** My colleague Andrew Kazama, a neuropsychologist, informs me that this fluctuation, which sometimes feels like instability, is pretty much hardwired. "I am often astounded by the fractal-like nature of our neurobiology," he recently told me. When I asked him over email to elaborate, he wrote, "our brain's hundred billion neurons are held in states of polarized, electrochemical imbalance, waiting to be stimulated by our inner and outer universes to achieve nanoseconds of perfect balance. This stimulation serves to create growth and change not only in each neuron, but also in our mind. Reflecting on my own struggles in life, I find it comforting to know that we are built to be in a near-constant state of imbalance. In fact, as Aristotle suggests in *Metaphysics*, imbalance is the catalyst for personal growth (*entelecheia*). Our neurobiology is thus consistent with the ancient philosopher's views on how we achieve *eudaimonia*, or well-being, balance, and purpose." Kazama pointed me to the following sources: A.L. Hodgkin and A.F. Huxley, "A Quantitative Description of Membrane Current and Its Application to Conduction and Excitation in Nerve," *Journal of Physiology* 117, no. 4 (1952), 500–44, and W.D. Ross, *Aristotle's Metaphysics: A Revised Text with Introduction and Commentary* (Oxford: Clarendon Press, 1924). (Andrew Kazama, Personal Communication, November 2023).

**My inner sense of sameness and continuity.** Erik H. Erikson, *Childhood and Society, Second Edition* (New York: Norton, 1963), 261. I especially appreciate Erikson's inclusion of the importance of career, the lack of which can contribute, I believe, to a fractured sense of self: "The sense of ego identity, then, is the accrued confidence that the inner sameness and continuity prepared in the past are matched by the sameness and continuity of one's meaning for others, as evidenced in the tangible promise of a 'career'" (261–62). This, of course, is tied to the notion, often attributed to Freud, that "Liebe und Arbeit," love and work, are the foundations of a psychologically healthy and fulfilling life.

# Acknowledgments

I am deeply grateful to the phenomenal staff at University of Massachusetts Press, especially Executive Editor Brian Halley, for his appreciation of both the content of this memoir and its methodology; EDP Manager Sally Nichols and Production Editor Ben Kimball, for their thoughtful and meticulous shepherding of my manuscript through editing, design, and production; Designer Adam Bohannon for the gorgeous cover; and Marketing and Sales Manager Chelsey Harris, for her wholehearted and professionally savvy support of my work.

As many memoirists know, memory is a co-authored affair. Through conversations, interviews, and letters, I have grown to appreciate others' versions of shared events, and I have intentionally or unintentionally woven evocative aspects of their memories into mine, fleshing out scenes with details I might have dropped or never mentally recorded in the first place, the flash of recognition and the pleasure of returned memory rendering the narrative more nuanced and rich.

This book owes more than I can express to the unfailing generosity and patience of two people who have long shared their memories and knowledge with me: my sister Thelma Blakeley, whose kindness and creativity ground our extended family, and Shirley Blakeley, my brilliant, witty, and at times heartbreakingly honest mother. Holly Dykeman Lajoie, one of numerous Wellfleet cousins, has an astonishing mind for details, and she added color and humor to many of our shared memories of childhood. Other relatives also offered stories or answered questions: Brian Blakeley, Judith Blakeley, Kenneth Blakeley, Pat Blakeley, Richard Blakeley, Vicki Blakeley Schmidt, Heather Dykeman, Ruth Anne Dykeman, Clyde E. Hersome, Charles Heudes, Mick Lynch, Lynda Provenz, and Bertha Hersome Myhr.

I've long felt that being born a Cape Codder is like being born Swiss, but without the self-congratulation. We recognize our luck in being raised in such a gorgeous and evocative landscape, but that natural beauty is only part of the story. Wayne Rhodes, a fellow Wellfleetian and writer, has helped me articulate the complicated relationship to a resort town called home, reading many drafts of this manuscript and talking with me over an endless string of lobster rolls and clam chowders at PJ's. His enthusiasm for this project buoyed me during the fallow writing years and inspired me during productive ones. Other Cape friends or acquaintances also shared stories or connections or expertise: Sheila Adams, Pam Puffer Anthony, Robert Anthony, Wendyll Behrend, Kiri Blakeley, Christina Brown, Lisa Brown, Fred Caldwell, Cynthia Letendre Cilfone, Julie C. Comins, Diane Moore Dodge, Ken Fettig, Joellen Harris Garner, Karen Gray-Karlsson, Katherine Ann Hartley, Maurice Glucksman, Gwynne Guzzeau, Paul Holbrook, David Kew, Kathy Schmidt Kuzminski, Karen Underhill LaVoie, Paul Mendes, Meredith Manni Meserow, George Milliken, Dennis Murphy, Nancy North, Jay Paine, Michael Parlante, Leslie Power, John Schmidt, Michelle Sutton, and Suzanne Turner. My mother's close friend Paul Sienkowski drew a witty portrait for me of my mother outside the home, especially in her role as a Marie Antoinette milkmaid at Chillingsworth, the haute cuisine restaurant in Brewster where they both worked in the 1960s and early 1970s, serving not only wealthy locals and tourists but also culinary luminaries such as James Beard and Julia Child, who helped develop the menu, and well-known actors in summer stock theater. (Joan Fontaine would sometimes show up in curlers, while Cesar

Romero would take Mom's hand and ask, "How are you, darling? How are the children?")

David Wright, curator of the Wellfleet Historical Society, offered helpful research assistance and materials, as did Anthony Sampas, archivist and special projects manager at the University of Massachusetts Center for Lowell History. Maureen Mahoney kindly facilitated my visit to the former orphanage in Lowell where my grandmother and great-uncle lived for four years. In the mid-1960s the Ayer Home became a convent, renamed Bachand Hall, and I was fortunate to converse at length with Sister Therese Forest S.C.O., one of the Hall's few remaining nuns. Sister Therese, who grew up near the Ayer Home, remembered as a child seeing the orphans walking in long lines of two, Madeleine style, through the large refectory windows.

As a member of the Atlanta Writers Club, a vibrant organization founded in 1914, I have participated in writing groups and the club's twice-yearly conferences, which feature editors, agents, and authors from across the country. I owe a big thanks to the novelist George Weinstein, who directs the conferences and offers unstinting support to AWC's diverse cast of both aspiring and accomplished writers.

Emory University supported the writing and publication of this book in a variety of ways. Emory College generously provided a subvention to offset production costs. The Emory Center for Faculty Development and Excellence, especially Allison Adams, the director of research and scholarly writing, offered pivotal mentoring through workshops and discussion groups for writers, as well as consultations with two outside editors, Christopher Lura and Michelle Tessler. I am forever indebted to John Morgenstern, Emory's scholarly communications librarian, for his detailed, vital, and encouraging advice on navigating the publishing process. Bailey Betik, digital publication specialist at the Emory Center for Digital Scholarship (ECDS), designed my author website with good humor and expertise; ECDS's geographer, Michael Page, provided valuable assistance in rendering damaged photographs publishable; and Megan Slemons, GIS librarian at ECDS, took my scribbled map of the Cape and made it beautiful, accurate, and relevant to my stories.

I am profoundly grateful to Emory's Institute for the Liberal Arts, where I have taught for the past ten years, for their enthusiastic support of my Memory and Memoir course, the annual teaching of which motivated me to resume the writing of this book after a long hiatus and, equally crucial, to revise its structure and focus. My colleagues—Rose Deighton-Mohammed, Arri Eisen, Robyn Fivush, Kim Loudermilk, Mark Risjord, Julia Tulke, and Peter Wakefield—have created a community of goodwill, engaging conversation, and genuine friendship, helping me to grow as a thinker and teacher. To my many Emory students over the years, I owe an incalculable debt; their honesty, insights, questions, and writing trained my eye, expanded my thinking, and pushed me to learn as much as possible about autobiographical memory and the craft of memoir.

Who are any of us without our own teachers? I was blessed with superb teachers from elementary school through graduate school, most notably Barbara Winslow, Elizabeth Hooker, Diane Campbell, Jean Emerson, John Gray, Borden Painter, Dori Katz, David Millikan, Virginia Hearn, Robert Paul, and Rebecca Chopp. Their exceptional gifts helped me to believe in myself and to pave my unlikely path to a profession in words.

I have been equally lucky in friends, many of whom have read parts or entire drafts of this book in its many versions over many years. John Howard and Darcy Dye were among my earliest and most generous readers. Darcy's astute editing skills guided me to the stories most worth telling, while John read multiple drafts of my manuscript and offered both unflagging encouragement and excellent advice on publishing. Elliot Gorn and Mary Frederickson generously read and commented on the most recent version of this book; their belief in its value kept me moving forward when optimism flagged. Other readers, some of them from my very first forays into memoir writing as a graduate student, include Bernie Adeney-Risakotta, Meg Ash, Malaga Baldi, David Balcom, Anne Bernays, Michele Bograd, Richard Bondi, Roberta Bondi, John Clum, Caroline Herring Crespino, Leslie Daniels, Phillip DePoy, Robyn Fivush, Cindie Geddes, Hollis Gillespie, Anna Grimshaw, Dalia Judovitz, Andrew Kazama, Nancy Koppelman, Kim Loudermilk, Michael Moon, Clara Mucci, Agnes Nairn, Lee Nowell, Jack Pendarvis, Seth Rolbein, Gary Romano, Bill Searles, June Akers Seese, Pat Strachan, Natasha Trethewey, Carla Trujillo, Candace Waid, Deb Watts, Sally West, Aimee Wise, and Ira Wood. For every kind word and constructive critique, thank you.

Conversations with still other friends, including Peter Ash, Anthony Clark, Grace Dyrness, Kate Ellis, Susan Gagliardi, Josephine Grant, Barbara Guttman, Sandi John, Clint Joiner, Evan Joiner, Megan Joiner, Jocelyn McWhirter, Cynthia Messina, Daniel Pollock, Maria Pramaggiore, Christine Ristaino, Barbara Rothbaum, Julie Sexeny, Stephen Smith, Nick Spitzer, Chris Suh, Aune Vanninen, Cecil Walker, and Daren Wang, refined my thinking and/or educated me on writing and publishing. Ideas explored in my many absorbing conversations with Robyn, an international expert on autobiographical memory, are woven throughout this book, though any mistakes are my own, of course. I am grateful to Natasha for her brilliant insights on the complex art of creating meaning from past pain, and to Sally for her steadfast friendship and keen understanding of human psychology. Thank you all, and thanks, too, to the many unnamed friends and relatives who have contributed in less direct but nonetheless meaningful ways to these stories.

To those closest to my heart—my husband, Allen Tullos, and our daughter, Hannah Rose Blakeley—thank you for listening to, reading, and living with these stories. My life is indelibly enriched by the music and poetry and art of your love.

CYNTHIA BLAKELEY was born and raised in Wellfleet, MA, a small fishing town on Cape Cod. A first-generation college student, she graduated Phi Beta Kappa from Trinity College in Hartford, CT, and taught for a year in Bordeaux, France, on a Fulbright. She earned her master's from New College, Berkeley, and her PhD from Emory University in Atlanta. She has worked as a freelance editor and writer for twenty-five years and teaches courses on memoir, interdisciplinary research, and theories of dream interpretation at Emory. Her creative nonfiction essays have appeared in the *Cape Cod Voice, Dreamers Magazine,* and *HerStry,* and she has been interviewed on family storytelling by Wisconsin Public Radio and the *Wall Street Journal.* She and her husband, who have a daughter, live in Atlanta, GA, where they write, teach, and garden.